WE DARED

WE DARED

THE BLOOD-SOAKED AUTOBIOGRAPHY OF BRITAIN'S MOST NOTORIOUS GANGSTER

By Danny Woolard with
Micky Gluckstead

JOHN BLAKE

Published by John Blake Publishing Ltd,
3 Bramber Court, 2 Bramber Road,
London W14 9PB, England

First published in hardback in 2003

ISBN 1 84454 001 4

British Library Cataloguing-in-Publication Data:

A catalogue record for this book is available from the British Library.

Design by www.envydesign.co.uk

Printed in Great Britain by CPD, Wales

1 3 5 7 9 10 8 6 4 2

Papers used by John Blake Publishing are natural, recyclable products made from wood
grown in sustainable forests. The manufacturing processes conform to the environmental
regulations of the country of origin.

Every attempt has been made to contact the relevant copyright-holders, but some were
unobtainable. We would be grateful if the appropriate people could contact us.

Oscar Wilde was in the machine shop,
sewing mailbags in Reading Jail, when a woman visitor from
the board of visitors said, 'What are you sewing, my man?'
Wilde replied, 'No, Ma'am. Reaping.'

WE DARED

The credit belongs to,
The man with courage,
Whilst trying his best
He's shed his blood sweat and tears

But still he strives boldly on, trying his upmost,
Even though the odds are
Stacked against him.

Who at the best,
He will triumph greatly,
And at the worst
Fail valiently
Whilst risking all.

But he does know his place
Will never be with those
Timid souls,
Who never tasted victory,
Or defeat:
'For they never dared'.

'TOUGH TIMES DON'T LAST, TOUGH PEOPLE DO.'

*Jason Hooper to Old Bailey Judge
Richard Hawkins February 1995 – After being
sentenced to 12 years for armed robbery*

CONTENTS

FOREWORD: THE SNOWHILL ROBBERY

Three men set out on 5th March 1995 from the East End of London towards the City's inner sanctuary, with one objective in mind. They knew there was a fortune being shipped in an 'Omega' security van and they were determined to take it. One of these men was a ½ English, ½ Maltese man by the name of Angelo (Festus) Hayman. He's the only one of the Robbers who ever had to pay the price of their actions. He is about 5ft 9in tall and almost as wide. With his shaven head, his looks would frighten the Devil.

As the armoured van came into view, Angelo got out of the van the bandits were in. Alone and with a road map in his hand he waved the driver down as though he was lost when the van slowed up, as by now Angelo was standing in front of it. He pulled out a sawn-off 12-bore shotgun, then forced the driver, a Mr Roy Adams, to let him in the passenger side. Incidentally, all this happened right outside the police station.

Once in the van Angelo made Mr Adams drive to some arches where the other two robbers followed closely in their van. When the security truck stopped, Angelo tied the driver's wrist to the steering wheel with bands. Then fate stepped in the way, as it does sometimes. Just the previous day the entire locking system had been changed on the van. So the homework these three villains had done was useless; there was no way the van could be unlocked.

The only solution was to smash a hole in the solid steel roof with jack handles, and lower the smallest member of the robbers into the van. It was so dark inside you could see nothing, but still he managed to pass out 48 bags before the police arrived, forcing the gang to flee with what they had got. The job had taken too long. There was £4 million left inside the truck in cash. What they did get was £400,000 worth of diamonds and £7 million worth of bearer bonds. So it was still a very good day's work.

They stashed the booty for a few weeks, then, when things quietened down a bit, they started making moves to cash the bonds and diamonds. Angelo and Danny Woollard knew all the right contacts. Danny and Angelo had a very powerful firm around them and money seemed no object. But the net was closing in, like a steel trap waiting to be sprung.

First, a leading light in their firm, Barry Dalton, an extremely hard man who had won over 40 prizefights, had been found shot through the head, laying slumped dead in his car in Hackney. Then, devastatingly for Woollard and Hayman, another important member of their gang, Del (Crocko) Croxson, who was on remand for shooting a man in Lincoln, died in Bellmarsh prison. He was only 32 years old, 18st 4lb of pure muscle – a real powerhouse. But he succumbed to the brown and he overdosed on heroin. Finally, another firm member, Turkish born Shaffi Ahmed, just disappeared.

THE SNOWHILL ROBBERY

The organised crime unit bugged Woollard's office and yard, which was their firms HQ trying to get some information on Shaffi's disappearance. Purely by accident they overheard Woollard and Hayman discussing the robbery and also the sale on the bonds plus possession of two sawn-off shotguns. Then Hayman got arrested for the armed robbery at Snowhill.

From the start neither man made any statement at all. Woollard, true to form, was cleared of murdering Shaffi. But he slipped up on the conspiracy charge after a trial lasting six weeks at Snaresbroke Crown Court. He got eight years and on the firearms charges he received another three-year concurrent sentence. The same Judge Medawar also sentenced Hayman to 16 years for the robbery plus 5-year concurrent again for firearms charges. Neither man made any statement or appeals for clemency to the court, as all around them were grassing and making deals trying to save their own skin. These two just kept silent and took it on the chin.

Hayman was immediately shipped to Swaleside Prison on the isle of Sheppey to start his sentence, whereas Woollard went to Norfolk to the end-of-the-line prison Wayland. Incidentally, the robbery both these men were involved in has been very well documented: it's the infamous 'Snowhill Robbery'. What made it worse, the driver Roy Adams died shortly after the raid. At Wayland Prison Woollard met up with his old pal Reggie Kray. Reg knew Danny very well and he personally persuaded him to write a book. Its called *We Dared*. It's all about the East End way of life, with no holds barred.

It was after this point that Reg Kray introduced me to Danny. As I listened to him, I knew his story was part and parcel with his way of life – prison was a certainty. So this is it, his incredible story.

Chris Brooks
September 2003

PROLOGUE:
IF I COULD ONLY HAVE FORESEEN THE FUTURE

I always rated Sunday afternoons and evenings as my highlight of the week. During the summer months Becky always used to have a massive barbecue laid on in my yard at the back of my house in Manor Park, when I used to come back from drinking in the Hathaway club. It would start off with me and Becky, plus my son Danny and his wife Tanya and my daughter Sharon and her husband Darren. There'd be my three grandchildren Becky, Georgia and Tanya running around playing, plus my mum and dad. My lodger Del Bather would also be there, playing all old records with his flat door open: Al Martino, Dorothy Squires, Nat King Cole – lovely music blaring out.

Then one by one there'd be Barry Dalton and Mary, Angelo (Festus) Hayman and his wife Tracey, Shaffi with a different bird every time, Del Croxon and Lynne, Dave De Freitas and Tracey plus his son Paul, and always Geordie Bill, Julie and his pal Fred

Higgleton with Janet, and, of course, Micky Gluckstead and Paul Foley with their partners.

We'd all finish up having an outdoor party and I always laid on whatever they wanted: food and drink, the lot. And many's a time the yard would be floodlit with music blaring out at 11 or 12 o'clock at night. If any neighbours wanted to call in everyone was welcome. They were great times. Little did we know what the future held in store for us. Myself, Angelo, Fred and Bill all finished up serving long sentences in prison – they gave us 444 years to share out between us. Poor Barry got shot dead in Hackney. Del (Crocko) Croxson died in Belmarsh prison. Shaffi went missing as he is to this day. The police nicked me for killing him, which was complete rubbish as he was a pal of mine. If I could go back in time I would love to spend a Sunday night with all my old pals now. Who knows? When I die perhaps it will happen.

The scene at the back of my house was like a scene from the film *The Godfather*. Yes, we were all villains, but good people and many a plan was hatched up on a Sunday night at one of my barbecues. There was more money earned there than in the stock market in London. There's only one way to tell our story, and that's from the start. So here goes …

ROUND 1

EARLY DAYS

Reg Kray and a few of us in Wayland used to sit and exchange stories nearly every night. Reg used to listen to my tales intently, and it was him who kept on at me to write this book, as he thought my experiences would be of interest to a good few people. So I started to write. When I'd done a few pages, I passed them from my window to next door, where my good pal John Waites would type them up for me. Then on visits I would smuggle the typed pages out for my daughter Sharon to put on a computer, as the prison authorities don't allow you to write books of any sort. So it took a lot of effort from me, John, Sharon and our proofreader, Reg Kray, to produce this book. I hope you like it. I've had to change the names in some of the stories, as I've no wish to hurt anyone's family, especially if the person I'm talking about is dead. Sometimes it's just to protect innocent parties. But I'm sure some people who read this will have their suspicions.

It's always difficult to begin a story, so I think the best way is to introduce myself. My name is Danny Woollard, and I was born in Manor Park, east London, over half a century ago. This story is fact and not fiction, unlike a lot of similar books I have read.

Let me set the scene for you. I had a very happy childhood. My dad (Len), my mum (Lil), my sister (Joyce) and myself lived at 2 Washington Avenue in Manor Park, and my gran lived at 86 Grantham Road, just over the way. There were 17 in my dad's family. My mum's family originally came from Stepney. She had eight brothers and sisters. Their family name was Pohl. They moved to Manor Park from Stepney, to Third Avenue, very close to us, so our house was always full of relations – cousins, aunts, uncles. The house was always full of laughter. We were never lonely.

My dad was a ragman, or 'general dealer' as they say. He used to work with a horse and cart, with my Uncle Ted, who had spent four years on the Burma Railway during the War. I never once heard Ted moan or complain though. As well as having alopecia, he still suffers with malaria to this day.

I never did a lot of schooling. Instead I'd go out ragging (or 'toting') with my dad and Uncle Ted. Occasionally my Uncle Ricko, who was also a dealer, used to work with us on the knocker, or dropping bills for rags. We'd drop off 500 bills, then go back the next day to see what we could pick up. Then it was back to Lilley's yard in Manor Park to sell the rags.

The rag yard was run by old Bill Lilley and his three sons, Harry, Lennie and Freddie. Harry married my dad's youngest sister, Gladys, so he was my uncle too. All the ragmen used to sell their stuff to the Lilleys. I saw the same faces every day.

There was a café just round the corner from the yard called June's. When we left the yard, everyone used to go in there. Sometimes my dad or one of my uncles would do deals in the café, buying or selling bits and pieces they had got that day. Any clothing they collected that was good enough to be resold, my gran used to buy off of them. They called it clobber. She would wash and iron the small bits, and get the coats and so on dry-cleaned. Then she would put all the small bits on a pram outside her house. The coats or shoes or boots went into her front room and all the neighbours would come and buy stuff from her. That was how she made her living. My gran's house was always full of people. I used to love it round there.

Every year around the end of June or the beginning of July, my mum would pack all our stuff. Then she, dad, Ted, his wife Doll, plus me and Ted's daughter Pauline and my sister Joyce would put all our stuff onto my dad's pal's lorry and we'd go to a farm called Cheeseman's in a little village called Yalding in Kent. There we would go hop picking or 'hopping' as we called it.

I loved it down in Kent. We were free to run and roam through fields and woods, and most of the people on the farm came from London. I also got to know lots of travelling people who are still my friends today. On Saturday nights, after the pub had closed, someone would fit a platform up and we'd all sit round a big open fire and take turns singing. They were great times.

When my sister Joyce was 16 and there was a very good-looking boy on the farm, a few huts along, who palled up with her. I was friendly with his brother, Chris. It was about the time Jimmy Young made that record 'They Try To Tell Us We're Too Young'. They got plenty of good-humoured stick over that record. He took up acting. His name was Terence Stamp. He went on to write a book called *The Stamp Collection*, and on the back cover is a picture of me, my mum, aunt Doll, Pauline, Chrissy Stamp and his mum, Ethell. I met Terence many years later and he remembered every detail of our times in Kent.

3

It was there, as a very young boy, that I saw my first proper fight. It was Teddy Hunt from Manor Park against two gypsies. He knocked them both out. Teddy Hunt, or 'Spring Hill Jack' as he was affectionately known, was a ragman like my dad, and even though he's been dead for over 40 years, he's still spoken about with reverence by the old folk. He was a natural athlete. He never used to train at all, but he could jump, no hands, right over a pillar box. At the Whippets in Manor Park on Sunday mornings, he would race anyone – but he would run backwards and they would run normally. He never once lost.

Levi Lee was the king of the gypsies. He was the best bare-knuckle fighter of all the travellers in the country and he challenged Teddy Hunt. A match was arranged. Literally thousands of people crammed onto a Yalding common called the Leas. That fight was legendary. My father saw it. He's seen many battles, but he reckons that fight was the best he's ever seen.

All the East End people backed Teddy and all the gypsies backed Levi. Thousands of pounds changed hands that day, which was a king's ransom then. An area was roped off, both men had seconds and a ref was present. The rules were that they had three-minute rounds with one minute's break between rounds. So it was similar to a boxing match – but without gloves. The fight was only over when either party was too injured to carry on. If either party was knocked out, their seconds could take them back to their corner and try to revive them. If they came out for the next round the fight carried on; if they didn't it was all over.

It was a cruel, violent battle, with Levi, the heavier man, bullying Teddy. But Teddy's sharp punching cut Levi to pieces, and after 50 minutes Levi could no longer keep fighting. Spring Hill Jack had won. Teddy and Levi both died young. Perhaps they killed each other that day many years before on Yalding Leas. They were two fine, brave men who deserve to be remembered and respected.

I lived with my gypsy friends the Boswell family at Sittingbourne one summer. We worked on the land, picking cherries, plums, pears and apples. Those days down in Kent were the best of my life. The work was hard, but I enjoyed it and it cleared the mind, and gypsy people are the salt of the earth. They took me in as one of their own.

For a while Sammy Boswell, was the best gypsy bare-knuckle fighter, but if Sammy was 20- or 30-handed and someone wanted to fight him, no one joined in. It was fair play given. Gypsies fight just fists: no kicking, head-butting or biting. And if a man goes down he is given time to get up. The fight is over if one or the other gives up or is too tired to carry on, or is obviously knocked out. The next day they shake hands and have a drink together. There is no malice in them at all.

I have met literally thousands of gypsies and they are my kind of people. The men are tough but fair, and the women are faithful to a fault. I don't know one gypsy girl that has betrayed her marriage vows. I think gypsy men and women are the best-looking people too. Later, when I was 20, I married a gypsy girl, Rebecca Boswell. We have two lovely children, Danny and Sharon, and she has remained faithful and loyal to me through all these years of trouble and upheaval from me.

Every year, after an idyllic summer, I began to get bored and restless. Once again, I would itch for London and some action. We came home from Kent each year about September time.

There was a gypsy site in East Ham, on the site of the old piggeries, called Bonny Downs. Ernie Harris, Jackie Harris and Joby Upton, three of the best bare-knuckle gypsy fighters in England, lived on the site. They used to come to Manor Park, and me and my dad would see a good fist fight nearly every week.

I think the best two fighters then were Teddy Hunt and my Uncle Jim though. Uncle Jim was a very powerful man who loved a straight-up fight. I think the only man who Jim was a bit wary of was Teddy, and Teddy was wary of Jim also. The conversation in Manor Park was very often who would win if they got fighting, but they never did. Teddy could move faster but I think Jim was a far heavier puncher, so it's anyone's guess who would have won.

Teddy's brother Freddie lodged at my gran's. He was a lovely man. Everyone called him 'Flash Fred' because he dressed so smart. Jackie Wright was another sharp dresser and another bold fighting man. I saw Jacko, as they used to call him, have many battles in the road and I never once saw him beaten. There was Billy Boyton too, another naturally strong, powerful man – although he only weighed about 12 stone – and another gentleman. Bill always tried to prevent trouble; he was a born peacemaker. Every fight he had, he was always hit first, but he was also very tough and no one ever beat him with their hands. Billy had 20 professional bouts: 20 wins, 19 KO's. Then he got nicked and done four years, which finished his boxing career. He is the only man I have ever seen bend a penny or half-penny in his teeth.

It was inevitable growing up in this environment that I would take up boxing. I went to St Bonaventure's school in Forest Gate. My best pal in school was Paul Foley. We both did a lot of boxing there and no one ever beat either of us in a street fight. We never fell out and he is still my pal today.

Our other friend went to a different school just down the road from us. His name was Micky Gluckstead. He also made a name for himself with his fighting capabilities. Micky had never done any boxing, he was just a rough, tough, hard boy. And he's one of the main stars of this book.

I left school at 15 with no qualifications at all. My dad had sold his horse and cart by then and had bought a 14.9 truck, which he and Ted used to work from. Myself, I didn't want to be a ragman. I had other ideas. Life was one big adventure which I was about to start on. And I didn't care for nothing or no one.

Me, Paul and Micky were virtually unstoppable by then. Like all young fellows in the East End we were up to anything and everything. We heard a few reports about the Kray twins but had never met them, as their toby was mainly Bethnal Green, Mile End, Stepney and Aldgate. We were always knocking about Forest Gate, Stratford, East Ham, Manor Park and Ilford, so our paths never crossed. But it was inevitable that we'd meet one day.

I like to train, so I started to go to Wag Bennet's gymnasium in Romford Road, Forest Gate to train on the weights. I got right into it. My training mates were Joe Camilleri and Brian Eastman. Brian became Mr Britain and Mr Europe; me and Joe – who had also done a bit of boxing – trained to keep fit. My dad, Paddy McGuinness, Old Pat McGuiness (Paddy's father), Bertie Coster and Billy Boyton all gave me tips. The best boxer at the gym was a lot older than me. His name was Terry 'Spud' Murphy.

Terry could really fight. Whenever there was a gym show, he couldn't get a fight. No one wanted to compete against him. He had a bit of a temper. Once, when Terry was a pro, a ref stopped a fight that Terry was winning. He was so angry that he hit the ref and lost his licence. Eventually he went into the pub business and discovered many stars at the Bridge House, Canning Town, including Chas 'n' Dave.

Billy Boyton learned me the heart punch. It's not used now as a few boxers died after receiving it. The idea was to throw a hook, then turn it into an uppercut straight into the heart. It is virtually impossible to stop. Everyone used to use it, as it took an opponent's breath away. Billy spent hour after hour with me, teaching me how to time the blow correctly. In later life it saved me on a good few occasions.

At that time Manor Park was a great place to live. It was full of characters, everyone knew each other and everyone tried to help their neighbours. There was Grantham Road, Walton Road, Selborne Avenue, Alverstone Road and Parkhurst Road – a little estate of old houses. No one had much money, but we all used to go into each other's houses and nothing was ever stolen. I had many pals. It was a real rough area but we all stuck together.

Everyone drank in the Coach and Horses. It was a good meeting place and everyone could be trusted. 'Battling' Ben O'Connor was often there with his three sons, Roy, Siddy and Brian. Ben was a right character who'd done a bit of boxing in his youth. Brian is a born comedian as are Siddy and Roy. Siddy did a fair bit of imprisonment. He went away with John McVicar and is one of the few men to escape from Parkhurst prison and get back to London. He stayed out for a few months but got captured in London – by a routine car check. John became known as 'Public Enemy No. 1' and Reg Kray's pal Bill Curbishly made a film of his life.

But Roy was the hardnut. I've never seen Roy cause trouble, but he had a fierce reputation and a lot of people tried him out, and Roy always won. I sparred with Roy when he was prizefighting. He said, 'Let's have a friendly spar.' Well, I'm glad it wasn't serious, as at the end of one round Roy had damage to his inner ear and had to have an operation. My nose was busted. I've never been able to breathe properly since.

Then there was another Roy, a great pal of mine, Roy Hunt. Roy's grandfather was known as 'Lion Hunt'. He used to take on allcomers in prizefights. Roy had a terrible temper, and he was very strong man of about 22 stone, so he wanted some stopping once he was upset. He used to get wild. Everyone just steered clear of him, because he was quite capable of killing you with his bare hands, but he used to calm down very quickly. It's only by luck that Roy never killed anyone.

The hardest hitting man I've ever seen is Jimmy Story. He lived in Alverstone Road. Jimmy married Lynne Boyton ('Heart Punch' Billy's daughter). They make a lovely couple. I've seen Jim hit at least 15 men and not one had to be hit twice. Jimmy is a joker. Just like his father-in-law, he's a real lovely man who never looks for trouble, but when it comes there's no one I'd sooner have up my back than Jim. He fears no man.

There was another Terry too, apart from the great boxer Terry 'Spud' Murphy: Terry Holden came from Forest Gate, near to where Micky Gluckstead lived before he moved to Manor Park. Terry worked as a dustman for a while, so everyone called him Terry the Dustman. Terry weighed about 26 stone. He was all fat, but he was so agile and nimble on his feet it was unbelievable. He was like a cat. Terry never used to train but he was a natural fighter. He had many prizefights and never once got beat.

He fought a fellow at the Rainbow Rooms. His opponent was supposed to be a killer, supposed to be unbeatable. Well, Terry knocked him senseless in the first round. The odds against Terry were 10–1 but he upset the odds that night. The thing I most remember about Terry was that, for a bet, he ate double pie and mash – that's two pies and two portions of mash potato and liquor – thirteen times in Cooke's Pie and Mash Shop at East Ham.

There was a gypsy family in Alverstone Road by the name of Attrell. There was another Sammy there – a man with the biggest pair of arms you've ever seen. Sammy was a gent and his wife Prissy is a lovely-looking gypsy woman, who always made you feel welcome. In her youth Prissy won the title 'Maid of Kent'.

Whatever the Attrells had, you could have half of it. Their son Matty is still my pal. Me and Matty got into a few fights and we always did well. Matty is like his father Sam, a real gentleman but not lacking in any way, especially when you're in a tight corner. Matty has got two sisters, Mary and Prissy, who I consider very close – more like sisters than friends. I don't see as much of them as I'd like to but the bond with all the Attrell family and me will never be broken. The Stockwells, who used to come to Kent with us, are like family too.

At the back of our houses was Little Ilford Park. Stevie Marriot, another Manor Park boy, made it famous by making a hit record about it called 'Itchycoo Park'. Behind the park lived the most talented man I have ever met, David Saich. He could make the impossible with his hands. He could do wood sculptures and carving, and antiques restoration. He really is a marvellous artist. He can paint a canvas equally as good as any old master. The master copy artist Keating was on the television once. 'You're the finest copy artist in the world,' the interviewer said to him. 'No, Dave from Dagenham is better than me,' he replied.

I could fill a book with stories of what Dave's made and painted. How the man has never been fully recognised I do not know. When Dave married Jackie, Steve Marriott and the Small Faces played at the wedding. Rod Stewart did a few songs as well. They were all unknown in those days.

Micky Reilly, was also a good friend of mine. His sister Phyllis, or 'Gypsy' as she was known, was the common-law wife of Billy Hill –

though I did not know it, the governor of London's underworld at the time. Billy was a thin, gaunt-looking man, but he had a ruthless streak and would cut anyone to pieces if they provoked him. So would Gypsy. I liked Bill myself. He had earned his reputation and money the hard way, but he would always help you if he could.

Two other top villains who used the Coach and Horses were the brothers Jimmy and Georgie Woods. They were known and respected everywhere. They were my dad's age. I knew them both very well. They were always immaculately clean and two of the most smartly dressed men I have ever seen. They were real big-time. I used to see them about in their flash cars, and they were always in the newspapers, with Jack Spot, Billy Hill, Frank Fraser etc. Although they were villains, they never once took any liberties with working people. They had no bullying way at all, and if my dad done any little job for them, they always paid him more than they had to.

Georgie got involved at one time in a couple of clubs with the Kray twins. The twins were real pals of Jimmy and George. My dad was a working man, a real family man, and him and his brother Ted had a greengrocer's business around that time. They had a horse and cart, and called on houses, mainly selling potatoes. Well, this one day, when I was very young, we was in Parkhurst Avenue and the horse and cart was in the middle of the road. All of a sudden, a big black car pulled up behind us, blowing the hooter.

'I won't be a minute,' my dad said to them.

Well, this tall, smart fellow jumped out of the car. 'Did you tell me to wait a minute? I'll cut your fucking head off,' he said. He had two women in the car, so I suppose he was showing off.

I was only about ten years old, but I picked up a weight off of our set of scales. If this bloke had cut my dad I would have tried to hit him with it.

As this fellow walked round the cart, a nearby prefab door opened. It was George. 'Leave these boys alone. If you've got a problem, I'll sort it with you – or just fuck off,' he shouted.

'All right, George. Sorry, mate. I didn't know they were friends of yours,' this fellow said, and got back into his car and backed out of Parkhurst Avenue as fast as he could. Then George just laughed as my dad waved his hand, and he walked back into the prefab.

In later life I was always looking out for that bully. When I found out who it was, it was too late. He had been shot dead and his photo was in the paper. He was the infamous Teddy Machin. George, Jimmy, Teddy, Siddy Cook and one or two others had attempted the bullion robbery at London Airport.

They had a guard straightened out to give the rest of the guards drugged coffee, but their man got cold feet and told the police. They had a terrific battle. Teddy got away but George and Jimmy both got caught and got ten years each. They both went to the infamous Dartmoor prison. It would have been the biggest robbery in history. There was even a film made about it.

So you could walk into the Coach and Horses some nights and you'd see Jimmy and George and sometimes Bill, three of the most important figures in London's underworld, just having a quiet drink.

Jimmy's daughter Josie married Bubbles Daltrey, a big man in every sense of the word – a big man with a big heart. Together they had three sons, Michael, Phillip and Peter. But a freak accident cost Peter his life at the age of 20. Bubbles just pined. He lost weight and died of a broken heart. It wrecked both Phillip and Michael as it did poor Josie. They never really recovered. They are the most feeling people I have ever known and have never hurt anyone, and they did not deserve the terrible hand fate dealt them.

In later life, me, my dad, Micky and Phil Daltrey, and George used to have some real good times. My dad and George were always talking about the old days. Jimmy had passed away by then but George always used to sing Jimmy's favourite song, 'Maybe', the old Inkspots number.

Not everything happened at the Coach and Horses. Frank Price was British Wrestling Champion at the time. He had two coffee bars: one in Upton Lane, Forest Gate and one in Manor Park. Hard man John Cotton, who had done ten years for shooting a policeman, was often there. John lived upstairs in the foam shop. There was a fire there one day and Johnny almost died trying vainly to get a little boy out. John was never the same man after failing to rescue that child, but he could do no more. He died shortly afterwards.

Frank Price had a mate called Gordon. This Gordon was a very formidable man. If there was ever any trouble in the coffee bar Frank used to call him down from the flat upstairs. Frank being champion of Britain at wrestling, it gives you some sort of idea of the calibre of fighting man that Gordon was. The only man he ever lost to was Micky Gluckstead.

Frank set about Micky's pal one night. The next night Micky went to the coffee bar to see what it was all about. Frank told Micky to mind his own business. Micky offered Frank out, as he had taken a liberty with Micky's pal. Instead, Gordon came down from upstairs. 'You take your pal's place and I'll take Frank's. How does that sound?' he asked.

'That's okay with me,' Micky said.

No one thought Micky had a chance. There was a big yard behind the coffee bar. We all went out to watch this fight. They tore straight into each other, like two gladiators. Five minutes later Gordon went down. He was finished. Mick said, 'How about you, Frank?' Frank wisely declined.

There was another late-night café just up the road in Ilford Lane. It was called Dave's Café, and a black fellow called Eddie Barret was always up there. There was a blacksmith's behind Dave's café with a big yard. If anyone had a row in Dave's it was always settled in the blacksmith's yard. Eddie Barret was built like Mike Tyson. He had many battles there, always proving victorious.

These are just a few characters and friends in Manor Park in those days. It really was a lovely place to live, but progress being what it is all the old houses were pulled down and replaced with flats. The Coach and Horses was demolished and we were all split up, everyone moving to different locations. This ruined the community we had. Even Dave's café went to make way for a superstore. It wasn't just the buildings that went – it was our way of life.

A lot of the truth about street fighting has been overlooked. For example, although Roy Shaw and Lennie Mclean are two very hard men, especially Roy, everyone seems to have forgotten a lot of facts and lot of hard people, but I haven't. Mclean and Shaw are talked about as if they were the only two hardnuts in the East End, but in reality it was full of them.

I've just received a copy of Roy Shaw's book, *Pretty Boy*. It was very good of him to send it to me. Lenny Mclean also gave me his book. They were both very well written and entertaining. As for myself, I have known all the hard men for the last 30 years, and I have read all about what Roy and Lennie have to say. Now I would like to tell you the story of three schoolmates: Danny Woollard, Micky Gluckstead and Paul Foley, all from the East End of London.

ROUND 2

MICKY MAKES
HIS MARK

The first time I saw Roy Shaw I was having a drink in the Plessey club at Ilford. He was bouncing there. I had heard about him on the grapevine. He was supposed to be able to have a bit of a fight. He was really drunk that night, but he looked awfully tough. What struck me was the size of his neck and his squinty eyes, which put me in mind of an English bull terrier: pig like eyes, and eyebrows that seemed to stick out, leaving his eyes sunken back in his head. I don't know how he ever got the nickname of 'Pretty Boy'.

What I couldn't understand was that Roy was a fine fighter, but when he was paralytic drunk a baby could have done him. About three weeks after this, me and a few pals were having a drink in the Greyhound at Chadwell Heath. And who should be there but Roy Shaw. Drunk as before. About 10 pm, two very pretty girls came over to us. One of them I knew – her name was Janet McQueen. We were having a good time.

This Roy Shaw character was legless by now, and he kept making remarks to the girls. When the girls went to the toilet, he walked up to me and my pals with his mate, and said, 'Right, lads, time for you to go home to bed as me and my pal are going to keep your girlfriends company.'

I turned and looked at him. Then I started to laugh. I really thought he was joking. But one look at his stern face and I knew he meant it.

I said, 'Roy, that is your name, isn't it? You ought to be a comedian on the stage, telling fucking jokes like that.'

Then he started hollering and hooting. Then he just sauntered away, mumbling. But he had ruined our night. When I turned round the girls had left.

I seemed to bash into Janet McQueen everywhere I went. We started to court, but unfortunately it did not work out and we parted. But I did think a terrible lot of her. If she reads this story, I don't know where she is, but I do wish her all the luck in the world, and I hope her life turned out a real success. She deserved it.

At that time of day, we used to drink in the Coach and Horses. One night Roy Shaw comes in with his wife, a very pretty Maltese girl by the name of Caroline, and with Rosie Enever and Frankie Turner. I thought Roy had come to see me, so I walked up to him. He said hello and we shook hands. He was a different fellow sober: quiet and sociable.

Billy Boyton was in the pub that night too, and Rosie started to dig him out over some money he owed her. It was only a small amount but she was showing off because Roy was with her, and she was trying to mug Billy off. She was putting Roy in the middle. I knew there was going to be trouble. Eventually Roy said, 'Bill, let's talk in private outside.'

MICKY MAKES HIS MARK

I walked outside as they were talking. Suddenly Roy exploded. He hit Bill with a tremendous punch, the original sucker punch – a proper surprise blow. The punch hit Billy square on the jaw. Bill immediately dropped to the floor on one knee, as though he had been shot. He looked up at Roy and said, 'Boy, if that is as hard as you can hit, you're in trouble.'

With that Roy set about Billy properly. Roy was one of the best street fighters I have ever seen. Bill never had a chance in hell. I pushed Roy off of him. Just then, Frankie Turner, Rosie Enever and Caroline hurried out of the pub and all four of them drove away in a Bedford dormobile. No doubt about it, Roy could have a terrible fight. I personally thought Bill would beat him, but Roy was a proper street fighter, whereas Billy was really just a very powerful straight-fighting boxing man.

The next I heard of Roy, he got three years for stabbing a bouncer in Seven Kings. Then he got a further fifteen years for armed robbery, with three years knocked off on appeal. Good luck to him. I still remember the night he fought one of the toughest men I knew, Billy Boyton. If Bill had fought taking every advantage he could, as Roy had, I still think he would have won, but 'if' is a very big word.

I'd got a flat in Romford Road, Manor Park. A bookmaker by the name of Sammy Bellson opened a betting shop opposite. He said to me, 'I've got a real hardnut in to look after me and my shop. He goes by the name of Donny Adams.'

Donny Adams – 'The Bull' – lived above Frank Price's betting shop. I met him in Rosie Enever's house opposite. He seemed quiet enough; a thick-set chap about 6 foot tall. Everyone kept telling me he was the best fighter in England, but he hadn't proved it to me. He gave Victor Horse a slap, but Victor wasn't a fighter at all, just a happy-go-lucky, very inoffensive bloke who owed Sammy a few quid. It was a real liberty.

Then one day Don beat up Harry, the comedian Tommy Trinder's brother – a little Jewish fellow. I was fast becoming convinced he was just a bully. He only seemed to fight anyone he thought was easy meat. In fact, when he hit Harry, my Uncle Ricko said to him, 'You couldn't hit a man.' And Don just walked away.

Anyhow, one Sunday morning we were in the Coach and Horses and he hit an unsuspecting elderly chap by the name of Andy Douglas. But Andy never went down. So Donny panicked and dragged him to the floor, and started to hit and kick him whilst he was down. Well, I just beat Billy Boyton to him and pushed him off Andy. As I squared up, I said, 'I'll fight you, Donny.'

He said that he didn't want to fight me as he knew my dad, but I knew Don was frightened. I said to my dad, 'He's a mug. That's Donny 'The Bully' Adams. That's how he got his name – not strong as a bull but a bully.'

After that, his bullying days were over in Manor Park, so he moved to Hoddeston and started bullying a few gypsies about. He was very muscular and browbeat a lot of people.

A while after this I heard the Kray twins were on their toes for something or other and I was at a place called Selly Oak, up near Birmingham. Well, Don was their pal, and I heard the twins had stuck up a lot of money for Donny to have a bare-knuckle fight with Hughie Burton from Doncaster.

I knew Hughie well. His brother-in-law was a fellow from Tonga, a very good professional fighter by the name of Kit Lave, and Hughie used to spar and train with Kit. But Hughie was much too much for him. Hughie was the best fighter amongst all gypsies. He was the king of the gypsies. He would have murdered Donny

Adams but Adams talked a good fight. It was in the *News of the World*.

Anyhow, it was the first week in September and Paul Foley had a horse for sale, and he was taking it to Barnet Horse Fair to try and sell it. So Micky and I went along for the ride. The place was a great big field with about four drinking booths on it and loads of stainless steel caravans and lorries. There were horses everywhere. And hundreds and hundreds of gypsies.

We had no luck selling Paul's horse. So we walked it about a bit, then tethered it to the side of this beer booth and went in to have a drink. And who should be at the end of the bar but Donny Adams and the Kray twins. They were all dressed up like city gents: very smart, immaculately turned out. They were standing near where our horse was tied up. Suddenly, our horse stuck his head inside the booth and nuzzled Ronnie Kray's arm, making a brown mark on his new suit. Ronnie just laughed and took it in good humour, but Adams said, 'Fucking horse,' and punched it right on the snout.

The horse reared up and pulled part of the tent down. It fell over amongst the canvas and we rushed out and got it to its feet. Adams said that we shouldn't have put it near them. Before I could say a word, Micky said, 'Would you like to try and hit me like that?'

Adams said, 'Put on four stone then come back and see me. In any case, I only fight for money, and you three don't look as if you have any.'

'Me, Danny or Paul will fight you. Take your pick. If you win, I will give you our horse – that's worth at least £500. If you lose, you give us £500,' Micky said.

As Micky was the smallest, Donny thought he would be easy. 'Okay, you'll do for me,' he said.

About 30 or 40 gypsies made a circle. To Ron Kray, I said, 'Will you make sure this fight's straight up?'

'Don't worry, lads. You'll get fair play,' he said. Adams had lots of gypsies with him, but I think secretly they all wanted this bully to get a good hiding.

Well, Donny weighed about 16 stone, Micky about 12. It was David and Goliath all over again. I was Micky's second, and another old fighting man Tommy 'The Bear' Brown was Adams' man. They used to call Tommy Brown 'The Tottenham Bear' – a giant of a man. Kenza Gumble was the ref, making sure this was a fair do.

'Make ready,' he shouted.

Micky looked at me and laughed.

'Go for it,' Kenza continued.

Donny was a southpaw and rushed at Mick. But Mick met him halfway. They started to trade really heavy blows. Donny couldn't move Micky – he stood his ground and took Donny's best punches. But whenever Micky landed, Donny went backwards and Micky was on him. Left, right, left combinations. He couldn't hurt Adams' body, but every time he caught Donny in his head it jarred him.

After about ten minutes, Donny went down on his knee. He got up, but then Micky caught him with a tremendous blow behind the ear. Adams was knocked unconscious. The gypsies could not believe it. Nor could the Krays. They walked up to us, and Ron gave Micky his £500 and said, 'Thanks, boys. You have just saved us a fortune.'

In the fight that was coming up, Hughie Burton would have killed Donny for much more money than that. Adams was unconscious for ten minutes. When he came round, he said, 'That was a lucky punch.'

'Yes,' said Micky, 'but who do you want to fight now – me, Paul or Danny? Fuck off, you bully.'

Then me, Paul, Mick and Kenza all got drunk, and then fetched Paul's horse home. We busted up the £500 three ways.

MICKY MAKES HIS MARK

When they say Donny Adams had 48 fights and 48 wins, I reckon he is only counting Harry Trinder, school playground fights and the fights he had with his wife. Or perhaps he just forgot about Micky Gluckstead.

After the episode at Barnet Horse Fair, I had the utmost respect for the Kray twins, or as their friends always referred to them 'the twins'. They had made sure we got a fair crack of the whip that day. I never saw Ronnie have a fight, but I was having a drink in the pub in Stratford one night in the early 60s, with Danny O'Leary and his brother, when I saw Reg and his stunning wife Francis come in. Reg and Francis were both dressed immaculately. They were an outstanding couple.

As they came in there were three men right there. One of them was a professional boxer. I didn't know the other two but they looked very handy fellows. One of them made a remark about Francis' bust and Reg heard them. I saw him go very white. He stopped in his tracks and said to the boxer, 'I heard that remark. Now I think you should apologise to my wife.'

He just looked at Reg, half smiling, and said, 'Obviously you don't know who I am. Anyhow, she has got nice tits, so just fuck off.'

Reg, realising the situation would result in a fight and that there were three of them, half turned as though he was going to walk away. Then he spun round like lightning and delivered the perfect left hook to the guy's jaw, knocking him spark out and breaking his jaw in the process. Reg knew instinctively he was finished so he laid into his pal, who by this time had grabbed hold of him. This fellow was trying to wrestle Reg to the floor, but Reg just punched him off and laid him out as well. The third man ran off.

This all happened in seconds. We never even had time to get to

Reg and help him, not that he needed any help. Reg just brushed his clothes down, combed his ruffled jet-black hair and said, 'Obviously he never heard of Reg Kray, either.' Then he said, 'Come along, Francis. We'd better leave before the police arrive.' Then the two of them just walked out.

Many years later in Wayland Prison I mentioned that fight to Reg and he couldn't even remember the guy's name. The truth is he was a top fighter, about Reg's weight, yet Reg had beaten him and his pal very easily. That's one of the reasons I truly believe Reg could have been a top fight proboxer, if his life hadn't taken him on a different journey. Make no mistake about it, Reg could really have a straight-up fight.

If you want to know about the hardest men in the ring, the ultimate accolade must belong to 'The Blonde Bomber' Billy Walker – another East End boy. I will never forget that feeling of national pride when Bill knocked out Cornelius Perry, the giant American, when England amateurs beat the Americans 10–0 a feat that has never been done before or since.

The greatest battle I ever witnessed in a boxing ring was when Billy Walker fought Ray Patterson, the Heavyweight Champion of the World. It was brutal, with Billy proving victorious. Billy Walker had many glorious battles in the ring, not only with Ray Patterson, but with the No1 in the world at that time from America, Thad Spencer. Billy, the underdog, gave him a good hiding.

Next Walker fought Henry Cooper, the British and European Champion. Cooper had previously all but knocked out Cassius Clay, later to be known as Muhammed Ali, with his famed left hook, known affectionately by the British public as ''Enry's hammer'. But Walker took Cooper's best punches and was coming on strong.

Cooper was in all sorts of trouble, have no doubt about that. He even started complaining to the referee, a sure sign of a loser. When an accidental clash of heads split Walker's eye wide open, the fight had to be stopped in Cooper's favour. This cruelly robbed Walker of the title. Cooper was a lucky man that night.

Billy had two rousing battles with Johnny Prescott who at the time seemed unbeatable, but Walker did him twice in wars of attrition – no skill, just bloody, brutal fighting. Both men were heroes, giving their all. It was a pity there had to be a loser, but Billy was a bit bigger than Prescott, the extra weight proving the deciding factor. At all Billy's fights, everybody from the East End turned up – he was a proper East End boy, one of your own. He had a real battle with the European Heavyweight Champion, a German by the name of Karl Milden Berger.

Billy had cut his eye in sparring with Peter Boddington, a useful heavyweight. Boddington was a heavy-hitting southpaw like Milden-Berger. The cut was not too bad, so Walker went ahead with the fight. The first punch Milden-Berger threw opened Bill's eye right up, but Billy fought gamely on. He was doing well, but in the fifth round his eye was a lot worse. So the referee had no alternative but to stop the fight in Milden-Berger's favour.

The next fight Milden-Berger had was a really tough bout with Cassius Clay for the Heavyweight Championship of the World. Clay won but Milden Berger gave him a right rough time, and Clay was in his prime then. But perhaps Billy's greatest battle was his last fight against a very awkward southpaw, a chicken farmer from Swadlingcote – Jack Bodell: country boy v city wide boy.

It was held at Wembley pool. As usual all the East End was there. The atmosphere was electric – you could feel it in the air. The band leader Billy Cotton, whose signature tune was 'Wakey Wakey', sat a few seats from me. The fanfares over, Walker and Bodell stood glaring at each other from their corners. At the bell it was total war. They stood toe to toe in the centre of the ring, neither man giving an inch. At the end of the first round, Bill took a tremendous punch to the stomach and, for the first time in his professional life, Billy was down. When the count got to eight he was up, then the bell rang, sounding the end of the first round. But what a round of action.

Round two, Bodell came rushing at Walker, thinking that if Walker was still hurt he'd finish him off. What a mistake. Walker hit him straight on the chin with a fierce right-hand shot. Bodell hit the canvas with a thud. He almost did a somersault, his legs up in the air, and his feet hit the ground above his head. Not one person in Wembley thought he would get up, but at the count of nine he some how managed to scramble to his feet. He held on for the rest of round two. Somehow he survived it.

By round three his head had cleared and the fight developed into a classic. First one man, then the other, getting on top. In the seventh round, as Bodell and Walker stood toe to toe, trading blow for blow the excitement proved too much for the celebrity Billy Cotton. He had a heart attack and he died. As the ambulance men stretchered him out of the Wembley Pool, the comedians, which you get at all the big fights, were calling out all around the arena, 'Wakey Wakey'. Billy Cotton was a happy man in life, a jovial sort of chap who would have appreciated the joke.

Meanwhile Billy Walker was taking a tremendous amount of punishment on the ropes, but he stubbornly refused to go down. He would sooner have died than give in – he has a true warrior's heart. But eventually the referee stepped in and stopped the fight in Bodell's favour. That fight had taken a tremendous amount out of Walker and he never boxed again, but he never did bad for an East End boy who started off as a bouncer at Ilford Palais. All the experts and pundits had reckoned he couldn't box at all.

Walker had heart and a big punch and no one ever had an easy fight with him. He always fought his heart out. The East End should always feel proud of him. It's important to recognise the difference in class between professional boxers and prizefighters. The best prizefighter at heavyweight was Cliff Fields. He knocked Mclean out twice and done Ron Redrup easily.

Then a Brazilian came over to this country, a professional boxer. He stopped Fields in five rounds at Ilford Palais. His next fight was with Frank Bruno, when Bruno was first on the professional scene. Bruno knocked him out in the first round. So consequently the best prizefighter would only be a mug in the real boxing world.

ROUND 3

MONEY AND TROUBLE

Working for other people has its pitfalls. I was in Rosie Enever's café one morning and my mate Jimmy Pike came in and had a bit of breakfast with me. He said, 'Dan, are you doing anything?'

'No, Jim, I'm nearly skint,' I said.

'If we go down to Albert dock tomorrow at 6 am and line up at the quay, if we get picked, we'll get a job unloading the cargo off of the ships. It's fantastic money. All cash in hand.'

'What if we don't get picked?' I said.

He said that we would go back day after day until we did – then they keep the same blokes on. It's only casual labour, he said, it is called the 'shore gang'. We could even get a stevedore or lighterman's ticket out of it eventually.

So at 5.30 am the next morning, I picked Jimmy up from his parents' flat in Custom House, Prince Regent's Lane. By 6 am we were lining up on the quay. This fellow, about 5 ft 9in, a real rough-looking man with a broken nose and bulging eyebrows, was standing on a bank above the other men, picking people out. He looked like an ex-boxer. He had a wooly hat on, a big black and red checked donkey-type jacket and big boots.

He picked about 25 men out, and left me and Jimmy standing on the quay. The next morning we drew a blank as well. Then on the third morning he picked us out. The dockers were a law unto themselves: at 6 am they had all been drinking heavily and they were all loud – hollering and hooting all the time. I did not like them at all. But I thought I would give it a go now that I was there.

Jimmy and I had to go down to the hold, and as a crane put pallets down, we had to load the pallets with bags of nuts – that was the cargo. When that floor was cleared, we had to load fresh pallets with dunnage. That is the wood or packing that holds the cargo still whilst the ship is at sea. We worked till about 3 pm – most of the registered dockers were in the pub by then. They had left the shore gang – us – to do the work, and their wages was four times as much as ours.

When we finished, we had to go to the tally clerk and he gave us a receipt. Everyone got paid by how much cargo had been shifted. As everyone was lining up for their money, I had already made up my mind that this was not for me. I reckoned the dockers were taking us for fools. Also, I noticed as everyone drew their money, this bloke in the wooly hat was talking to them and they was handing him money. I thought perhaps he was an illegal bookmaker.

We got 50 bob, or 2 pounds 10 shillings. That was a lot of money in those days. Today its £2.50 – enough to buy a child's ice cream. As me and Jimmy drew our money, this fellow came up to Jimmy and said, 'You've got to give me five bob – two half-crowns.'

'What for?' said Jimmy.

'That's the rules for picking you out and giving you a day's work,' he said.

'Leave it out,' said Jimmy. 'I ache all over. I've worked hard for this money. In any case, I don't want you to pick me out any more. It's a matter of fact that I won't be here any more for you to pick me out.'

'Okay, have it your way,' this fellow said, then turned to walk away. But quick as lightning he spun round and cracked Jimmy straight on the jaw, knocking him right out.

As I bent down and lifted Jimmy's head up, I could see his jaw was broken. His mouth was laying wide open, all limp. When Jimmy regained his senses, I got him to his feet.

'Now I'll have your five shillings,' said this fellow. 'Your mate's paid his. Now you can pay your dues.'

'I'll tell you what I'll do,' I said. 'Let me take my mate to the hospital and see to him. Then tomorrow I'll come back and fight you. No sly punches, you coward. You win, I will give you your two half-crowns; if I win, you pay me.'

This bully let out a belly laugh. 'Listen, fellas, I've got to fight Jack Dempsey here tomorrow for my money,' he said.

'Listen, big head, you won't be laughing tomorrow,' I said. 'What time do you want me here?'

'Okay, 2 pm if you've got the guts.'

'Don't worry, I'll be here.'

So I got Jimmy into My Vauxhall Cresta and took him to East Ham Memorial Hospital. They kept him in to have his jaw set. I went to Jimmy's parents' flat. When I told his dad (a retired docker) what had happened, he went white. 'Dan, you're not thinking of going back are you?'

'Of course I am,' I said.

'The man who broke Jimmy's jaw is called Jack. He's got a quite a reputation. He'll kill you. Take my advice and don't turn up.'

The next morning I picked Jimmy up from hospital. His face was a real state. He couldn't see out of one eye it was closed. He had lost four teeth. His jaw was all wired up, keeping his mouth closed. I felt really sorry for him. When we got to his flat and his mother saw him, she started to cry. I was boiling over inside. What a liberty this Jack had taken. At about 12 pm I said goodbye to Jimmy and his mum and went home.

I sat indoors by myself for a while. Then I phoned about six of my pals, but none of them wanted to know. They had all heard about this Jack character – they wouldn't even come with me to see fair play. So I thought I'd give it a miss. Then at 1.30 pm, I thought about poor Jimmy's face and his mum crying and my temper started to rise again. So I got into my car and drove to the Albert Dock – on my own.

As I went through the gates, I saw Jack and three of his pals waiting by the quayside. I pulled up and walked over to them. They all smelled of drink and Jack had a roll-up in his mouth. I thought to myself, 'It must be a good sign. He is most probably not very fit.' As I got to them, Jack said, 'Boy, you've proved you've got a lot of bottle just by turning up. Just pay me my money.'

'This doesn't have to be,' I said. 'I've come here to collect, not pay. I've come here to fight you. But I am on my own so will you guarantee me a fair fight?'

Jack gave a deep-throated laugh. 'You cheeky bastard,' he said. 'You think I need help? Come on, just you and me. No one else will interfere.' And with that, he waved his arms and a crane lowered a pallet. The five of us got onto it and were lifted up onto the ship, then down into the hold, which had been emptied the previous day.

As we got to the bowels of the ship there was an electric light on a cable which ran right down to the hold from the deck. There was 40 or 50 dockers there – some sitting, some standing, most drinking. There was smoke everywhere. They had a square in the middle for me and Jack. It was about 12 foot square. I asked Jack what the rules were.

'Just country rules, boy.'

'What's that?' I asked.

'You use just your hands – a straight-up. No rounds, last man standing, or if any one of us quits the other one wins.'

When Jack took his shirt off he surprised me. He had massive biceps and a very deep chest, but I noticed a bit of a belly.

'Are your ready, boy?' he shouted.

We met in the centre of this square. I threw a straight left at Jack as quick as a flash. He sent a counter punch over the top of my guard and split my eye open. As I went back he hit me in the face and head four times.

I grabbed his arms and tried to hold him but he pushed me off and opened up again on me, this time to the body. I half turned to save myself and he hit me in the spine. I felt a sharp pain run down my leg.

I grabbed him again. This time he shoved me off and attacked me to the head once more. I managed to hit him twice in the stomach but he didn't even feel it, so I grabbed him again and tried to tie him up. He was giving me a terrible mauling but I kept holding him, trying to wear him out. Tiring tactics was the only chance I had.

By now we had been fighting for about ten minutes. Although I had soaked up plenty of punishment, I hadn't gone down, but I was losing a fair amount of blood and I was getting weak.

I noticed Jack was beginning to blow a fair bit. 'I bet he wishes he hadn't gone for a drink before fighting me,' I thought, but Jack was still strong. He bored into me and pushed me back, then he crashed a right hook into my jaw. He was in full flow now but he got careless. He made a bad mistake. He thought I was finished and he left himself wide open as he rushed in. I didn't think. I automatically crashed a perfect blow into his heart; I had delivered the perfect heart punch. The punch stopped him in his tracks. He gasped as his heart missed a beat. Before he could recover, I crashed a left and right straight into his heart.

His mouth came open and I attacked, left, right, left into his face, then a terrific punch onto his heart again. He was not hitting back now, he was trying to hold me, but I wasn't going to be denied.

I split both his eyes then I crashed a perfect straight right-hander to his nose, splitting it right across – and Jack was down. He staggered up. There was no count – just last one standing or one quits. And it was not going to be me.

I smashed him right round that ship's hold. He was down again, his face smashed to pieces. My hands were like raw bits of meat, my eye was pissing with blood and the pain in my back was excruciating. Jack was all but finished.

As he struggled to get up, I looked around at the men watching us fight. Jack's pals were pointing at him and laughing. They were laughing at this brave fighting man. I knew one more attack would finish Jack. He knew it as well. He was up, standing there, waiting for me to finish him off. I just couldn't do it. This was Jack's world: this life, the docks, dockers, drink, ships and the whole scenario. I couldn't take it away from him.

Instead of going in for the kill I wiped the blood from my eye and said, 'Jack, I give you best. I quit. I cannot carry on.'

I managed to get to my car and drive to the hospital. They stitched my eye up and gave me some X-rays. As I was passing blood, they kept me in overnight. The next morning I went straight home to bed.

The following morning I felt a little bit better. I drove down to Albert Dock to see how Jack was. This time the dockers shook my hand. They called me Jack, as Jack had said he had to fight Jack Dempsey for his money.

That day, as I got to the shore gang, Jack was sitting down. When he saw me, a broad grin went across his battered face. 'I hope you don't want a return,' he said.

'Not likely, Jack. You're too good for me.'

'Any time you want a job, come and see me,' he said.

I said okay and we shook hands. He then gave me a little leather pouch and told me to look at it when I got home.

When I got home I went to bed as I was still passing blood, but before I got into bed I looked in this leather pouch. There were two half-crowns. Me and Jack both knew I had beaten him, but I think it finished up right, as I didn't want to work down the docks anyhow and Jack still had the respect of all the dockers and his life.

It was time to start working for myself. Before long, I got a smelt going, running down beer barrels for their aluminium content. Me, Paul and Micky used to go to different pubs and pick them up, then take them to our smelt to melt them down.

One day me and Micky went to a club in Barking. We paid for a hundred barrels at £3 each, then loaded them onto the truck. As we went to drive away, this thick-set ginger bloke came up to us. 'Where are you going?' he said.

'What's it to do with you?' said Micky.

'Are you fucking deaf?' said the ginger bloke. 'Where are you going with my barrels?'

Micky said that we had already paid for them.

'Now you have got to pay me or else you ain't leaving this yard,' he went on.

Just then, two other blokes walked up to the motor. I winked at Micky and said, 'All right, mate. We will pay you. We don't want any trouble.'

This arrogant ginger bloke smiled and said, 'That's more like it, girls.'

I started the motor up and quickly pulled away, smashing the club gates down and running one of these blokes down. Then I pulled up. Two on two – I fancied that.

As they ran at us, I hit my man with a spanner right in the nose. He went down straight away, screaming blue murder.

Micky was fighting with this ginger geezer. As I grabbed ginger, Micky screamed, 'Keep out of this. One on one.'

Well, Micky gave this fellow a systematic hiding. He got up five times before he was knocked right out. That same fellow was to get brutally killed a while after this. His name was Davy Elmore. He was a real horrible man, a proper bully.

One day, me and Steven Savva, or Savva as everyone knew him, went looking for a yard out of the way a little bit, to start up another smelt. I saw a small goat farm advertised at Cold Norton in Essex, so me, Sav and Del Croxson went down there to look at it. As soon as I saw it I knew it was unsuitable, as it wasn't on flat ground. It was situated up on the side of a hill – ideal pasture land.

Not wishing to seem ignorant, I let the lady show us around. Now, Sav had always lived in Stepney. He knew nothing of country life. The woman showed us some big machines with long pipes attached to them. 'This is a proper licenced goat farm,' she said. 'Here is where we milk the goats. I don't know what you have in mind to do here?'

Being polite, I said, 'I thought I might keep some chickens here.'

'Oh, that would be okay,' she said. 'The council wouldn't object to you having chickens here at all.'

Savva, trying to look as though he knew a bit about livestock, joined in. 'Would these machines be all right to milk the chickens with?' he asked.

The woman looked at him as though he was mad, and said 'Milk chickens? You can't milk chickens, you fool. Now, you three time wasters get off of my farm, or I'll call the police.'

Needless to say, Savva was ribbed endlessly over his comments on milking chickens.

He showed his mettle on another occasion around the same time though. A pal of ours, I won't say his name, was dealing in drugs. But unbeknown to him, the police were watching him one day as he picked up some stuff and drove his new Mercedes to the long-term car park at Heathrow Airport. There he parked his car and flew straight out to Europe for a holiday at his holiday home. He figured his car and goods would be ultra-safe in Heathrow, continually under camera surveillance.

Unfortunately, the police at Limehouse knew there were some drugs in the Merc, so they went to Heathrow and took our friend's car back to Limehouse police station – at that time you had to search a suspect's house or car in their presence. Then they just waited for our friend to come home.

But we had a bit of help in those days. We got a phone call telling us all about our friend's predicament. The information cost us £1,000. So I rang and told our friend at his holiday home. He started panicking, but I told him to keep cool, asking if he had a spare set of keys to his car.

'Yes,' he said. 'They're in my house in Barking. If you contact my son, he'll get them for you.'

So that night me, the guy's son and Savva had a meet. I knew Limehouse police station quite well, and I knew the cars were kept in an open compound behind the nick. I was sure we could get the Mercedes. Anyhow, Savva supplied us with two stolen cars. I drove one and our friend's son the other. We drove down to Limehouse. I had Savva in the car with me.

Now, there's an alley on each side of Limehouse police station, which allows vehicles access: one lets them in, the other out. The yard and compound is directly behind the main building. This is where any vehicles under investigation are kept.

Savva walked straight through the alley into the compound. Once inside, he simply got into the Mercedes and drove it straight out, smashing through one of those barriers you usually see in car park entrances.

Immediately, I pulled one stolen car across one entrance and Billy did the same thing at the other entrance. Then we locked both the cars, thus blocking Limehouse police station right up and stopping any police cars from following the Mercedes. We brought the nick to a complete standstill.

Then Barry Dalton picked me and Bill up in his cab, just down the East India Dock Road – if anyone did take Barry's number and report it to the police, all Barry had to say was that as far as he was concerned it was just a normal fare.

Savva drove the car into a lock-up garage, took the drugs out and locked the garage door down. We met back at my house and gave our friend's son the drugs to hide. Limehouse police went potty, but there was nothing they could do. Our plan got our friend right off the hook that night.

Sad to say, much later, while I was in Wayland, the news had come through the prison grapevine that our friend was now in Brixton prison waiting to be extradited back to Australia for a big gold robbery they think he was involved in. I was in Wayland; Savvas was in Wandsworth; and our friend was in Brixton. So I suppose in a way justice had its way. It seems no matter how many years pass by it catches up to you. But I do think Savva showed plenty of bottle that night by what he did.

Shortly after this episode, our furnace blew up, so we had to pack up smelting beer barrels down. So me and Paul became partners in a night club called Antics at Stratford.

Soon after, I was at Barnet Horse Fair with Levi Smith. Now, Levi could really fight. Since Hughie Burton had died he was the best fighter of all the gypsies – as that other Levi, Levi Lee, had been all those years ago. Smith has never been beaten.

Then who should turn up but Ronnie Smith – Levi's cousin who is also a gypsy – and Roy Shaw. Ronnie is a thick-set man who takes everybody on for their money and then has to have someone like Roy Shaw around him to look after him in case he gets into any arguments. Ronnie is a very clever businessman and hates violence of any sort.

It was good to see Roy after all those years. He looked tremendous. It looked like he had been body-building all the time he was in the nick; he had put on loads of muscles. Me and Ronnie had previously fallen out over a real good-looking girl from Manor Park called Linda Driver. So we did not speak at all to start with.

Well, I stayed with Roy and Ronnie all day, laughing and drinking. And after a while, when the drink started to take hold, both me and Ronnie started talking, and happily we finished up the best of friends. Roy acted like a real gentleman all day. We all had a good drink and I went home happy after a good day out, with no violence at all. I later heard that Roy had got a few challenges from some gypsy fighting men after I had left, and sure enough he beat allcomers for good side-stakes. So Roy earned a good few quid that day.

Personally, I'd have given a year's wages to see Roy and Levi fight. I would hate to pick a winner. Donny Adams, who Micky had beaten at the horse fair, was also at Barnet that day, but he kept very quiet. Micky Gluckstead was in prison at this time doing a bit of bird for knocking two police officers out. So for once he wasn't involved in the action.

Well, about two weeks after seeing Roy at Barnet, my good friend Joe Carrington came into our club. He told us Roy Shaw was going to fight Donny Adams.

'Adams has no chance. He is a mug,' I said.

'I know,' Joe said, 'but it's being billed as the hardest men in Britain, and we are selling tickets like hot cakes. That fight will earn a fortune.' Then he gave me two tickets, so me and Ray Harman went along to Great Winkfield near Windsor to Billy Smart's winter headquarters, to see 'The Fight of the Century'.

Adams came out first, with his old pal Tommy Brown, then Roy came out to the music of Gary Glitter: 'Do You Wanna Be In My Gang?' I was at ringside. I'd tried to get a bet on Roy, but no one would have it. Some drunk got in the ring and challenged the winner. Adams and Shaw threw him out together. The bell rung. Roy threw one punch and Adams went down. Roy hit him on the floor but there was no need; as I said, he was a real mug that people thought was hard. Lots of people paid hard-earned money to watch a forgone conclusion. It was a right rip-off.

Donny Adams did have one more prizefight – with Steve 'Columbo' Richards. Richards was no more than a middleweight fighter, but he knocked Donny out in the first round. So Adams' prizefighting record reads: two fights, two knockouts – both in the first round. Not very impressive, is it? Donny always trained himself to perfection. A very strong man but unfortunately he had a glass jaw.

Roy's handlers were very clever. All of his opponents were very strong, powerful brawlers who came to fight. What they didn't want or need was a fancy Dan boxer, one who would just keep away for a few rounds. By this time Roy must have been 40 years old – very strong and not old, but against a 25-year-old skilful boxer, I think Roy would have found it difficult to win.

Also, people went to prizefights to see a real battle. This suited Roy as he was earning a fortune by doing what he did best: having proper tear-ups. Roy was a good showman. He used to come into the ring like a madman, and Roy's gang all said if anyone beat him he would kill them afterwards.

Anyone who had plenty of boxing experience was bypassed, not by Roy I might add but by his advisers. After the Adams fight Roy and his manager Joe Carrington were looking for opponents – easy money, preferably someone who had a big reputation but had no experience in a boxing ring. Roy had done a fair bit of boxing so he would have the advantage – a pair of boxing gloves to a street fighter, is like swimming with your clothes on, something not many of us experience.

Well, first Roy and Joe went to Barking and challenged Davy Elmore, the ginger bully who had tried to charge us for the aluminium barrels, who Micky had also sorted out. Davy said, 'Roy, I will fight you right now in the car park, but I have never been in a boxing ring or even had a pair of boxing gloves on – never mind worn a gum shield. But I will fight you for what you like on the cobbles.' Joe was having none of it.

The next place they went to was Twilights in Stratford Broadway. Micky was now out of prison and in there having a good drink, when Joe walked in with Roy. Joe asked Micky if he would fight Roy for £2,000.

'£2,000?' Micky exclaimed. 'I haven't got two bob.'

Alan Sewall stepped up. 'I will back you, Mick,' he said.

'Come on then, outside,' said Micky.

But Joe said no, at Seven Kings Hotel. Micky asked when and Joe told him in three weeks' time, on Tuesday at 8 pm. Micky agreed.

Micky had never even spent half an hour in a gym. He was always in the pub drinking. Still he thought he would beat Roy easily.

The fight was postponed for a week due to police presence at the Seven Kings Hotel. Eventually it took place at Dagenham working men's club. The place was packed. A big hall upstairs was full, with a boxing ring in the middle. When Micky was in the dressing room, Joe Lazarus came in and said, 'Mick, there are a few police in the audience. You will have to wear these gloves.'

'Okay, I don't mind,' said Micky.

'One more thing, Mick,' said Joe. 'We have heard you fight dirty. If you start that game, Roy will tear your head off.'

Micky replied, 'Tell that Roy if he wants it that way I will get in the ring and take these fucking gloves off, and, see this finger? I will stick it in his eye and pull his eyeball out of his fucking head.'

A few minutes later Joe came back into the dressing room. 'Mick, the place is crawling with old bill so keep it cool,' he said.

'All right, as long as that Roy does.'

'Bring on the lions,' shouted Nosher Powell.

Micky was first into the ring. One person walked into the ring with him, carrying a bottle of lemonade. Micky had ill-fitting gloves on with no bandages on his hands, no gum shield and a pair of trainers, a shirt and vest which he had borrowed. It was the first time Micky had stepped into a boxing ring.

The lights went off and a spotlight came on directed towards Roy.

He ran into the ring, with the music of Gary Glitter blaring out. Roy looked twice as big as Micky. Roy was about 15½ stone and Micky was only about 12½ and a half. Roy was jumping around the ring like a maniac, stirring the crowed up. He was some sort of showman, that Roy.

Micky's corner man said, 'Micky, I'm glad you're fighting him and not me,' and jumped out of the ring leaving Micky on his own. Micky just looked at Roy and laughed. They were just having a prizefight with gloves on, that's all right, thought Micky.

The ref called them to the centre of the ring. Micky was still laughing. Then it was show time – the bell rang. For round one, Micky and Roy got to the centre of the ring and stood toe to toe for three minutes. Trading good, fast, terrific shots to the body and head, they were like two pit bulls fighting, neither giving an inch. This action went on for the first three rounds.

Although they both slowed down after the first round, Joe and all Roy's mates were looking worried. With all the advantages in Roy's favour, he still couldn't knock Micky over. Micky never even had a corner man and was just drinking lemonade between rounds. They were both punched out.

Now round four started. Micky was laying on the ropes. He was no boxer. He didn't know how to pace himself. Roy was punching him but just could not seem to hurt him. Micky even drunk some lemonade during the round which someone had given him from the crowd.

Round five, Roy could hardly stand but was still trying to punch. Micky was just standing there exhausted but laughing at Roy's punches. Between rounds five and six, neither of them could hardly breathe. It was a long break.

'Come on,' said Micky Cahill to the timekeeper, one of Roy's pals.

'Ring that fucking bell,' he went on. 'I've got £1,500 on Gluckstead.'

Round six, Roy was nearly dropping with exhaustion, but Micky was still standing. Roy was nearly finished. Micky was taking no notice of Roy's punches, he was just waiting for him to collapse. Micky got a towel from his corner and wiped his forehead halfway through the round. The thing was Micky wasn't fighting back, just standing there breathless.

The ref suddenly stopped the fight to save more embarrassment, or so I thought, to both fighters. Micky thought he had won the fight, as Roy was finished also, but when he went to get his money, the promoter said, 'What money? You lost.'

'How did I lose?' Micky replied. 'I never even went down. A prizefight is the last one standing.'

The promoter told Micky that this was a boxing match and Mickey's corner had thrown in the towel.

'I never had anyone in my fucking corner,' Micky said, 'So how could they have thrown the towel in? I want my fucking money.'

'Sorry, Roy's taken it.'

Micky asked where he was. The promoter told him he was down the Epping Forest Country Club celebrating. Micky went straight down there, and asked the doormen, 'Is Roy Shaw in there?' Yes, they said, he was celebrating after just winning a prizefight. Micky asked them to get Roy for him.

As Roy came out, he was at least ten handed.

'Roy, you haven't beat me yet. Let's finish it out here now,' Micky said.

'Do me a favour,' said Roy, then he laughed and gave him a handful of notes, adding, 'Here you are, Mick. I don't really think any of us won.'

Micky went into the club for a drink, and a few of Roy's pals gave

Micky money as well. He got £3,000 altogether, so he was satisfied.

Both Roy and Micky grossly underestimated each other. But that first round of pure warfare is still spoken about in the East End of London to this day. In his book, Roy said he thinks Micky Gluckstead is a mongrel. Well, he found out that that particular mongrel bit like a pit bull.

After Micky's fight, Roy had a one-round win over a fellow called Terry Hollingsworth. Frank Warren was ringside with his cousin, Lennie Mclean. Lennie had never done any boxing. He was just another hard boy from the East End.

After watching the Roy Shaw and Hollingsworth pantomime, Lennie jumped into the ring and challenged Roy to fight him for £20,000. Roy accepted. Micky had already beaten Lennie in a bare-knuckle brawl in a pub at Hoxton, but Lennie was a hardnut who would have a go at anybody. What he didn't realise was it is a different game in the boxing ring.

The fight was held at a night club in Streatham called Sinatras. It was a full house, with many stars in the crowd as well as villains. The Hollywood actor Gene Hackman sat ringside with his entourage.

At the first bell, Mclean and Shaw went toe to toe in the centre of the ring as Shaw and Micky had done previously. At the end of the first round, Lennie was out of breath. He had never been in a boxing ring before – he had shot his bolt. He was completely knackered. Round two saw Lennie just standing in the corner, too exhausted to fight back, but Roy could not hurt him. He stood in the corner waving Roy onto him, but as hard as he tried he could not put him down.

Round three, Lennie was still standing in the corner, not hitting back at all by now. Roy gestured to the ref to stop the fight as Lennie was not defending himself, but he had not gone down either. So the ref stopped the fight. No one was more pleased in the hall then Lennie Mclean to get pulled out of there. I think Roy had acted like a gentleman to just stop hitting Lennie. In the next fight, Lennie never showed Roy the same courtesy.

After that Roy fought a few more pub fighters. Lennie in the meantime started training for boxing. He got Kevin Finnegan, a very good professional boxer, to train him. Finnegan knew the boxing game backwards; he was a world-class fighter. He really trained Lennie – pushing him to the limit, sparring with him daily, teaching him all the tricks a boxer knows, especially how to pace yourself and bandage your hands in the correct way, and how to use a gum shield. All these things Lennie had never used before.

And where was Roy? He was living off the fat of the land, drinking more than he should, getting soft. When the time was right, Lennie challenged Roy to a return match, for big money. Roy accepted immediately. He thought what he had done before he could do again, but Lennie was a different man now. Now he was a well-trained fighting machine. And a much younger fighting machine at that.

The return fight took place in Sinatras as before. Again the venue was packed. The atmosphere was electric. I was ringside. The old fighter Larry Gains had a special table right at the front near the ring apron – he was the guest of honour. Lennie came in first, already gloved up, which I thought was strange. Fighters always glove up in the ring.

Roy left Lennie in the ring for ten minutes, but this did not seem to upset Lennie at all. Roy came into the ring to the same roaring Gary Glitter song, the crowd going mad.

The bell rang for the first round. Roy rushed out as usual, but just one clubbing punch from Lennie knocked Roy right across the ring and through the ropes. He seemed to take off and landed slap bang on top of Larry Gains' table. That was the hardest I have ever seen anyone get hit in the ring. It was as though Lennie had hit Roy with a sledgehammer.

Roy's shocked seconds scurried him back into the ring all but unconscious. Lennie started to kick Roy; he was frightened Roy would get up and have a go back. Roy was helpless, taking a kicking in the ring. Joe Carrington jumped into the ring, pushed Lennie away from Roy, and Joe squared up to Lennie.

'No, I don't want to fight you,' said Mclean. He was frightened of Joe, I could tell that.

The official rung the bell to end the round, to stop the trouble. Roy's seconds got him into the corner and tried to fetch him round as best they could, but in reality that one punch had knocked the life out of Roy. The bell rang for round two. Roy gamely staggered out, Mclean threw one more clubbing blow to Roy's head and Roy was gone. The ref could have counted to a hundred, but he just said, 'All over.'

Lennie jumped straight out of the ring and ran back to his dressing room.

Mclean never punched as hard as he did that night again, and I don't think anyone in the country could have knocked Roy Shaw out twice with just two punches. Roy could take a punch. Now Lennie was prizefighting's new champion, so it was his turn to earn as much money as possible trying to get the easiest opponents available.

Micky challenged Lennie to a prizefight in the ring or on the cobbles, on a winner-take-all basis, but Lennie declined the challenge.

ROUND 4

BULLDOG PROMOTIONS

Just after this I started Bulldog Promotions, staging kick-fighting and prizefighting in partnership with a man called Terry Butwell. A few years later, his young son Terry became kick-fighting champion of the world at five different weights.

Me and Terry staged 27 tournaments, but I think the saddest sight I ever saw in prizefighting was when arguably the greatest fighter ever to come from Britain, Scotsman Ken Buchanan, who had all but beaten Roberto Duran, resorted to prizefighting for a pittance.

Duran had fouled him with a low blow. Then when Buchanan could no longer continue, the Americans gave the fight to Duran, even though he was losing by a mile at that point and it was very near to the end of the fight. Buchanan had been robbed and Duran knew it. He would never fight Buchanan again.

Buchanan had previously beaten Ismael Laguna, an all-time great lightweight, to win the Championship of the World, in Puerto

Rico, Luguna's back yard. Just what a great feat this was cannot be overestimated. One must think of what Terry Downes, another world champion, said: 'In America, you have to knock the guy out to get a draw.'

Have no doubt in your mind, Buchanan was an all-time great fighter, but with bad investments he had gone broke and came down to London prizefighting to get a bit of money. He always won – as a matter of fact he toyed with and carried his opponents to make them look good – but a man of that calibre shouldn't have been prizefighting in any case.

When Ken Buchanan first came down to London, he fought a fellow at Ilford Palais. Ken carried this fellow for a few rounds, then put him away. Ken got a measly £1,500 for that fight. Then he boxed a good south Londoner by the name of Jimmy Revie at York Hall. Ken came into the ring to the sound of bagpipes. Same procedure – after a few rounds Jimmy was asleep.

An old pal from school days, Alan Williams, had the Elm Park Hotel back then, with his lovely wife Sylvia. As Ken had nowhere to live, Alan let him live in a room at the hotel, as Ken was on the floor – skint. Alan never charged him one penny rent. Ken had literally hundreds of boxing video tapes and we all passed many a happy night watching them. He must have relived the Duran fight a thousand times.

After the Revie fight, Ken had £4,000 altogether. So with Alan's help they got in touch with the brewery and Ken invested his money and took over the Church Elms pub in Dagenham. Before Ken took over as licensee, my old pal Frank Jackson was the governor there with his wife Franny. Frankie's a giant of a man, an ex-boxer himself.

Well, me and Micky had our own good idea to earn a few quid at Frank's new pub. I went and got films of Roy Shaw, Lennie Mclean,

BULLDOG PROMOTIONS

Micky Gluckstead, Donny Adams, plus all the other prizefighters I could lay my hands on, then I got them all put onto one tape. We put a few posters up advertising a film night of prizefighting. Most people then had never seen a prizefight. They imagined it was bare-fisted fighting, they didn't realise that both contestants wore boxing gloves.

We charged a £5 entrance fee. The deal was, me and Micky had the door money and Frank had the bar. Then we hired a big screen and video for the show that day. We had the screen and video delivered to the pub. Then we took the film of the fights there, so we were all set to go the following evening.

The next night, 350 people crammed into the hall of the Church Elms pub. We let everyone start drinking early, so Frank could take a few quid. Then at 9 pm we dimmed the lights and started the film. Everyone was waiting for this. The air was full of expectancy. The show began.

Then, halfway through the first round of Roy Shaw v Mad Mullin the Irishman, I heard 'Da Da-Da Da-Da, Da …' It was the theme tune from *Coronation Street*. I was dumbfounded. So was Micky.

Everyone started shouting. I put the lights on. I asked Frank what was happening. Well, Franny had only taped *Coronation Street* over our tape by mistake, but worse than that she had just left the video to keep taping, whilst she was working in the pub downstairs. So the tape had all the previous night's programmes on it.

It was so embarrassing. Everyone was hollering and hooting. I stood up and said, 'I'm sorry about this, but I will just go and get a copy tape.' I just said that. We had no copy tape. So me and Micky said, 'We won't be long,' and left the pub as fast as we could. No one got any of their money back. We had already spent it. But a couple of Frank's punters stole the screen and video equipment. We didn't care. It didn't belong to us and we had signed up for it in a wrong name.

Anyhow, Frank said one or two of his customers were looking for us for their money back, but they couldn't have looked very hard as we never hid ourselves. Me and Micky earned a nice week's wages each, although it was very embarrassing at the time.

In the early days of Bulldog Promotions, Barry Dalton had stabbed Solly Francis in the stomach at a pub in Woolwich, almost killing him. Solly was a big fellow, so Lennie decided to fight him. Solly had still not got over his operation, so Lennie said he would take it easy with Solly. He said it would be easy money for the both of them, so Solly agreed.

But nothing had changed. Once they were in the ring it went off for real. Lenny set about Solly. Then they decided it was time for a third fight for Lennie with Roy Shaw. This fight was a guaranteed sell-out.

It was billed as the 'Close Encounter of the Third Kind', after the Steven Spielberg film which was out then. It was a promotion at the Rainbow Rooms in Finsbury Park.

This time Roy was in the ring first, waiting for Lennie, but Roy did not look his old self. He had put on a bit of weight and his knee was bandaged up. Then Lennie came into the ring to the record 'Daddy Cool'. He paused and looked at Roy before he got into the ring. I noticed that Roy looked away; perhaps the memory of their last encounter was on his mind, or perhaps, as he said in his book, he had taken too much ginseng – I don't really know.

As the bell went for round one, Roy got close to Lennie, but he was slapping with the inside of his gloves, fighting like a complete mug or a man on drugs. Lennie's boxing tuition from Kevin Finnegan paid dividends that night. He hit Roy with a right hook, and as Roy staggered back, Lenny followed him. Left, right, left, right

– every single punch was on target, hitting Roy in the head. But Roy didn't go down immediately.

Lenny must have hit him at least 30 times before he went down. Not one punch, like in their previous encounter. Funny, it took one of Lennie's punches to knock Roy out when he was on top of his game in the previous fight, but in the rematch when Roy, in my opinion, was half the man he had been, it took 30 punches.

When Roy was lying on the floor, Mclean was up on the ropes shouting, 'Who's the Guv'nor now, then?' And all the crowd was shouting out Lennie's name. As we left the Rainbow Rooms to get to our car, I saw Lennie and two other fellows talking. Then out came Joe Carrington and Roy Shaw. Roy was carrying a big sports bag. Lennie and Roy never even looked at each other.

Lennie may have knocked Roy out in their third meeting, but the real Roy Shaw wasn't there at all. Lennie only beat a shadow of the real man. I think Roy's estimation of events, taking too much ginseng, is absolutely right. Roy was fighting like he was in a dream. After his third fight with Roy, Johnny Waldron, who was a much lighter man than Mclean, knocked Mclean spark out twice – on both occasions in the first round.

Cliff Fields knocked him out twice and Kevin Ruddock beat him on points, but Lennie stopped that other good fighter from the East End, Ron Redrup. Mclean wouldn't fight Micky, and there was not enough money in it for Micky to fight anyone else – Mclean was the only one who could draw big crowds. He was the only prizefighter being promoted properly.

Some time after Lennie defeated Roy Shaw for the second time, Roy made a comeback. He had kept himself to himself and had started to look after himself properly, and trained his body to perfection. He had honed himself once more into a fine fighting machine. He had taken a couple of warm-up fights, against stiff opposition, and had come through with flying colours. The real Roy Shaw was back.

Lennie Mclean was off the scene and the champion (Guvnor) was the gypsy champion Harry 'The Buck' Starbuck. Roy issued a big-money challenge to Harry to fight him, which Harry had accepted. The Buck had never lost a fight and, as he was both bigger and younger than Roy, he would be a hot favourite to win. But I had seen Roy's two comeback fights and I was sure Roy would win. I didn't think any prizefighter in the world could beat Roy Shaw now.

Our plan was to go to the fight and bet all our money on Roy. I'd seen Roy on the day of the fight at Joe Carrington's house, and he looked superbly fit and confident. This fight was to be held at Dartford Football Stadium, an open- air event. The place was full of Starbuck's supporters, there was a licensed bookmaker there and the gypsies were having fortunes on Starbuck. He was 2–1 on to win. We punted about and managed to get odds of 3–1 against Roy, so we put £10,000 on Roy. That was all the money we had. If I'd had a million pounds, I would have put it on Roy.

The first fight on the bill was an old mate, Micky May, fighting a fellow called Vernon Shaw. Micky unfortunately got knocked out that night. After a couple more fights it was Roy's turn.

He entered the ring with little applause. Then 'the new Guv'nor', Starbuck, arrived to a massive roar. The noise was deafening. You could hardly hear the bell sound for the first round

As it did, Roy sprung into action. He was like a cat. He was so fast that he smashed 'The Buck' into complete oblivion. Inside one and a half minutes of the first round, it was all over. Roy had defied all the odds. He was 'the Guv'nor' once more.

We picked up our money: £40,000. Micky was all excited. He

thought another money spinner now could be him to have a return with Roy – but it wasn't to be. Roy had another couple of fights against two good men, then retired as the undefeated champion.

I still could not get Micky any big-money fights on our promotions, because as soon as his name was mentioned no one would fight him.

Years before, someone who was about to become a big name had found out what it felt like to be unpopular throughout the East End. It all happened at Wag's gym. Wag fetched an Austrian fellow to the gym and let him live there. He was like a father to him. This Austrian chap got really massive. His arms were huge and he became Mr Universe. When I first knew him he couldn't even speak English. But he went to America and became a huge film star by the name of Arnold Schwarzenegger.

When Arnold used to train his biceps, it looked like his skin would tear open. I thought, 'If he hit anyone he would kill them.'

When Arnold had first come to live with Wag he was unknown. A big lad but still unknown. His main sport was curling, on the ice. But he took to body-building like a fish does to water.

His muscle gains were tremendous and after coming second in the National Amateur Body Building Association (NABBA) competition, he won it the following year. Wag Bennet was a powerhouse and him and his great rival from Forest Gate Bill Stevens, who also had a gymnasium, were the first two men in this country to bench press 500lb. When you consider these two powerful men only trained on weights, no special machines either, it makes you realise just how strong they were.

At the judging of Mr Universe held at the Royal Hotel, Russell Square, only NABBA photographs were allowed. Anyhow, some

French fellow kept taking photos after being warned twice. Bill Stevens grabbed this man, who was a previous Mr Universe winner himself, so he was very large and strong, but Billy just grabbed him easily and manhandled him out.

At the Miss Britain judging, which was held on the same day at the same venue, Arnold was a guest judge. Kathleen Winstanley from Wigan easily won it – she far outshone her rivals.

Bill Stevens' real name was Threadwell. He had a few florist shops in the East End. One day at a cemetery in Manor Park he asked a worker if he could have all the old wreath steel frames, which were being dumped anyhow. This fellow said, 'Yes, just give me a drink.' So Bill loaded up these frames and gave this cemetery worker £50. The frames were only rubbish to the cemetery.

Anyhow when he was driving out of the cemetery, a security man stopped him at the gate. He asked Bill where the frames came from. Bill told him he had paid the worker for them. They got the man who Bill had paid for the frames, who promptly denied any knowledge of the transaction, so Bill got arrested for stealing these unwanted frames.

As usual the newspapers reported it all wrong, calling Bill a graverobber etc. and saying he had stolen flowers off of the graves to sell in his shop. Bill went to court and got acquitted. But he never got over his ordeal and died shortly afterwards of cancer. The worry of it all and the shame and indignity the newspapers had caused had started off the dreaded complaint and now Bill lies next to my Uncle Jimmy in Manor Park cemetery.

Wag had taken Arnold under his wing and Arnold owes everything he is to Wag, because Wag picked him from obscurity.

Let's hope when he's sitting alone sometimes he realises what he owes to Mr Wag Bennet. I don't know if he's altered now, but in the

60s Arnold Schwarzenegger didn't care who he trod on to get on in life. A very selfish individual. I think everyone was pleased to see the back of him when he finally went to America, especially Wag. Arnold proved to me that size doesn't matter, it's what's in your heart that counts.

I still had the club Antics going with Paul. At this time we had Johnny Cooney, a real hard man and a thorough gent with it, running our door at Antics. We were having a drink in there one night, when John called me down to the main door. He said some people said they knew us and wanted to come in without paying.

When I got there, there were two blokes who I never knew, so I said they would have to pay. These two looked drunk, so I didn't really want them in the club. Anyhow, they started to get nasty, saying they knew the owner Paul, not me, the hired help. I said, 'Well, when Paul's here you can get in free, but if I am here you pay.'

One of these fellows said, 'Do you know who I am? Shortly, you'll be paying us to come in here.' Then he pulled a blade out of his pocket. I had a sixth sense that this was going to happen. I was ready for it. I belted him straight on the jaw, knocking him out. His mate jumped on my back. Micky smashed him in the back of his head with his fist, knocking him off of me. Then Micky tore into him with a left, right, left combination. That finished him off. We just left them laying there.

The next day we had a phone call: what they were going to do. They did nothing. Them two people were Franky Salmon from Barking, whom I had knocked out, and Paul Edmonds from Canning Town, who Micky had done.

After this, Frank Salmon got a long stretch for demanding

protection money from clubs and Paul Edmonds got shot dead in the Sultan pub in Plaistow. Tony Argent got a life sentence for this killing. But on the whole, except from one or two little bits of trouble, we were doing quite well.

ROUND 5

DAMSELS IN DISTRESS

Whilst I was away Micky got himself into some real serious trouble. There was a motor dealer in Stratford – a short, fat fellow, very flash, always wearing loads of gold. He was into debt collecting, property development, in fact anything which earned money. He drove a Rolls Royce, had a big fortress-like house, and always had at least two minders with him. I won't say his real name, as I don't want to embarrass his wife, so we'll just call him Tim and his wife Tina.

This fellow thought he was the King of England. He thought he could buy everyone and everything and if you crossed him, his minders would beat you up. A lady traffic warden kept sticking tickets on his cars outside his car site. Every day he would argue with her, a big blonde lady, but he was taking liberties. It was a main road site with no parking, but he just ignored it, giving the warden no option but to give him tickets.

What this bully did was to get a plastic bucket with a screw-on lid, and him and his cronies pissed and shit in it till it was full – they even ejaculated in it. Then one morning as the warden was sticking a ticket onto one of his cars, one of his men ran up behind her and put the bucket, with its contents, over her head and banged the top of it.

Well, she screamed: the mess was up her nose, in her mouth, in her hair, everywhere. An ambulance came and the woman was taken to hospital to get cleaned up. Her nerves were shattered after that it completely ruined her confidence. She was never the same woman again. Then, one day, in a fit of depression she killed herself. She left a husband, a very inoffensive, quiet man who wouldn't say boo to a mouse, and three lovely children. When the police interviewed Tim about the incident he denied all knowledge.

Well Micky, had just come out of prison when she died. He was related to Vera, the poor woman who had killed herself. So he rang the car dealer's site up.

'What's been going on, Tim?' Micky said, as he knew Tim personally – he had collected a few debts for him in the past.

'It's got fuck all to do with you, Micky,' he said. 'You're only a plastic gangster, so keep your fucking nose out of it. It's over your head.'

'Listen to me,' Micky said. 'That woman has left three children. I want £10,000 off of you for them. You killed her so they're entitled to it.'

'That seems fair enough, Mick,' Tim said. 'I don't mind paying for the children's future. Come over and I'll give you a cheque right now.'

When Micky got to the site, they shook hands and Tim told him to come into the office. As Micky walked in, one fellow squirted him with ammonia and three others gave him a fearful beating. It was an ambush. Micky was put on a life-support machine and was blinded in one eye. When the police asked Micky who had done it, he told them he had been mugged and he did not know who they were. As Micky started to get better he got a visit from Tim. He had two heavies with him.

'There you are, Mick. Perhaps now you will mind your own fucking business. No one tells me what to do.'

'Okay, we'll leave it at that. I've had enough,' said Mick.

Well, it was two months before Micky felt okay. Then, one by one, he got the people who had attacked him. He always managed to get them when they were alone and beat them terrible with his hands. Then he would disappear. He wasn't at any of his local haunts, so they could never find him to set about him or get their revenge. He got all of them except the main man, Tim, who would not leave his house; he had managers in all of his businesses. We got to him in the end and got £20,000 out of him. Micky gave all the money to Vera's husband to help fetch up the children, so it was a job well done.

She wasn't the first or last innocent woman to suffer because of a big bully. A fellow called Vic Bellamy came to see me one day. He said, 'Dan, I know a fellow whose just been made bankrupt. He's still got a few quid owing to him from his business deals, but if any money goes into his business account he will lose it.

'If you know anyone who can accept a £50,000 cheque into their account, this fellow will get the cheque made out in your man's name, and when it's cashed, you can return £35,000 to my man. So I'll have £5,000, you'll have £5,000 and the fellow who cashes the cheque will have £5,000.'

'Don't worry, Vic. I will find somebody,' I said. So I rang an accountant who knows all the moves. I explained the deal to him and he said, 'Give me a week.'

Within the week we had found a candidate, who was okay with everyone. So we got the cheque made out to a Mr B Berge. The accountant said we should wait ten days for the cheque to clear, because if we had it specialled it would only draw attention.

I phoned the accountant after a week. He said everything was on course.

But unbeknown to us, Mr Berge had financial problems himself, and had owed some £4,000, for some time – and the people were getting impatient for their money. He intended to pay his debt with the money he got from our deal. In the meantime, he had a visit from Big Lonnie and some massive body-builder. Mr Berger's debtors had employed Lonnie and his mate as debt collectors on a 10 per cent basis.

Mr Berge invited them into his house to try and explain the situation, but Lonnie assumed Mr Berge was either messing them about, or not going to pay at all, and in his own words, 'No one fucks with Big Lonnie.' Mr Berge said he had no money at all at the present time, but was expecting some in a few days, and he could have that. Lonnie went potty and said, 'Right, I want that money tomorrow. You find it somewhere. In the meantime we'll give you something to think about, and this is only a taste of what you'll get if you don't pay up.'

He grabbed Mr Berge and bent him over a table. Then he pulled his trousers and pants down whilst his pal held him. Lonnie then pushed a stick of Ralgex up his bottom. The pain must have been excruciating. All this was done in front of his wife. When she tried to stop them, Lonnie's pal said, 'Sit down or we'll do the same to you.' Lonnie shoved this stick of Ralgex in and out of Mr Berge's bottom, as Mr Berge screamed in terror and pain.

Sid phoned me up and told me what had happened. Me and Mick drove down to Mr Berge's house as quick as we could. Sid was supposed to come with us, but he never turned up. I didn't really expect him to, as Sid hates any sort of violence. We eventually found Mr Berge's house. It was at a lovely place called Denham in Buckinghamshire.

When we got there, Mr Berge was in bed. His wife was still in a state of shock – she was 35 years old, but she looked 60, and looked like she had been crying for a week. 'Don't worry,' I said. 'I will see Lonnie for you. I've got his phone number on me.' She gave a sigh of relief. I rang straight away, in front of her, so she could hear my conversation and it would take a load off her mind.

When the phone was answered the other end, I said, 'Could I speak to Lonnie, please?'

'Speaking,' said a big bear's breath.

'Hello, Lonnie, Danny Wollard here.'

'What can I do for you?' he said.

'No, Lon, it's what I can do for you. I am at Mr Berge's house in Denham, and I have picked some money up. Mine and yours.'

'Lovely,' he said.

'I'll meet you at my office at 10 am in the morning.'

'Great. I'll be there.'

So I said to Ruth, Mr Berge's wife, 'Tell your husband that there'll be no more trouble from Lonnie. I have got him off your back. I'll clear it up. I will do all the dealings with Lonnie in the future. In any case, our cheque will be clear in a couple of days so there's no problem.'

Next morning at 9.30, me and Micky are down the office waiting for Len. At exactly 10 am the doorbell rang. It was Lonnie and his big mate. They were very intimidating, like a pair of giants. This other fellow wasn't as tall as Lonnie but was extremely broad.

We sat round a table. 'Lon,' I said, 'I have got an ongoing deal with Mr Berge, and I have got to collect some money in two days' time off of him.'

'Yes, but that doesn't concern me,' he said. 'You said you have got money, so I want it.'

I gave him a piece of paper. Written on it was 'IOU £4,000 signed D Woollard.'

'What's this? A fucking joke?' he said.

'No, Lon,' I said, 'my credit's good everywhere. I'll give you your money in two days' time once we've been paid.'

This other geezer jumped up and said, 'Lon, they think we're mugs.'

I knew it was going to go right off, so I snatched a squeezy container from my pocket and squirted this big fellow with ammonia straight in this face. He reeled back and I was on him, left, right, left, Down he went, his face smothered in blood.

Lonnie was on his feet, bellowing and screaming. Micky hit him straight on the jaw. He staggered back. He nearly went down, but he managed to throw a couple of wild swings back at Micky, then tried to grab him to stop Micky hitting him, but I could see Lonnie was in trouble. He was gasping for breath. I thought he was going to die.

I stopped Micky from hitting him. I thought perhaps it was the ammonia fumes affecting him. I got him a chair, and opened the front door for him, to let some air in. After a while he could breathe again. I roughly pulled his mate up. He could hardly see. 'Lonnie, you should go somewhere about your chest,' I said.

'No, Dan, I've had the flu and it's left me short of breath, that's all.'

'Lon, there really was no need for all this. I'll give you your money in two days' time.' Then Lonnie and his pal left. His pal was taking Lonnie to hospital.

I phoned Ruth. 'I've seen Lonnie and co. It's all sorted out,' I said.

'Dan, I have some bad news,' she said. 'My husband hung himself last night in our garage. I found him this morning.'

DAMSELS IN DISTRESS

I was flabbergasted. Whether it was fear of Lonnie and his mate coming back or the humiliation of what they had done to him in front of his wife, we'll never know, but he was dead. Our £50,000 had been paid into his account and when he had died our money had gone into the estate. He'd left quite a few debts as it turned out, and our money was taken up to clear them.

I phoned big Lonnie up, and told him what had happened. Him and his mate made themselves scarce for a little while after this episode. Lonnie was then diagnosed as having cancer, and he died. I didn't really mind Lonnie, but he was a terrible bully and he bullied Mr Berge to death, him and his pal. I told Vic Bellamy about what had happened. He took the news well. He just said, 'We'll make it up on another deal.'

ROUND 6

TOP DOLLAR
DOGS

At this time I was into pit bull fighting in a big way. I bought one of the first pit bulls ever to come to Britain. We used to fight him mainly up north against Staffordshire bull terriers – until the penny dropped. Pit bulls are far superior to any other fighting dog in the world. Soon they wouldn't fight us any more, so we used to fight anyone who was game enough to take us on with any dog.

We had a dog fight arranged at the Elm Park Hotel. There was me, Del Croxson and Paul. Micky wouldn't come.

The bloke that owned the dog turned up with his girlfriend plus about 20 other men. The girl was a real looker – about 22, blonde hair, short white mini-skirt and bright pink tight T-shirt showing every curve. Everybody was drinking and taking loads of cocaine, and as the dogs were fighting this girl was going crazy, leaning right into the pit. It was really turning her on. After about 40 minutes we were victorious. We won £1,200, a good day's work, so we all stayed there drinking and snorting cocaine.

The general opinion of dog fighting is that it is a cruel and barbaric sport, with two dogs being made to tear each other to pieces by unfeeling people who deserve to be horsewhipped themselves. But the reality is that dog fighting is the fairest sport in the world, covered by strict rules that are hundreds of years old and carefully adhered to.

The dogs are fought in a pit approximately 14 foot square, so there's plenty of room for them both to manoeuvre. They are fought under strict Cajun rules, which means both dogs have a corner each. They are both released at the same time. When one of the dogs turns his head away from the heat of the battle, the referee calls a 'turn', which means as soon as both dogs are out of holds, the handlers pick their dogs up and the one which has turned his head has to go and grab hold of his opponent.

After both dogs have been refreshed and had a 30-second break, if the handler pushes his dog towards his opponent's corner he is disqualified immediately. The dog has to cross the pit and grab his opponent of his own free will, with no enticement at all, within ten seconds. Once the dog has done this, the fight carries on. When one dog gets hold of another, this is known as a 'scratch'. That's where the old saying, 'coming up to scratch', comes from.

After the first scratch, each time both dogs are out of holds, they're picked up and refreshed, the same as what happened on the first scratch. They then have turns each at scratching. So each dog has plenty of opportunities to pack up. Most dog fighters, if their dog is getting a real hiding, will pack up the battle for him.

Dogs are fought weight for weight. When the contracts are drawn up, a stipulation is made with it – and if a dog is a few ounces over, the fight will not go on and the offending side has to pay a forfeit, usually half the amount the dogs are fighting for. This is paid to a neutral third party. Unless, of course, a match is made at 'catch weight'. Then there is no weight limitation.

Before pit bulls were put on the dangerous-dogs list, and people were stopped from owning them, lots of people fought their dogs, and most were good people, proper characters. There was one fellow who was on rescue manoeuvres and a flare blew his eye out. He had a solid gold eye made, and was known as 'Gold Eye'.

In the shady world of dog fighting, no one uses their real name on contracts or letters as it is an illegal activity. You are always referred to by a chosen pseudonym. Mine was 'Out', short for 'Outlaw'; Micky's was 'Bi', as everyone knew he was game as a beagle; Paul's was 'Blue', after the legendary old fighting dog from Scotland, the Blue Paul. There was also 'Big Jeff', 'John the Dog', 'Dirty Harry', to name but a few.

Dirty Harry's father was a tattooist in Piccadilly. He reckons he earned most money by cutting fellows down the face with a razor. They thought it made them look hard. I didn't believe him, so one night I went to his tattoo parlour and watched. Sure enough, some of his clients wanted a 'chiv mark'.

The south London boys all clubbed together and sent £8,000 out to a dealer in America for a dog. They had all heard of this dealer's exploits in the dog fighter's bible the *Sporting Dog Journal* and thought he would sell them a good dog. This dog was supposed to be a real killer.

Well, the dog arrived at the quarantine kennels in due course. The kennel's bill added another £2,000 onto the total cost, but at long last they had this fine example of a pit bull home. After about a week, me and two East End lads went to where this dog was kennelled to have a look at him.

'Have you gave him a roll yet?' I said to Big Jeff. That's not a fight, just a little dust up with another dog, to see his worth. Just a bit of a test – the equivalent of a professional boxer sparring.

'No,' said Jeff. 'We were frightened he will kill any dog we put with it.'

'Don't be silly, Jeff. That's impossible.'

'That's what Don said.'

'I'll go and fetch a roll dog,' I said. That's a dog that's not match quality, but he gives the up-and-coming dogs a little roll.

'Okay, but it's your funeral.'

We went home and got our dog, then we all went out into the yard.

'Let your dog off, Jeff,' I said.

This killing machine took one look at our dog, then ran around Jeff's legs, scaled a wall and ran away.

Me and my two pals creased up laughing. The south London boys were all running after their dog – one jumped into his car and caught it. So Don Mayfield had them for £10,000.

My two pals fared no better. They saw an advert in the *Sporting Dog Journal* for a quality-bred pup for £4,500. They sent their money off and all they got was a card saying, 'Thanks, mugs – you've just paid for my holiday in Florida.'

The only way was to go in person to either America or Holland. That's where the best dogs were. Or you could breed them yourself from proven stock. I always did that.

It's all about getting a game dog that will keep on scratching. As the rules go, if it's your opponent's turn to scratch and he's already killed your dog in the pit, it's still his turn to scratch. The gentlemanly thing to do is to concede defeat, but I once saw the Scots boys' dog Bill kill a dog in the pit and their opponents wouldn't concede defeat until the Scotsmen's dog had scratched to a dead dog.

It was a real gruesome scene. The handler stood his dead dog up and held him upright for Bill to scratch to. Thankfully, these sort of situations are few and far between.

There are lots of tricks involved in the sport. One is to wear black trousers if you've got a black dog or brown trousers if you've got a brown dog. If it's a long fight and the dogs are in shock, they sometimes can't see the dog in the opposite corner, because it's camouflaged by your trousers. So they won't scratch. I remember once my pal was in the opposite corner and put his hand through the boards in my opponent's corner and held their dog's tail so it couldn't scratch, and we won. There are a million tricks which a good handler knows. Still, in the main they are all good people enjoying their sport with no vindictiveness, but as in all walks of life there are a minority of very wicked people involved with pit bulls that get the rest a bad name.

On one such occasion we clashed with those types. They had paid a fortune and got a dog imported from America. This dog had apparently killed a few class dogs in short time out there. In order to establish their dog's reputation in Britain, they challenged me to fight my champion Nilsen with their imported American champion Costa, for £6,000 a side. We accepted. The fight was to be held in a big barn on a farm just outside Rayleigh. It was a catch-weight affair.

Well, their dog was 3lb heavier than Sam (Nilsen was only his kennel name). It was a terrible battle with neither dog giving any quarter. The fight was fought at a tremendous pace. After 1 hour 50 minutes, Costa quit – he refused to scratch. That is the worst defeat a dog can suffer, because no one will use a quitter for stud even, so this match had cost these boys a fortune. I personally think they were stupid to risk their investment by fighting Sam. They should have just got the dog home and opened him up for stud, saying he was retired, as he already had a mighty reputation in the States. They would have earned a fortune in stud fees.

When Costa quit, they were understandably annoyed at the outcome, but what they did was barbaric. We were in our corner seeing to Sam. They were all in their corner, when I heard Costa let out a terrible yelp, then silence. I walked over to their corner and what one of them had done was to lay Costa down and put a 6-inch nail to his ear and hit it with a club hammer, driving it through his ear into his brain and killing him.

I couldn't believe it. This dog had just fought his heart out and because he lost, these animals killed him in a terrible fashion. My first instinct was to vomit. My second was anger at these fools – not just anger, raging fury.

Before I had a chance to do anything, Micky had picked up a bailing hook and hit the fellow who had killed Costa, opening his face right up. The others didn't do anything. They were just a bunch of cowards. They were the ones who should have been put to death.

I drew our £3,000, as £3,000 had been paid in forfeit money already and we picked up Sam and left. The fool that had killed Costa was just laying on the floor moaning with blood pumping out of his face. We had won the match, but it had left a bad taste in my mouth.

My dogs were doing well. I was using my best dog, bred from Sam, for fighting. His kennel name was Dirty Bertie. He was a grand champion, which means he had won five big-money, proper-contracted fights, under Cajun rules. A separate judge had reported these matches to the *Sporting Dog Journal* in America and the English equivalent, the *Pit Bull Gazette*.

Sam was five and a half, and well past his best. He had won nine matches without defeat. So I had retired him to stud, and was using his offspring in matches instead. Sam's reputation was worldwide. He was known all over: America, Holland, everywhere. Before I retired him I challenged all the top dog fighters, but had no takers. He was four and a half at the time. Since then, he had just lazed around and got fat and mated bitches. I reckon Sam at two and a half to three and a half was unbeatable, but little did I or he realise his biggest challenge was in front of him.

There was a group of dog fighters from Broadwater Farm Estate in Tottenham. It is a rough area, where Constable Blakelock had been hacked to death in a riot. A black man called Winston Silcott got the blame. It is common knowledge in London that he was innocent, but once a police officer gets killed all hell lets loose. His nickname didn't help his cause either – it was Stix, after the mythical river which flows by the gates of hell, because when you cross Stix you get hell.

These dog fighters called themselves the Barbarians. Our kennel was called East Enders – long before the TV series started. Well these Barbarians started to slag Sam off in the *Sporting Dog Journal*, saying his fights had all been hand picked, that he was inferior to their dogs and that I had had these easy fights to get a name for Sam, to push up the price of his stud fees and make his services more popular. All this was, of course, a load of rubbish.

I never took any notice at first, but after a few months it started to annoy me. They put an advert in the *Sporting Dog Journal* and in the *Pit Bull Gazette* challenging me to fight Sam with their champion for £10,000 a side. Well, I knew Sam was a better dog, but he was five and a half, their champion was only three years old – in his prime, in fact. I phoned my pal up, who used to help me condition Sam for all his fights. 'Come over, Joe,' I said. 'I want a word with you.'

Joe was an Asian and his nickname was 'The Doctor' as he was like a doctor around dogs. He knew everything there was to know about conditioning a dog and also the main thing – getting them better afterwards. When he arrived I showed him into my sitting room. 'Joe …'

He stopped me then and there. 'I know what this is about,' he said. 'It's about Sam fighting again with the Barbarians' dog, Commander.'

'What do you think? Can we win?'

He thought for a minute. 'I don't know,' he said, 'but Sam's a born warrior. Yes, he's mating bitches and loafing about, but he yearns to fight. Now, I think he's a better dog than Commander, but he's well past his best. We would have to pull all the stops out to help him. The only way we could get him fit again is to put him on a course of steroids. That still might not be enough though and he would no longer be any good for mating, as these steroids would make him sterile.

'But, Dan, the dog is living a life he doesn't want. If he dies in a pit battle, that's how he would choose to leave this world. But as I have said, he would be no good for mating, so you'd be out of pocket. Plus the other dog would be odds-on favourite to win. He is in his prime, and they never come back – just look what Larry Holmes did to Mohammed Ali. If you decide to go for it I will help you.'

I thought long and hard. After a week I was still undecided. Then one day I walked out to my yard. Sam was chained up. He was just sitting there staring into space. I know that look. I have experienced it myself, looking out of a prison cell window, many times.

All of a sudden a dog walked past my gate. Sam sprang to life. He went mad, jumping and screaming to get out of his chain at this other dog. It was driving him crazy, this life. He needed to fight. This fighting instinct had been passed to him from his forebears for over 200 years. Now he was being denied the chance to do battle. I understood Sam's feelings that day. Our minds were as one. So Sam had made my mind up for me.

I phone up Joe. 'We're in business,' I said. Then I phoned up the *Pit Bull Gazette*, put an advert in accepting the challenge and told the editor to make a meet with the Barbarians for me as soon as possible. As soon as the magazine was printed the Barbarians phoned the *Gazette* and a meet was arranged on neutral territory.

We met at the Blind Beggar pub in Whitechapel. The pub had become famous as Ronnie Kray had shot George Cornell in there a few years before. Me, Micky and Joe were there before these Barbarians. As we were waiting we sat in the garden and had a couple of drinks.

All of a sudden a tall black fellow came up to us. 'Are you the East Enders?' he asked.

'Yes,' I said.

He called two other blokes from the bar. One I recognised as the editor of the *Gazette*, Dave. The other one was a massive man I didn't know, but he looked mean, with his head shaven, a flat nose and a scar running down the side of his face. They came and sat at our table. The black fellow said, 'Look, we all know what were here for – to discuss the fight, not niceties or smalltalk.'

'Right,' I said. 'What weight do you want to fight your dog at?'

Sam usually fought at 47lb but I knew we would be hard pressed to get him to that weight after his lay-off. The black fellow said 50lb, which was ideal for us. He though Sam still fought at 47lb, so we would be giving weight away. That was a bad mistake by them.

I asked about a venue. 'I run a community centre at Broadwater Farm,' he said. 'It's the safest place in the country. The police won't dare come there.'

'Sounds good to me,' I said. 'Just one thing I insist on. No money at the venue. I will give Dave the editor £10,000 this week. You do the same. If either dog pulls out, the opponent takes half the prize money.'

'Agreed,' he said.

We also agreed that it should take place in seven weeks' time, and signed a contract – 'Outlaw' and 'Ebony'. Then I shook hands with Ebony, as did both Micky and Joe.

The white fellow, whose name was Cribb, and who hadn't said a word up to that point, then said, 'I don't want to shake your hands. I'll shake hands after my dog Commander has killed your mongrel stone dead.'

'We'll see,' I said. 'We'll see.'

For the next seven weeks, me and Joe had a full-time job. First we stripped Sam out: we fed him tomato puree and bran to get all the fat out of his system. We then started to build him up with pure beef. These steroids enabled him to work much harder and longer. After four weeks Sam was looking good and the strength he was getting was unreal. He was nearly back to his old self.

At six weeks Sam started to get to peak fitness. Another week would be just right. I phoned Dave asking if everything was in order. 'Yes,' he said. 'I have got their cheque. Cribb has got another £5,000 to bet. Can you match it?' I told him the money was on its way and put the phone down.

Then Joe came to me and said, 'Sam's had £400 worth of steroids and in a week he will be as fit as he ever can. But I have heard this dog Commander breaks dogs up – early fitness won't come into it. Have you seen the state of Sam's teeth? Some are broken, some are worn down from the battles he's had.'

'I know Sam's teeth are not what they use to be,' I said. 'And just as a boxer or prizefighter only has his hands to fight with, a dog only has his teeth. Without his teeth for weapons he cannot win. Just leave it to me.'

The day of the fight arrived. I fed Sam late the previous night so that he'd clear out and be fighting with an empty stomach. I got up at 6.30 am and walked Sam for half an hour. I phoned Joe and told him to be there by 8 am. The fight was at 3 pm.

'You're up early,' said Joe when he arrived. 'Can't you sleep?'

'It's not that. We've got a visitor at 9 am.'

My visitor arrived with his little case. 'Good morning, chaps,' he said. This man was a dentist I knew. He had been struck off for molesting women whilst they were under general anaesthetic. He'd always denied it, saying that the drug they used to knock people out makes women randy and they imagined all the things they said had happened. I didn't believe him at that time, but I found out later that this drug actually does have that effect.

Well, this morning he was operating on a dog, so we had no such worries. He gave me the syringe to inject Sam, as he wouldn't let the dentist do it. I injected Sam in the hindquarters, and within two minutes he was sound asleep. We laid him down on the kitchen table. The dentist knocked three nails in the table and wound string from one to the other and through Sam's open mouth to keep it open. Then he put some paste on an electric tool for sharpening teeth.

After about ten minutes, Sam's teeth were like razor-sharp chisels and his canines like spears. Sam started to come round, so we untied him and just let him sleep. I gave the dentist £500. Now we were favourites to win. Before the dentist left he gave me two morphine-based pills – the strongest painkillers he had.

At 1 pm, I took Sam for a short walk. He was buzzing, raring to go. At 2 pm, me, Micky, Joe and Sam set off from Manor Park heading for Broadwater Farm. This was the talk of the country, with most people thinking Sam was going to lose. When we arrived at the estate Ebony greeted us on his own and took us to the community centre. Inside there must have been about 200 people, all black, waiting at the pit side. The pit had already been put up.

I gave the two painkillers to Sam, so that if Commander bit him hard it would lessen the pain and stop him going into deep shock. Then we weighed both dogs – dead on 50lb. I think Ebony and Cribb were surprised we wasn't a bit lighter, but we was right on the weight. Then I gave Sam some speed, so that he would come out fast and lively, as I knew Commander would. This Commander was a bundle of muscle, with an enormous head. He was red and Sam was black, so we could easily identify which was which.

Commander was going mad to get at Sam, but Sam had seen this many times before. He just stood in the corner staring across the pit at Commander, concentrating. I was in the pit as Sam's second; Cribb was Commander's second; and Dave was ref. Then it was time. Everyone went quiet.

'Right, gentlemen,' said Dave. 'Face your dogs … Release your dogs.'

The two dogs ran at each other, colliding at the centre of the pit, both vying for holds. Sam was down with Commander on top, as Commander was the much stronger dog. Sam grabbed his chest from underneath, whilst Commander was shaking Sam's front leg like crazy. He was really shaking Sam up, but Sam had a hold on his chest and he wasn't letting go.

His sharpened teeth were going in real deep, but poor Sam was being shaken to pieces by his front leg, which was taking some terrible punishment. After about 15 minutes, Commander started to slow up. His chest was a mess and Sam was biting deeper and deeper. All of a sudden deep red-coloured blood, almost black, started to come from Commander's chest. Sam twisted him over, still keeping the chest hold, but now Sam was on top. Instinct told Sam to keep working the chest. He wasn't letting go.

By now both dogs were bleeding badly, Commander the worst, but Sam's front leg bone was broken, piercing right through his skin. But Sam was still working hard – the morphine was doing an excellent job.

At 40 minutes, Commander just lay there with Sam shaking him by the chest. All of a sudden Dave said, 'Cribb, your dog's dead. The match is over.'

I picked up Sam. He was close to death. Ebony came over to stroke Sam and felt his teeth, but I knew in a fight a dog's sharpened teeth go blunt at ten minutes. Joe put a saline drip straight into Sam's leg and got him warm, because we knew if he got cold he would die. Cribb couldn't believe his dog was dead.

'Not bad for a mongrel, eh, Cribb?' said Micky, and started laughing.

This enraged Cribb. 'Yes, your dog is game,' he shouted. 'Are any of you three as game as your dog?'

I told Joe to look after the dog. 'Yes,' I said immediately, as I had taken an instant dislike to this Cribb character. 'I'll fight you now.'

'He's talking to me not you,' said Micky. 'I'll fight him.'

So all the people stayed to watch Micky and Cribb have a fight. Well, Cribb shaped up and he was very quick. He gave Micky some real hard punches, but Micky is one of those people impossible, it seems, to knock out. It was like the scene in *Raging Bull*, when Sugar Ray Robinson gave Jake LA Motto a terrible hiding, but LA Motto refused to go down in one of the most savage fights in ring history. Cribb was beating Micky mercilessly – he could really fight. Micky was smothered in blood. They were fighting in the same space as Sam and Commander had just fought in.

I thought, 'Micky has got to go down in a minute,' but Micky is a real warrior – not much on skill but a throwback to the old bare-knuckle fighters. He is all heart. He can and will take fearful punishment without wilting. All of a sudden, out of the blue, Micky hit Cribb with a tremendous blow to the stomach as he was rushing in. This winded Cribb. Now Micky was on the attack, left, right, left, right. Then Cribb dropped. As Cribb rose, Micky stepped back in and landed a peach of a right hook on Cribb's jaw, knocking him right out.

As they dragged Cribb from the pit, Ebony jumped in. 'Out,' he said to me. 'Your dog's killed our dog. One half of East Enders has beaten one half of the Barbarians. That just leaves me and you, and I think somehow you cheated with Sam. That leaves you and me to sort matters out.'

'I thought you'd never ask. I'd love to oblige you,' I said.

'This is all in,' Ebony screamed. 'To the finish.'

'Great,' I said. Then, just to get him wild, 'You can think what you like of me and call me a cheat, but you're far worse. You'll always be just a black cunt.'

Well, that was silly thing to say, as most of the people that were there were black, but it was too late. Ebony was fuming. As I got into the pit he rushed me. I am about 5ft 10in; he was about 6ft 2in. I saw him coming and we smashed into each other. As I was the shorter man, my head crashed into his mouth. His mouth seemed to explode, teeth and blood everywhere – more by luck than judgement.

He reeled back. He'd lost two teeth plus there was plenty of blood coming from his mouth. My head was pouring with blood and where his teeth had crashed into my head there was a huge lump just below my hairline. As he was staggering backwards, I kicked him straight in his private parts. He gasped and fell to his knees. Before he could get up I smashed about ten punches into his face. He was helpless to hit me back, but he'd said to the finish – all in. When I stopped punching, he went over sideways, unconscious. I was bleeding heavily from my head wound and I was dizzy.

Then three of Ebony's pals jumped into the pit. One of them pulled a knife and said, 'Black cunt, is he?'

All of a sudden there was a loud crack and this black man was on the floor screaming, with blood pouring from his leg. There was pandemonium. People were screaming and running all ways. I looked round and Joe was at pit side with a revolver in his hand. 'I thought we might need this,' he said. 'Come on, the dog's already in the car outside.' By this time Micky was in the pit with me.

So the three of us went out to the car. No one would get near us, as Joe was waving this gun about and he'd already shot one person. When we got back to my house, we all looked a sorry state. We got the dog settled in my kitchen first, then I cleaned myself up. My head had stopped bleeding by this time, but I was still giddy. I had concussion. I'd had it before. I knew I needed rest. Micky went home to Forest Gate. We hid the gun, but we knew those black people wouldn't say anything to the police. I left Joe with the dog and went to bed.

The next morning I was woken at 10 am by Micky knocking at the door. His face was all swollen, but other than that he was all right. I felt much better, but I was still a little bit giddy. When we walked through to the kitchen, Joe was asleep. So was Sam – his leg was twice its normal size. I woke Joe with a cup of tea. 'Dan,' he said. 'Sam suffered shock in the night. His old heart just gave up.'

'What? You're telling me he's dead?'

'I'm sorry. I did all I could,' he said, and broke down in tears.

I put my arm around his shoulder. Micky was wiping his eyes also. So the three of us buried Sam in my garden. The next thing I phoned

Dave at the offices of the *Gazette*. 'Hello, Dave,' I said. 'I didn't see the goings of you yesterday.'

'Dan, it got too heavy for me,' he said.

'Right, we'll be there at 12 pm for our money.'

'Fine,' he said, then asked how Sam was.

I told him he was all right. 'He's sitting in front of me now,' I said. Joe and Micky looked at me in amazement.

I put the phone down. 'Don't ask me any questions,' I said. 'I'll explain later. But if anyone asks how the dog is, he's fine. All right?' They both nodded.

I went and collected £30,000 from Dave, and took my original £15,000 out. Then I gave Dave £2,000 for his efforts, Joe £4,000, and me and Micky had £4,500 each. When we got back to my house, I said to Joe and Micky, 'Come into my yard. I want to show you something.'

In one of the kennels there was a black dog, the same size and build as Sam, with Sam's yellow eyes – some people call them evil eyes – and a fair few scars on him. He was Sam's litter brother. My cousin owned him. I had given him to him, he had two fights with him and got beaten. That's how he got his scars. Just after we'd signed contracts for Sam's fight, I got him back off my cousin. He no longer wanted him because he had bitten his wife. I didn't know what to do with him at the time, so I was just using him as a guard dog, to let me know if anyone was about.

I knew he was a good guard dog by what my cousin had told me. But now everyone wanted to use Sam at stud. As he'd done the impossible and beaten Commander, his stud fee was £500, so my cousin's dog would have to change his name from Gus to Sam. I was sure he wouldn't mind.

I got Dave to phone the Barbarians up. They had all recovered, no police got involved and they said to Dave, 'You win some, you lose some. Just tell any of them East Enders never to come to Broadwater Farm or they are dead. And we'll stay out of the East End. There's room for all of us, but we'll never be friends.' So even in death, Sam was still serving me. What a dog.

Soon I was concentrating on dealing with pit bull terriers, fighting them, using my champion dog at stud and selling pups.

Some years later my dog Bertie was contracted to fight a dog from Wales by the name of Tyler, so I arranged for the fight to take place in the back hall of a club. Well, the dogs had a tremendous tussle. After 1 hour 45 minutes, both dogs were in holds, but Bert was winning easily, as Tyler was in shock. It was only a matter of time before Tyler died.

So the handler of Tyler said, 'That's it. I give you best. It's over,' and we shook hands. I got my breaking stick, which is a wedge-shaped stick made of the hardest wood in the world. I used it to get a dog's mouth open so as to break the hold. As I bent down and grabbed Bert, this other fellow said, 'I have forgotten my stick.'

'Okay,' I said. 'Hold your dog.' Then I broke Bert off but this other fellow's concentration wandered for a moment and he looked away momentarily. Tyler was in shock. He turned his head round and grabbed this bloke's jaw. He screamed and stood up with the dog – which weighed 55lb – still hanging onto his jaw. In his state of shock Tyler thought he was biting Bert, but he was doing this guy plenty of damage.

Everyone jumped back. I gave Bert to Joe, pulled a knife from my pocket and stabbed Tyler just under his front leg, near his chest, straight into his heart, killing him instantly. Tyler's grip was still holding onto this bloke's face so I had to break it off. There was blood everywhere. It was a bad ending for a game dog, but I really had no option. We took the dog handler to East Ham Memorial Hospital and left him outside. I had won £9,000 but it was a hollow victory.

Dogs were not the only fighting animals we encountered. In the early days there was a fellow knocking about with my crowd by the name of Fairsy. I'm not sure what his first name was. I know his second name was Fayres. He was a big blond-haired fellow, who had done a fair bit of boxing. He was always immaculately dressed and had a way with women. He could charm them out of the trees.

One night, me, Fairsy, Roy Hunt, Danny O'Leary and Micky Gluckstead all went for a drink over the Mitre pub, just through the Blackwall Tunnel. In the Mitre, we met four girls who lived in Blackheath. As we were driving across Blackheath in Fairsy's big American Buick car, we saw a massive fairground. So Fairsy pulled up and we all went to the fair for a laugh.

There was a boxing booth, and there was a boxing kangaroo next door. I suppose the same fellow was running both shows. The roo was all kitted out with gloves etc. They were offering anyone £5 to go three rounds with this kangaroo. Well, Micky was getting in the ring, but Fairsy beat him to it.

This kangaroo was really spiteful. It knocked Fairsy round the ring in the first round. I noticed he was leaning back on this massive tail and balancing himself and springing forwards and upwards, using his great big feet to really hurt Fairsy's lower body. I thought to myself, 'The tail is his only weapon. Without it he's useless.'

During the second round, this roo had his back to us, so I could reach his tail. I lifted it off the floor, as I thought this rendered him helpless. Fairsy started to punch this roo's head. It screamed blue murder. The fairground people went mad. We had one hell of a fight with them. The girls went from laughing hysterically to screaming and crying. They ran off and we never saw them again.

The boxers ran from the booth to fight us. We made short work of them. They might have been boxers but they weren't any good at street fighting. By this time the fight had spilled out from inside the sideshow tent to outside. It seemed like all the fair was fighting. All the sideshow workers joined in; there were loads of them. We just couldn't win.

All of a sudden a big black Buick, hooter blaring, crashed through two sideshows, smashing them to pieces. One of these was a hoopla stall, offering a goldfish in a bowl to anyone who could throw a hoop over the bowl – there was goldfish wriggling about on the floor everywhere. The other one was a bingo unit. As the Buick smashed into that one, the people who were playing all scrambled to safety, all panicking and screaming. There were pots and pans and broken china everywhere.

We all scrambled into Fairsy's car and he tore off, like a bat out of hell. There was chaos and mayhem everywhere, but Fairsy saved us all from a real hiding. I know them fairground people can be rough and the sheer force of numbers would have done us. As it was, we all had a fair few injuries. The next day we met up in Rosie Enever's café. We all looked a sorry state.

Danny O'Leary's face was a mass of bruises, his head looked twice as big as it normally did and he had a job to talk, as the inside of this mouth had been badly damaged. Roy Hunt's jaw was swollen out of all proportion and he had a broken arm. Micky Gluckstead's eyes were both swollen grotesquely out of shape. My nose was twice as broad as it should have been, the blood had been seeping out all night running down my throat and both my eyes were black and swollen.

Fairsy was the last one to arrive. He could hardly walk. He turned up on crutches – a bit drastic, I thought, but that was Fairsy for you. He had massive bruises all round his ribs and lower body. But the funniest thing was Fairsy trying to explain to Rose that a kangaroo had caused his injuries.

We all just sat there listening, trying to look serious and stop ourselves laughing as we were in so much pain. It hurt to laugh, but it was impossible not to, and once we started to giggle we all finished up in hysterics. I reckon Rose must have thought we'd all gone mad.

I hadn't seen Fairsy for years. Then, last year I visited a pal one day and a young fellow said to me, 'Are you Danny Woollard?'

'Yes,' I said.

'You used to know my dad.'

It was Fairsy's son. He said Fairsy had gone to live in America, but his son re-enacted the story of the fighting kangaroo exactly how it happened. I thought to myself, 'I bet Fairsy has told that story all-round America by now.' But he did save our bacon that night.

ROUND 7

CASH IN CORNERS

While I bred and sold my puppies, Micky had to earn a living. So, with Roy Neal, he concentrated on his business of cornering people. Everyone else steered clear of Roy Neale; he was a very hard, violent man who had been to prison on a manslaughter charge. Him and Micky were a very formidable pair.

'Cornering' is either: tricking someone into buying something you haven't got; tricking someone into giving you a commodity they're trying to sell without you paying for it; or tricking someone into paying you for a service you cannot provide. Notice how the word 'tricking' comes into it all the time. The corner job is a confidence trick. Anyone can be cornered and Micky is the best there is at it.

A pal of his, Arnie, who was also in the corner game, came up to me and Micky one day, as we were having a bit of breakfast in Pellici's café in Bethnal Green.

'Mick, I am knocking about with a prostitute who's bought a big house in Green Street, Forest Gate,' he said. 'She has heard all about you and reckons you and no one else could trick her out of her money.'

'So what?' said Mick.

'She's taking her driving test at Barking test centre next week,' he continued. 'I told her I knew an inspector there, and for £500 I would guarantee she would pass. She agreed but she would only pay the inspector on completion of the test. She wouldn't give me the money. She's cute this bird. I don't know any inspector, I was just going to take her money and disappear.'

'Okay,' said Micky. 'What is the date and the time of her test?'

'Next Wednesday at 10.45 am.'

'Right. You take her there at 10.15 am and walk in with her. Make sure she has the money in her envelope.'

So at 10 am on Wednesday, Micky makes his way to Barking test centre with a nice pair of glasses on and a clipboard under his arm. There were about four people in the waiting room waiting to take their test. Micky stood looking at the noticeboards.

As Arnie and this girl walked in, he just walked up to them, clipboard under his arm. 'Miss Wilson?' he said.

'Yes.'

'I am Mr King. Shall we go?'

Once outside the centre Micky said, 'Right, Miss Wilson, where did you park?'

'That's my car there. A blue Ford Escort.'

'Lovely,' said Micky, and then to Arnie, 'We won't need you, sir. Go into the café along the road. We'll be about half an hour.'

Arnie said okay, and Miss Wilson and Micky drove away. After ten minutes, Micky said, 'Park here, please, Miss Wilson.' Then he looked at her and said, 'Have you got an envelope for me?'

'Yes, here it is,' she said eagerly.

Micky opened it, checked the money and put it in his pocket. He spoke to her for about another ten minutes. He told her that her driving was nowhere near up to standard, so to take it easy for a while, as he didn't want to lose his job if it came out he was passing people not qualified to drive.

'No, sir,' said Miss Wilson. 'I'm driving so badly because my nerves have got the better of me.'

'That's all right then, but be careful and don't tell anybody else about this transaction.'

'Of course not,' she said.

'Right-oh. Just drive back and park in the same spot where we came from.'

When they got back to the driving centre, Micky said, 'Miss Wilson, it's my pleasure to tell you, you've passed your driving test. Wait here, I'll just go into the centre, fill in the appropriate forms and get your pass slip. Your friend is waiting in the café just along the road there. If you join him, I'll fetch your pass slip to you in about five minutes.'

'Lovely. Thank you very much, Mr King.'

Micky walked into the test centre, gave it a minute of two, then walked out again into his car and drove off with Miss Wilson's £500. He met up with Arnie in the Square Ring coffee bar in Upton Lane, Forest Gate, and gave him £250.

Arnie couldn't resist it. A few days later he rang Miss Wilson up and rubbed her nose in it.

'I've got two minders working for me,' she said. 'And we know Mr King is really Micky Gluckstead and they know where he drinks. They are going to kill him.'

So Micky phoned her. 'Hello, Miss Wilson,' he said. 'Mr King here.'

'You bastard. You're dead.'

'Am I?' said Micky. 'Well, you tell your fucking minders I am looking for them now. We'll see who's dead.' And he put the phone down.

By this time I had got another club. It was the Hathaway at Manor Park, a lovely little family club. Well, the phone rings one day. It was my mate Angelo. He's half Maltese with a shaven head and massive shoulders – scary-looking, but I knew he was a good man, a man of his word. 'Dan, you're friendly with Gluckstead, ain't you?' he said.

'Yes, I am.'

'Can you make a meet with him at your club? There's no bother, it's only to sort something out.'

'Okay,' I said. 'When for?'

'8 pm tomorrow night.'

So I phoned Micky and told him. The next night Angelo turned up first with a dwarf. But this wasn't a midget or a normal dwarf, he was just like a little man with massive shoulders and bulging biceps. Like a small version of Arnold Schwarzennegar. It was Royston 'Little Legs' Smith. A real hardnut who first introduced midget wrestling to England. He had worked for the Kray twins for a long time. They trusted him implicitly. He had been in prison for murder and all sorts of villainy. I knew him by reputation, and he'd been to America and acted with Tony Curtis and Burt Lancaster in *Trapeze*. I knew he could have a terrible fight. He was the union leader Jack Dash's personal minder for years with Angelo. They were a very formidable pair.

After 15 minutes, at exactly 8 pm as arranged, Micky arrived. As he walked in, Angelo got up and I introduced him to Micky. They shook hands.

'Mick,' Angelo said, 'Roy's been minding a brothel in Green

Street, and the woman who runs it told Roy she wants someone to shoot you. So I went and saw her and told her I would do it for £4,000: £2,000 up front and £2,000 when the job was done. So I drew the £2,000, and me and Roy had £1,000 each. Then I just disappeared. She didn't know me from Adam. Roy just says I've been nicked and I'm in prison. So there's no one looking for you and I have heard your looking for us. I've come to tell you the score. You've not got the patent on cornering. We've cornered her as well.'

Micky roared with laughter. 'I like it,' he said. And the five of us had a good drink together.

But not all our antics finished so amicably. Near the entrance to Hathaway Crescent, where my club was situated, stood a phone booth. It was one of those with just the back and sides, with no front.

Well, early each morning at 3 am, a big, fat black woman used to go to the phone and she would spend about 30 minutes screaming and shouting, swearing and yelling all sorts of obscenities into it. She was keeping everybody awake on the estate and if anyone complained she'd scream threats and abuse at them, and the next day her three very large sons would visit the people that were complaining and threaten them violently.

A pal of mine had two children and this woman was keeping them awake. Their schoolwork was suffering and my pal's wife was heading for a nervous breakdown. They were in a very awkward position, so me and Micky went down to the phone box one night at 2.50 am and put superglue over the earpiece and the handle.

Sure enough, at 3 am up she waddles. She picked the phone up, and I noticed she never put no money in the box, so obviously she was talking to herself. She put the phone straight to her ear and started shouting, then all at once she realised she was stuck to the phone. Her hands were stuck to the handle and her ear was stuck fast to the earpiece.

She immediately panicked. She screamed, hollered and cried, 'til eventually the police turned up. I saw one of the police officers crease up laughing. Anyhow, the police called an ambulance and they cut the phone cord and the last I saw of her was being led into the ambulance still holding the phone to her ear, yelling threats to the police and everyone else. It was hilarious. Me and Micky were hysterical.

The next day the joke turned a bit sour, as her three sons were running wild all around the estate trying to find out who had put the glue in the phone box. They were running riot, bashing people and threatening everybody. They were really mad. They frightened someone into telling them they'd seen me and Micky laying the ambush for their mother.

Up to this point I had never actually seen the brothers, but I had heard all about them. I knew they were three very large, violent young men who were fast making a name for themselves as villains and bullies. So that afternoon, me and Micky were playing pool in the club when the King brothers walked in.

I had expected them, as my pal had phoned me and told me they had found out that me and Micky were responsible for their mother's plight and they wasn't happy about it. They were coming after me and Micky all tooled up. They had heard all about us and in their own words they were going to hurt us badly and then bury us. I told Micky. 'Can't they take a fucking joke?' he said, and started laughing.

As they walked in they walked straight up to the pool table and said, 'Are yous the two arseholes who fucked with our mum last night?'

Micky looked at the one who was speaking as he was about to take his shot. Instead of taking his shot, Micky stood straight up and in one movement he crashed the pool cue across this very large black guy's nose with a horrible crunch. The blood spurt out of his face.

Before anyone could move, Micky hit him twice more across the back of the head with the broken cue as he was going down. It had happened so fast the other two had just stood there dumbfounded. Micky was like greased lightning. Meanwhile I had two pool balls in a sock which I had in my trousers pocket in readiness for the King brothers. I swung the sock as hard as I could. The second brother turned just at the right moment and the perfectly aimed missile hit him straight in the mouth with a deep thud. He screamed and immediately fell to the floor as though he'd been pole-axed. There was blood and teeth everywhere. I had no need to hit him again.

The third brother tried to run out. He was screaming for help. Micky chased him and caught him just outside the club and knocked him spark out with his hands. This African giant had a bit of a fight, but he was no match for Micky. His fist opened his face right up before knocking him out. We dragged the other two brothers out of the club bodily, then we locked the club doors and called an ambulance for them on an untraceable mobile phone, as they were losing plenty of blood.

The first ambulance called for another ambulance, and the police came as well. They were knocking on the club door. We sat inside all quiet watching what was going on outside on our latest security camera and video equipment. A fire engine turned up as well. We thought they were going to break the door to the club down, but instead the firemen started to hose the pavement down. There was so much blood, it looked horrible – like a little river of blood flowing along the gutter. There was a hell of a fuss, but eventually it quietened down.

We thought the King brothers wouldn't grass on us as they were up-and-coming villains, hurting plenty of people. We were wrong. The next morning at 6 am I got raided, same time as Micky. They had said it was us. The police were confident we were going to be nicked really heavy for this. They gave us three weeks' police bail, pending further inquiries. Mysteriously, two weeks after this incident, the King brothers never picked me or Micky out in an identity parade. They said the two people they thought were Danny Woollard and Micky Gluckstead were nothing like us two. I never heard any more of the King brothers. They obviously decided that they didn't want to be villains after all.

There was a Scotsman knocking about the East End at this time by the name of Eddie Jamieson. Everyone knew him as Scotch Eddie. I liked Eddie a lot. I always found him a complete gentleman – but once upset, this quietly spoken man was the Devil himself. He'd cut people absolutely to pieces. He was merciless, but he never once started a row. He was easy to talk too. He also had 11 sons who all tried to live up to him, but believe me, Eddie was a one-off.

Well, his son Micky started performing in pubs – cutting people, acting the bully, nothing like his father at all. First of all my pal Phil Daltry knocked him out, then Phil got out of Eddie's way for a while. Then Phil got nicked and went to prison. So Eddie couldn't do anything about it, but he didn't like it.

I had to meet Micky Gluckstead one night at the Duke of Edinburgh pub in Green Street. I was late, but Micky had got there on time. Micky Jamieson and his pal were in the pub half drunk, and they both started to dig Micky out, as he was on his own. Micky Gluckstead said, 'Leave me alone.'

With that, Jamieson pulled out a knife and lunged at him. Micky Gluckstead hit him straight on the chin, knocking him out. His mate threw a glass at Micky, cutting his head. He didn't take any notice of the cut and knocked his mate out as well, just as I arrived.

I took Micky to hospital. He had to have 15 stitches in his head. When we got back to the pub, Scotch Eddie was there. Obviously someone had phoned him to say his son was in a bit of trouble. As we walked in, Eddie said to Micky, 'My boy's in hospital with a broken jaw. I've been told three of yous done him. Is that right?'

'Eddie, he tried to stab me first,' Micky said. 'Then his mate done me with a glass. Why don't you ask anyone in here?'

Eddie, always the gentleman, understood the situation and we had a good drink, instead of a fight.

I didn't like his boy at all, and a few months later I was proven right. An old couple in Canning Town won £1,000 on the Bingo. Eddie's Micky and his mate, by the name of Anderson, followed this old couple to their house in New Barn Street, Canning Town, and they tortured them to death for the money. Then him and his pal killed five more people, all working-class people, for peanuts. Then, when the police cornered them, Jamieson laid on the floor pleading for mercy, the coward.

He had a gun. He was all right shooting innocent people. The newspapers called him 'Public Enemy No1'. The old people he tortured to death were a policeman's mother and father. The police must have been sorely tempted to shoot him, as I would have been. But TV cameras were there so they couldn't. Anyhow, Jamieson got life with a recommendation of 25 years. His mate Anderson got a bit less. Micky Jamieson was certainly hated by a lot of prisoners doing long sentences, and with good reason.

Lifers sometimes keep budgerigars as pets. These men doing very long sentences, some even natural lifers, really do think a lot of their birds. These convicted murderers, killers and armed robbers were so very gentle with their animals, and when you think of it, they were their companions 24 hours a day. Yet Micky used to make a habit of creeping into their cells and pulling their heads off.

Although it was well known he did it, no one could ever catch him. Then the prison authority let my good mate Del Croxson have a pet budgie. They thought it would calm him down a bit. Del taught this bird all sorts of tricks. It could pull a car along and it was beginning to talk. Anyhow, he found it one day upside down in a cup of tea. Jamieson had drowned it. Del went mad, although as usual no one had seen Micky kill the bird. Del would have still done him, but Micky got himself put down the block and shipped out of the prison. He was just a very nasty, spiteful man. When Micky had killed the old man, he cut a budgie's head off and choked the old man with its body. It seems in his twisted mind he had a thing against budgerigars. I think he needed help. He should have been in a mental home, not a prison. A few years later Jamieson hung himself in prison.

Meanwhile Micky Gluckstead was still busy living on his wits and loving it. And as Paul had bought a smallholding in Upminister and settled down with a lovely girl by the name of Tracey, none of the original crew was available. So I got a fellow called Terry McCarthy to help me run my club. I also bought a small office block and got Mrs Jacqueline Beatty to help me as well, along with Dave Defreitas. Terry also used to sell T-shirts at Petticoat Lane. Terry was always laughing and joking, but he was also 'No1' at karate in Great Britain, and him and his partner Tony Price used to teach karate and grade students up to black-belt standard.

He lived at Warrior Square, Manor Park in an eighth-floor flat. There was a girl who lived near him. She must have weighed 25 stone. She was massive and aggressive with it. She was a horrible, rough person, but she had never done any real harm. She was all mouth. In the same block as Terry lived a fellow who had been convicted of raping a young teenage girl that we knew. He was a tall, thin fellow with a shaven head and little round glasses. He'd served a measly five years for ruining this girl's life, and not only did he rape her, but he beat her terrible as well, knocking her teeth out and pulling out her hair. As usual, he had received treatment in the mental hospital. It must have driven her family mad just seeing him. I waylaid him one night, masked up, and smashed him across the nose with a baseball bat. The police questioned me about it but had to let me go. Still he came back to torment this young girl.

Well, this large lady – Carole was her name – was getting married this day. As I looked over Terry's balcony I saw her walking to the Lita Club in her wedding dress to the reception. 'Quick, Tel, give me the gun,' I said, as he had a highlypowered slug gun, a rifle with sights on it. He gave me the gun. I lined up Carole in the sights, then 'Zap', a pellet hit her right on her massive bottom, hitting the left cheek. She screamed and screamed. Then straight away 'Zap', another hit her, this time on the right cheek. She hollered and ran up the road with both hands holding her bottom.

Me and Terry were in hysterics. Afterwards we found out that Carole had to gone to East Ham Memorial Hospital as the slugs were embedded in her flesh, so the joke had gone a bit sour. I saw Carole's husband, a Scotsman called Jim. He was going on about it. 'Look,' I said, 'don't say it came from me, but that rapist George in Terry's block shot Carole. I saw him do it. I was in Terry's flat and I saw him firing off of his balcony.'

'Okay, thanks,' he said. 'I'll get rid of him. He wont be able to live around here any more. I'll get a few of my relations down from Glasgow to deal with that piece of shit.'

Anyhow, after about a week, as George went out to get into his car to go to work, he was hit over the head and bundled into his vehicle by three strange men. Two of them took him to a garage behind the flats, and in the meantime the third man got the lift up to his flat and let himself in with the front door key, which he had taken from George's key-ring. Once inside, he completely wrecked it. Every bit of furniture was smashed up – TV, stereo, everything. After about 30 minutes he left and met his two pals outside the Victoria Cross public house, and the three of them drove off. The police had a call telling them there was something in garage No58 they would be interested in.

When the police opened the garage they found George screaming and blood everywhere. He had been castrated. He nearly died, but he survived. All he could tell the police was it was two Scotsmen. The Scotsmen had just left him to die, but Jim thought a murder inquiry would involve his wife. So in a moment of thinking sensibly or of conscience or perhaps fear that he would get caught, he had phoned the police. But there was no report in the paper. The police interviewed everybody, including me. They couldn't find one witness, and we never saw George again.

Just after this, Terry said to me, 'I was teaching karate last night and one of my fellow instructors offered me a marvellous deal. He introduced me to this fellow who owns a factory in north London manufacturing T-shirts. Well, they're going to set the place alight for the insurance money. They have got about £25,000 worth of T-shirts already made. I can have them for £5,000.'

'Terry, do you mean sell them for £25,000 or what?' I said.

'No, they would cost us £25,000 to buy,' said his partner, Tony Price. 'We sell them for double.'

'Where are the T-shirts now?'

'What we've got to do is this,' said Tony. 'We'll hire a lorry in the morning. Then we've got to meet them at Mile End station at 11 am. Then we go to Manor House and pick the shirts up.'

'Right. How about payment?' I said.

'I've got to take the money with me and pay them there and then,' said Terry.

'Terry, listen to me,' I said. 'It's a corner.'

Him and his partner looked at me and said, 'What do you mean by that?'

'There are no shirts,' I said. 'You'll lose your money and, being as I'm giving free information away, I'll tell you who set you up. Terry, it's always the person who makes the introduction. You trust him so it puts you at ease, off guard. Terry and Tony, you're what's commonly called "the mark".'

'That's rubbish,' they both exclaimed. 'We've known this fellow instructor for years.' Funnily enough his name was Micky.

'Take my advice and don't go,' I said.

That night at about 7 pm Terry phoned. 'Dan, would you come with us tomorrow?' he said.

'Yes, I'll come,' I said. 'But, Tel, come tooled up. Be prepared for trouble.'

He just laughed.

Next morning at 10 am Tony and Terry pulled up outside my house in a big hired yellow lorry. They both came in for a quick cup of tea.

'Right, I'll come,' I said, 'but you have to do as I say, okay? Or else just leave me out.' They both agreed. 'Right. Who's got the money?'

'Here it is,' said Terry. I told them to give the money to me, and under no circumstances to tell anyone who was holding it and at all times to stay together. They agreed, so off we went.

At Mile End station a short, thick-set man with a beard ran across the road. 'No car to check the number plate,' I thought straight away. He looked at me and said, 'Who are you?'

'I'm the driver. Who are you?'

'I don't like this,' he said. 'Let me look in the back of the lorry, to make sure there's no old bill in the back.'

I opened the back shutter. 'Okay,' he said, 'but I thought there were only two of you.'

'If you don't like it, call the deal off,' I said.

'No need for that,' he said, 'but they wont like it.'

'I don't suppose they will,' I said, and grinned at him.

As we got on the East Way he said, 'Pull up. I want to check the mirrors, so we're not being followed.'

I pulled up and said, 'Terry, you do know this is a load of old bollocks, don't you?'

Terry never answered. Before we could pull away he said, 'Right, whose got the money?'

'One of us,' I said.

He asked which one.

'Listen to me,' I said. 'Once the T-shirts are on this lorry you'll be paid, and not before.'

'No, it don't work like that,' he said.

'No, I didn't think it would,' I said.

'You never have the goods and money together,' he said, 'because if the police turn up you'll lose the lot. What we'll do, whoever has got the money will wait in the Manor House pub with my mate, and the other two will come with me and load the shirts up. Then we come back to the pub and you pay for them.'

I just laughed. 'Listen, mate, you're wasting everyone's time,' I said. 'There's no fucking shirts. It's a corner. For a start the T-shirts are not supposed to be stolen anyhow, so what if the police do come?

And also we're all staying together.'

'All right,' he said. 'Have it your way.'

'Don't worry, I will,' I said. 'Let's go to the Manor House.'

When we got there he said, 'Park down this side street.'

As we walked into the pub, I saw Roy Neale up at the bar with two other mean-looking men. I looked across the bar and spotted Micky's mate. 'Listen, Tel,' I said, 'have you ever heard of Roy Neale?'

'Of course,' he said. 'He's a killer.'

I said, 'Well that's him at the bar. This is Micky Gluckstead's firm, but Micky's not here. I know Arnie, but Roy is running this. There are no T-shirts.'

In the meantime, the bloke we arrived with was talking to Roy up at the bar.

'If it comes to it, I'll take Roy out,' I said. 'Are you two tooled up as I said?'

They both went white and said no.

'Well, once Roy's down the others most probably won't want to know,' I said.

'Dan, give them the money,' Terry said. 'We can always get money. We can't get a new pair of legs.'

'You two are both black-belt karate experts,' I said. 'You're teaching young people how to defend themselves every week.'

Tony said that it was only a sport; it didn't work in real life.

'Look, Arnie will not fight,' I said. 'So once Roy's done, that leaves that mug in the lorry we came here with, and the other two blokes with Roy.'

'Just give them the money and let's get out of here,' said Terry.

'Listen, you two,' I said. 'When I said I'd come with you, you agreed to do what I say, my way. I'm not giving these mugs fuck all. You two go back to the motor. I'll be down in a little while.'

They both scooted out of the pub. Roy called me up to the bar. 'Hello, Roy,' I said.

'Hello, Dan,' he said. 'Where's the money for these T-shirts?'

'Roy, you know and I know there's no fucking shirts,' I said. 'You owe me £200 for hiring the lorry and wasting my time.'

'No, Dan,' he said, 'truly the shirts are only round the corner in a lock-up.'

'Right, Roy,' I said. 'I'll go and get the lorry and we can load them up. Then you can get paid.'

'All right. My pal will go with you.'

I told him there was no need for that.

'It's no trouble and he knows where the lock-up is. Saves you coming back to the pub. You can go straight there.'

I agreed, so me and this right handy looking chap walked down to the lorry. I knew the only thing that stopped them robbing us was that they didn't know who had the money. I walked in front, he was behind me. As we got to the door of the lorry, I spun around and hit him right on the nose. He reeled back and went inside his pocket to pull a tool out, but I was faster than him. I had a jiffy bottle with ammonia in it.

I squirted him right in the eyes. He screamed and held his eyes. I jumped straight into the lorry and tore off. We had to drive past the pub to get away. As we got to it, Roy Neale and the rest of them were rushing about getting into cars. A BMW pulled away from the curb just as we got to them. They were going to try to stop us, but I just smashed into the front of it, pushing it out of the way.

On the way back I said, 'Here you are, Terry,' and gave him his money back. 'Put it back into your bank,' I said.

'Dan, you never gave them a chance to show us if there was any T-shirts,' he said. 'I still think there was. I know Micky wouldn't con us. I have known him for years.'

'Terry there was no T-shirts, but if you think there was I'll get out here, and yous two can go back. But you'd be making a terrible mistake.'

That night I phoned Micky Gluckstead. 'I've heard all about it,' he said. 'Why didn't you just drop out and earn a few quid?'

'Mick, you know that's not my style,' I said. 'I'm loyal to pals. Who put the bit of work up?'

'Their pal Micky the karate instructor,' he said, 'but don't tell them.'

Well I did tell them but they both refused to believe it. Micky didn't have too many of his corners go wrong and no doubt if I hadn't been there that one would have worked.

Mick continued to do well and one day he did the impossible. Him and his mate dressed up like farmers, wellington boots and all, lent a Range Rover and sold a Pakistani the cows that graze on Wanstead Flats. When the foreign gentleman turned up with his float to pick them up, the police were called and he was arrested. Micky had taken £7,000 off him as a deposit.

He used to put people at ease about the many scars on his face by fetching into the conversation that he'd been involved in a car accident. And Micky doesn't talk like a villain; he talks with a good speaking voice.

Micky always seemed to find trouble when he was out of prison – like me, often through his loyalty to pals. One night, him and his mate Billy 'The Fonz' Gibney went to the Regency Club in Hackney for a drink with the Kray twins. They left early and called back for a drink in a little drinking pub in Station Road, Forest Gate.

As they left, three young policemen stopped them and started to have a go at The Fonz, as he dressed rather loudly. Bill was scared of dogs. One police officer, realising this, said to the dog, 'Attack,' then held his snarling beast back, just inches away from Bill's face. He was terrified.

'You're not so flash now, cunt, are you?' said the officer. 'So let's see what's in your car. I'll stay here with the dog guarding you to stop you running away, while my two colleagues go with Mr Gluckstead to search the car.' Obviously the officers knew Micky and they wanted to search the car for either drugs or weapons.

Whilst searching the car, one of the officers said that they suspected them of having drugs in their possession. Now, up to this point, Micky had put up with all their cheek and given them his right name and details, so his car checked out down to him. Billy had also given his right name and address, so he also checked out clear. In fact, Micky and Bill had been ultra-polite up to this point – but enough was enough.

'Look, officer,' Micky said. 'My pal is terrified of dogs. Could you please hold the dog, as you have checked us out thoroughly.'

'What, so he can run away?' the officer said.

By this time, Billy had pissed himself with fear. Ever the gentleman, Micky said, 'If you don't hold that dog back, sir, I will have to get it away from my friend as quickly as possible. As you can see, he's in a very distressed state.'

All three police officers started to laugh. As quick as lightning Micky declared war, and went into action. He kicked the dog straight in the ribs. The dog yelped in pain and rolled over. Micky was on it before it could recover and kicked it three times in the body. The dog just lay there whimpering.

The dog handler hit Micky with his truncheon. Micky belted him straight in the face, breaking his nose. He punched one of the others straight in the spine – he went straight to his knees, screaming. Just then more police arrived. Obviously they had been waiting nearby, and they gave Micky and Billy a real good hiding.

CASH IN CORNERS

Micky went away for 12 months, Billy for 6. The police dog had to be put down.

Micky had a fight with Johnny Seagers in prison. No one had ever beaten Johnny. Micky broke three of his ribs and done him good and proper, but Seagers bit half his ear off. Micky had to go in front of the governor. 'What's happened to your ear?' he said.

'I'm working on an outside party,' Micky said, 'and there's a horse near where we're working. I went up to it to stroke it and it bit my ear.'

'It's funny,' The governor remarked, 'we had Seagers up here earlier on, and that same horse broke his ribs as well.'

'Some strange things happen in prison, sir,' said Micky.

'I can't nick the horse so no action will be taken.'

A bit later on in his life, Seagers was a supergrass for the chainsaw security gang. He put them all away, but that was the only fight he lost.

When Micky was released the police were really after him. When the drink-driving law first came in Micky was nicked within 15 minutes and got 6 months in Pentonville. He got 18 months for the burglary charge. In every nick, Micky was top dog. By this time his reputation preceded him and he had plenty of challenges. But Micky never ever lost a single fight.

Every time he came home he had to get a living, but the police would not leave him alone. One night they pulled him up but this time Micky exploded. They immediately called for back-up, and at the end of the day Micky had put four of them in hospital. Still, as they had beaten him almost to death with their truncheons, and as Micky had only used his hands, Micky's barrister managed to get him off with an 18-month jail sentence, so it was back to prison for poor Micky. It seemed in or out of prison Micky was always fighting.

At the time Micky went away, he was courting a girl named Maureen Wright. They were engaged to be married. Then, after about six months went by, Maureen deserted Micky and started living with a police officer. Micky was devastated but he had to accept the fact. When he was released from prison he tried to make a fresh start, so he went away to sea for a while, so that he could forget about Maureen and also so that the police would forget about him. Some chance of that now – they were really after him.

When he got back from sea, The Fonz told Micky, 'I have got to go to Tilbury docks to pick up some money that's owed to me. Would you like to come?'

'All right,' said Micky.

When they got to this yard near Tilbury Docks, the man who owed the money didn't want to pay and was arguing, saying he didn't owe it. This man had two nasty Alsation dogs chained up. Bill was sweating with fear. The bloke said, 'Get out of my yard. You can whistle for your money.' With that, he let one of his dogs loose and it ran to Bill.

Micky stepped in and punched the dog with a tremendous blow to the ribs, cracking them. Just then, Bill shouted, 'Look out.' The other dog was off his lead and in the air, leaping at Micky. He grabbed the dog in mid-air, threw it to the floor, and started to kick and punch it. Soon both dogs were lying there crying and whimpering.

'Can we have the money now, please?' Micky said to the fellow, all calm. The fellow immediately paid up.

'Micky, if I hadn't seen that with my own eyes, I wouldn't have believed it,' said Bill.

Micky laughed. 'Don't tell anyone, Bill,' he said, 'or people who hear the stories that I'm mad will start to believe them.'

CASH IN CORNERS

About this time Micky met Janet who he really fell madly in love with and was to marry. Then one day out of the blue Maureen phoned Micky and said, 'I'd like to meet you. I have got something to say to you.' Micky arranged to meet her on the Woolwich Embankment where they used to meet when they were courting.

When they met, Maureen said she realised she had made a mistake, and she really loved Micky and wanted to make a new start with him. 'I'm sorry, Maureen,' said Micky, 'I'll always have feelings for you, I can't help that, but I am about to marry Janet whom I dearly love.'

He kissed her and said goodbye. As he walked away, she shouted, 'Micky, if you leave me, I'll kill myself.'

Micky told her not to be silly, turned and carried on walking. Then he heard a scream and a splash. She had thrown herself in the Thames.

Micky dived in after her, but the current was too strong, Micky couldn't get to her. He almost did three times but he failed. Some lightermen dragged Micky from the Thames almost dead, but still trying to reach Maureen – but she was gone for ever. To make matters worse, the police held Micky in custody and tried to say he'd murdered her. They made his life a living hell.

ROUND 8

THREE GOOD MEN DOWN

I had a phone call one morning. It was Peter Morris. He wanted to borrow some beer barrels for his club, the Gallions, in Custom House, Prince Regent's Lane. I liked Peter, he was a tough man and a good professional boxer, but not a bully at all, so me and my son Danny delivered three barrels of lager to his club. I spoke to Peter and his pal Micky O'Shay, then I left them at about 1.30 pm.

Then, in the early hours of the next morning, I got a phone call. I hate early morning calls. They're never good news. It was my pal Dicky Hills. 'Dan, have you heard the news?' he said.

'Dick, it's 1.30 in the fucking morning,' I said. 'What are you talking about the fucking news for?'

'No, listen,' he said. 'Peter and Micky went drinking over Tony Weedon's pub the Telegraph last night. They had a fight and Peter's dead.'

I was dumbstruck.

News started to leak out through the grapevine over the next few days. Apparently Peter had been shot and hit in the head with a machete. The murder squad came to see me because I was with Peter that day, but I couldn't help them.

Peter had had the top of his head cut off, and under a car they found a cat with the top part of his scalp, licking and eating it. I heard Peter had done plenty of damage himself. Peter would put up a good fight with anyone, but you can't fight bullets and machetes with fists. No one was ever convicted for killing Peter. That was a sad end to a good, brave fighting man.

It wasn't just bad news for Peter's family and friends. My friend Tony Weedon, nicknamed 'Tucker', ran the pub where it happened. His uncle Bert – one of the finest guitarists in the world and teacher of Eric Clapton, John Lennon and Joe Brown to name just a few – had lived in Ruskin Avenue when I was growing up.

Tony has been unlucky in his life. He wasn't even there the night Peter got himself killed, but he lost the pub all the same. From then on, his luck was on a downward spiral. He couldn't seem to do anything right. The strain of it all broke his marriage up. He went round to see his wife one night, as they were living apart. They had a bit of a row, his wife stabbed him in the leg, they had a struggle and his wife fell onto the knife. It killed her instantly.

The police arrested Tony for murdering his wife. The CPS said to Tony, 'If you plead guilty to manslaughter you'll walk out of the court as a free man, and as you've done a bit of time on remand already it will be time served.' Tony said no, it was an accident.

Tony unjustly got a guilty verdict on a manslaughter charge and got six years. When he came up for parole, the parole board officer said to him, 'Say sorry for killing your wife and you'll get parole.' But Tony insisted it was an accident so he did the full time, because he would not own up to a crime he never did.

He is a free man now and he is trying to rebuild his life. Tony really is a lovely chap, who has had hard times. I hope they are over for him.

There was another sad loss during that time. Johnny Cooney had my good friend Del Croxson helping him on the door at Antics. Del was a powerful man who had been in prison with Barry Dalton, but whereas Barry was a bit of nuisance on drink, Del was always a pleasure to have round you.

When Del came home from prison he tried to get off heroin, but it was a hopeless task. He robbed a post office with his pal Steve Steph. They both got caught once again – a grass finished them. They appeared before the infamous Judge Greenwood at Chelmsford Assizes.

Del knew in front of Greenwood they had no chance at all, and he also knew Greenwood would give them as much as possible, so Del went to the toilet and fetched a bar of soap into the court room with him. At the first opportunity he threw it at Greenwood. The High Court Judge saw it coming and moved out of the way. Del's barrister got straight up and asked for a different judge, as he said, 'Mr Croxson will not get a fair trial now.'

Judge Greenwood stepped down, but all them judges work hand in glove, so Del still finished up getting eight years. By a strange quirk of fate, when Barry Dalton was finishing off his five years, which he got for demanding money with a gun, he got sent to Eastchurch on the Isle of Sheppey, the same prison Del was in.

They became close friends training together, but Del was always the Guv'nor. They got released about the same time. Barry looked up to Del as he was so big and strong. When Barry had a prizefight, Del always did his corner, and if he got into any trouble he always used to call for him to help him out. Del never ever accepted one penny for his work, he truly was a gentleman, but his addiction started to get the better of him.

Then Del started to lose weight and lose his strength. When this happened Barry started to dig him out, which he would not have been capable of doing earlier on. Barry by this time was doing well: he was selling drugs in a big way. Del was working at Antics but his money was all going on heroin and Barry was rubbing it in. One night Del said, 'Can you lend me £30?'

'I wouldn't lend scum like you six pence,' said Barry. 'You're just a fucking idiot.' I told Barry to get out of my house or else me and him could settle it in the yard. Barry wisely left it.

By this time Del was desperate for money, so a bit of work was put together to rob a drug house of drugs which had just been delivered there, worth £400,000. The information was good, but everyone would have to go armed, as these drug dealers were dangerous people. The only problem was, Barry and Del were both involved. Both were on drugs and a hatred was building up between them.

The idea was that three people would go in Barry's straight car to avoid a mug pull. A stolen van would go behind with dodgy plates on it, to load the drugs in. And another crooked car behind that would drive to the bit of work, and if things got nasty, it would smash into anyone following them. This could have been either other members of this drug gang or the police.

Barry's car would be driven to near the drug house, then he would transfer to the stolen car, then drive the stolen car and van to the drug house. The drugs would then be taken and loaded onto the van, Barry would come away in the stolen car, then get back to his own vehicle and drive home in a safe car following the van containing the drugs straight back to the lock-up. Then the drugs

Top left: Happy days. This one's of me arriving in Spain to soak up the sun.

Top right: Me and Bill, my brother in law. Tragically, he died in a car accident some years ago.

Bottom: The love of my life. Me with my wife, Becky, at a boxing dinner show.

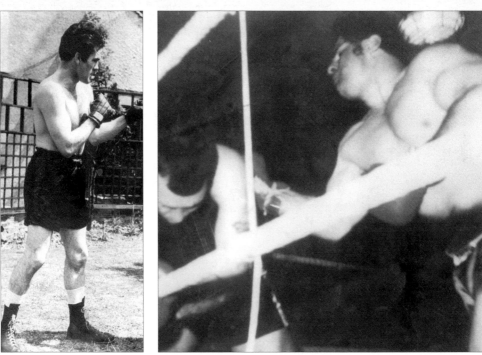

Top: Freddie Mills, ex light heavyweight champion of the world, enjoying himself.

Bottom left: Fooling about in Freddie Mill's Garden.

Bottom right: Micky Gluckstead at 29 head to head with Roy Shaw in his prime.

Top Left: Micky with Billy Gibney (middle) and Micky Tucker (right).

Top right: Micky still looking well and meaning business in 2001 age 53.

Above: Micky after a good night out.

Right: Micky with Jazz singer Jimmy Herring.

Top Left: The listeners advert in Wayland. A sad sight.

Top Right: One-eyed Jackie Clifford, Georgie Woods and the great Rocky Marciano at the Astor Club back in 1960.

Bottom: Some artwork I had done in prison.

Pit bulls are one of my life's passions.

Top: Danny and Sharon, my kids, with two beautiful American Pitbulls. I was the first to import them into this country.

Bottom: Two of my champion dogs. Sam and Bad Company. Sam finally made the front cover of pit bull news – the best dog in the world!

PIT BULL NEWS

CH NEILLSON

XMAS 1989

Top left: Dave Defreitas with Savva.

Top right: Roy Shaw with Roy Hunt.

Bottom: Georgie Wood with his Nephew Mickey Daltrey.

Reggie Kray. Need I say more?

Top: (*left*) Tania proved a loyal pal to Reg, as did Jacquie Williams (right). In the centre is Reg's lovely wife, Rob.

Bottom: Ronnie and Reggie's final resting place and (*inset*) the letterhead that Reg used for business when was inside.

Terry Butwell, 5 times kickboxing champion of the world, in full flow at the finals. (*Inset*) Terry after the fight, holding his title.

could be checked, and one man was going to come down and buy the lot. It had all been arranged.

When they got about a mile away from the drug house, Barry said to Del, 'I don't like this plan. I reckon all the cocaine should be loaded into my car, all the grass in the van. That way if we lose either one, we don't lose the lot. I'll sell the Charlie and see yous all later on with the money.'

Well, most of the money was in the cocaine and it wasn't bulky, it was easy to shift. Barry was obviously trying to cheat everyone out of their money. 'I don't think so,' said Del. 'We stick to the original plan. That way everyone is happy.'

'Listen, cunt,' said Barry. 'I run all of London. What I say goes, you scumbag.'

'Bollocks,' said Del. 'You're not taking my coke.'

Barry in his drug-fuelled state pulled a revolver from his pocket as he was driving along. As quick as lightning, Del shot him twice in the head with a shotgun, killing him instantly.

Barry's car crashed into a wall. Del and the other fellow got out of Barry's car and jumped into the car behind. The van shot off. So no one got any money. Del made himself scarce.

The murder squad interviewed me, as they knew Barry had been with me a few days earlier. They went and saw Paul as he had thrown Barry out of the club. They interviewed Micky as he'd had a fight with him.

They could not find Del, but he was not a suspect. Anyhow, everyone thought they were the best of pals. Eventually the fuss died down. Barry was only 35 – too young to die. Drugs destroyed Barry, nothing else. But Del still needed the heroin.

One night, a fellow said to him, 'There is a grass in Lincoln. He is a drug dealer who's just put my pal away. We can't do nothing about it as he knows us, but if you go to Lincoln and cut him, just give him a few stitches across his face, we will give you £2,000.'

'Consider it done,' said Del. He recruited two fellows – I don't think they even knew what they were going to Lincoln for. I do know that the driver never had a clue. He was only running Del to Lincoln for a favour.

When Del got to Lincoln, it all went wrong. The driver waited in the car around the corner from the house. Del told him he was just collecting a debt for someone. Del and the other fellow knocked at the grass's house. A lady answered the door, and he asked for the grass.

He must have smelt a rat, and would not come out. But he stuck his head out of an upstairs window and said, 'What do you want?'

Del pulled a 9mm automatic pistol from his coat and shot him in the head. By a miracle, the way the grass's head was angled, the bullet travelled round the inside of his scalp, but did not go through him. It made a circle right round the inside of his scalp and out the back.

Obviously Del thought he was dead. Him and his mates ran back to the car but, unbeknown to Del, the police had been keeping observation on the grass's house for drug dealing. A terrific chase ensued. Del opened fire on the police, so they kept well back.

Del jumped out of the car in Lincoln and made his own way back to London. He got away and the other two got caught. When he got back to London, he was given a car, a flat and £1,500 to help him lay low, but he had to steer clear of Romford as he was so well known in that area.

Within three days he could not resist it. He went back to Romford to his sister's house for some heroin. The police obviously had observation on all his family's houses, so he was arrested for attempted murder.

Whilst awaiting trial in Belmarsh, Del started training and was getting really fit. He was getting off heroin. Then some idiot smuggled some heroin in to him. It was pure. Del took it and it killed him. He was only 32 years old.

His co-defendants both got 18 years, which was terrible as they didn't know what they was going to Lincoln for in the first place

Poor Del left a lovely wife, Lynne, and four children. One of them he had never seen as Lynne was pregnant when he got nicked. Heroin killed a fine man. So drugs killed both Barry and Del, old cellmates at an early age.

I took Del's death very badly. He was more like a younger brother or even a son to me. I received a letter from him. I had news of his death before the letter arrived, so when I opened Del's last letter I knew what to expect. It broke me up.

ROUND 9

ME AND MICKY
ARE NICKED

Micky was really down too. He married Janet and had a little boy, Michael, but he still felt responsible for Maureen's death. His mind was in a terrible state. He turned to drink, but every time he went out somebody tried to get a quick reputation by beating him. There was always someone who wanted to fight him.

At a party in Canning Town, a big lump started digging Micky out. 'You don't look that tough to me,' he said. 'I reckon I could do you.'

'You most probably could, mate,' Micky said, 'but you won't get the chance tonight, I'm going home.'

This fellow wouldn't pack up, and jumped up out of his chair as Micky was leaving, grabbing hold of Micky in a bear hug, trying to crack his ribs. Micky's patience finally snapped and he bit this fellow right on the nose. The big lump immediately let Micky go and was screaming. There was blood everywhere. Micky just grabbed his head and bit harder. He bit this fellow's nose right off.

Then he said, 'Anyone else think they can beat me?' You could have heard a pin drop.

Again the police picked up Micky, but no one, including the big lump, would give evidence, so they reluctantly had to let him go. The police hated letting Micky go, but they had no option.

Micky's reputation was getting bigger and bigger. He went to meet some people at a pub in Bow in the East End of London one night. As he was waiting, he bought himself a drink. Then five drunks tried to set about him, just because he was Micky Gluckstead.

The first one smashed him in the face with a glass, which later required 28 stitches. Well, Micky took all five and the bar apart. The pub was cleared, people running everywhere. The next day the pub was boarded up, closed for business. The police nicked Micky for it, but the witnesses didn't turn up in court, so once again Micky stuck his fingers up to the police. But Micky was still always in trouble, fighting or trying to corner someone.

He had a fight with Kenny Johnson who had the Two Puddings in Stratford. Kenny had never lost a fight before, and Micky done him and his minder with just his bare hands. But Mick got a terrible stab wound and the doctors said he would never use his right arm again. Three nights later a Zodiac just like Micky's drove past and shot the Two Puddings up. The police said it was like a Chicago-style drive-by shooting. Again the police picked Micky up, but there was no evidence against him.

Janet, although she loved Micky, couldn't stand this way of life any longer and they broke up. Micky still loved her tremendously, and she loved him, but she couldn't stand no more trouble as it was making her ill. But it wasn't Mickys fault, his reputation went before him and everybody wanted to take it.

At this time Micky met up with a girl called June, who had a son.

She seemed to make Micky happy, and after a little time they moved in together. She was a highly strung girl. Hardly Micky's type, but he must have seen something in her.

They had a volatile relationship. One minute they were together, then they were apart. It seemed like they were always rowing, but Micky was doing well at the cornering game, so when he had a good score, everything seemed all right between them.

A drinking club opened up in Forest Gate about this time that only catered for black people. It was what they called a blues club. The proprietor was a big African about 6ft 4in tall and full of muscle. He was a fearsome character. One night Micky – half drunk, half out of his head – walked into there alone and asked for a lager. This big African came charging around the counter. 'Out,' he said.

'Listen, Golliwog,' said Micky, 'I'll go because there's so many of you, but I could take you on your own.'

This big giant just roared with laughter, showing four gold teeth. 'You fucking white midget,' he said.

'If you're so confident, come outside,' Micky went on. 'Just me and you, man to man.' This African shouted out that on no account was anyone else to get involved and laughed. So Micky walked out of the club with about 15 Africans following him.

Well, Micky and this black giant went toe to toe for 15 minutes, surprising some passers-by who stopped to watch this fight. Black and white were cheering and clapping in unison. Then suddenly the big black bloke dropped to his knees. He had never been beaten in his life, but he had had enough. The shock of seeing this stunned the black people and they went deadly silent.

Micky was black and blue. He had two broken ribs and a broken wrist, but he just walked away. That same night, a Zodiac six-cylinder car, just like Micky's and just like the one that did the Chicago-style shooting at the Two Puddings, did the same thing at this club. A few black guys got hurt. They picked Micky up for this shooting but there was no evidence against him.

About a month after this shooting the police picked Micky up and nicked him for burgling an office and stealing a safe with £6,000 in it. The only evidence they had was a fingerprint. Micky said he was innocent and was nowhere near the office that night. But he was found guilty and got two and half years in prison. I felt sorry for Micky, but I felt the bit of bird he got would straighten his head out.

What with the Hathaway club and my small office block I managed okay but, just like Micky, I had a job keeping out of trouble. First David Brown stabbed me in Manor Park. I beat him half to death as soon as I realised he had wounded me badly – in fact, the injury nearly cost me my life. We were both picked up by the police at East Ham Memorial Hospital, where we were both treated. We said we'd been mugged by a gang of blacks, so no charges were ever made.

A few years before, I'd seen a television programme about a debt collector from over south London by the name of Dave Courtney. I thought, 'What a lairy, flash bloke he is. Then I saw him on TV another time spouting off. I really thought, 'This geezer is potty.'

Well, me and Dave Defreitas were in the Hathaway club one morning when a big, flash BMW pulled up. Two fellows got out, both wearing dark glasses. I nudged Dave. 'Who're these pair of jokers?' I said. It was Dave Courtney and his pal Ian.

As they walked in, Courtney said, 'We'd like a word.'

'Go on,' I said.

'Well, we've got a club in the West End,' he said. 'It closes at 5 am Monday morning. Could you have all our punters here till about 12 noon on Monday, to chill out?'

'We could,' I said, 'but what's in it for us?'

'You can have the bar plus half the door money,' he said. 'You can charge at least £5 entrance fee.'

'That sounds okay to me,' I said. As the Hathaway was sound-proofed, we wouldn't disturb any one.

So Monday morning me and Dave Defreitas and Black Del were in the Hathaway at 5.15 am. By 7 am we were packed – with all good spenders. Courtney and his pals all looked either ferocious or weird, but they were all really lovely people, no trouble at all. It was a really successful Monday.

'Leave the money,' Dave said. 'We'll square up later. I've got to dash off. I'm in a hurry right now.'

The following week it was the same procedure, but black Del stole all the two weeks' door money. Well, after everyone had left the club, and Dave and Ian had run a couple of people home, they came back for their money.

'Dave, it won't take long to count what's here,' I said. 'Del's nicked it all.'

Dave just laughed. 'Never mind, Dan,' he said. 'I hope he enjoyed himself.'

I thought he was going to go potty. It surprised me, his reaction. Well, we had a few complaints from neighbours and the police stopped us from doing it any more, as our licence didn't cover us for early morning drinking. But I reckon Dave Courtney should be nicked by the trade description act, because he advertises himself as a real flash, horrible man. He is a hard man who's no one's fool but he's also a very nice man, who is easy to get on with. I found Dave and Ian both thorough gentlemen whom I would gladly put myself out to associate with.

At around this time I had a fight with a giant of a man reputed to be the strongest man in Essex, over Janet McQueen, who as I said, I used to go out with. Luckily I caught him just right and knocked him out. When he came round he pulled a bowie knife on me, and would have done me a lot of damage, but my old pal Danny O'Leary shot him in the stomach. The big man did get over it. The police pulled me in, and again I made a 'no comment' statement. This giant made no comment as well, so no charges once again. But they wanted the gun man badly, so Danny O'Leary went back to Ireland for a while until things cooled down.

Next there was a man in Manor Park called Brian Childs. I had known Brian for years, but we never spoke. I didn't like him and he didn't like me, but he was built like a bull, a short but very broad man. Then he started a row with my dad, on purpose, to get at me. So the next morning at 9 am I went to see him at the greengrocer's where he worked in Romford Road. To cut a long story short, me and Brian had a right battle. We finished up toe to toe in the middle of Romford Road stopping all the traffic. People were getting off of buses to watch us, it was like in Roman times – a big crowd watching two gladiators fighting to the death if need be.

At the finish there was at least a hundred people watching us and no traffic moving in either direction. No one dared to try to stop us. Brian is a very powerful and game man. His face was pissing with blood, but he was so strong. Eventually, after about 15 minutes, I hit him. He went down and broke his ankle. No one was more pleased than me. I knew it was impossible for him to continue fighting. I was exhausted. I could hardly breathe. I really don't know how Brian stood up to my punches. I was catching him right as he was boring in. He went down twice but twice he got up. He was out of work for a year on crutches.

Afterwards my hands were in a terrible state – smashed to pieces.

An ambulance took Brian to hospital; I got in my grey and white Humber Hawk, went round my mum's to have a bath and change my bloodstained clothes, and went to the café for a breakfast.

As I walked into Rosie Enever's café, Rosie came up to me. 'Dan, you'd better make yourself scarce,' she said. 'The police have already been here looking for you.'

'Rose, first things first,' I said. 'I will have egg, bacon, beans and a fried slice.' So she took me out the back room and fed me. Then the phone rang. It was my mum. She said that the police had been to her house as well.

So I went down to Yalding in Kent and stayed with my gypsy friends for about a month to let things die down. When I came back to Manor Park, I walked into Ilford police station with my solicitor, Mr Riley from Breeze, Benton and Co., in Bow, and asked the police why they were looking for me. They said that they had witnesses who saw me do terrible damage to a Mr Brian Childs. Full marks to Brian, he said nothing. And I said nothing. So the police could do nothing as by this time all the witnesses had developed amnesia.

I saw Brian in the Lita club with two of his friends a while after. He was up at the bar having a drink. I had to go up to him. I didn't want to, but pride being what it is, I said, 'Hello, Brian. I think you're looking for me.' He just glared at me. 'Right, Brian,' I went on. 'We can have this one of two ways. You and me can go outside now and we can have another go or we can have a drink. I am not bothered, one or the other.'

'Let's have a drink,' he said. And was I pleased? I didn't fancy fighting him again. Me and Brian will never be bosom pals but I do respect him and his courage, and a lot of people reckon we had one of the best fights ever seen in the East End of London.

Then one night me and my old gypsy pal Matty Attrell went to

Brentwood for a drink with some other fellows. We got into a fight in a Chinese restaurant. Well, the Chinese put me and Matty in hospital, but there were 12 of them in the hospital with us. One lost an eye. They all had stitches. I was hit with a meat cleaver across my head. The police gave us bail pending further inquiries. Surprisingly no witnesses could or would make any statements again, so once again the police work came to nothing. But they were beginning to hate me.

They arrived at my house at 6 am, searched it and found nothing, but took me to Bishopsgate police station and charged me with obtaining firearms by deception. I knew nothing about any deception. What happened was that my pal Ronnie Baxter had said a church verger had some guns for sale at the Dutch church in the Barbican. I thought, 'I can buy them and we can take them to my mate Bill Stevens' farm down Kent and have some target practice, just a bit of sport.'

Well, we went to the Barbican and had a look at these guns. 'How much are they?' I said.

'£1,000 for the three.'

'I'll give you £750,' I said, and he agreed.

As I went to pay him, he said, 'Can I see your firearms licence?' I told him I didn't have one. In that case, he said, he couldn't sell them to me. I only wanted them for target practice on a farm, I said, but he still refused. 'Well, if you change your mind here's my name and phone number,' I said.

Apparently after I left, a fellow called in there and bought the guns on a forged licence. When the verger reported it to the police, they nicked me and Ronnie Baxter for it. They said that we had sent somebody there with a forged licence – as if I would leave my name and phone number if I was getting the guns on a dodgy licence. They also nicked Terry Palmer from Manor Park. I really don't know how Terry got involved, he knew nothing about it all. But we all got remanded to Wormwood Scrubs.

The police let Baxter and Palmer out on bail after the first week but they kept me. Nine months later, I went to Knightsbridge Crown Court and got acquitted – but I had done nine months in prison.

Wormwood Scrubs was filth: three men to a cell, and we had a bucket each to go to the toilet in. The plastic bucket had a screw-on lid, and when you undid it, the smell made you vomit. On the landing was a big white sink with a hole in the middle of it. At 8 am it was slop-out time and we all queued up with our buckets to empty them into this sink, with a tap running all the time. Sometimes you would stand there and the bloke in front of your bucket would splash up on you. I've seen many a fight over that.

If anybody wanted a shit in the night they would do it in a piece of paper and throw it out of the window. The next morning you had what you call the shit patrol; someone who went around with a screw collecting this shit up. As the inmate doing this job was always a goody-goody – or as we call them 'screw boys' – most mornings they would get pelted from cell windows by shit wrapped up in paper.

Frankie Fraser's boy Patrick was my neighbour in the Scrubs. He is a good man. He'd got nicked with a lot of money and was accused of dealing in cocaine. His explanation of how he had got hold of this money was that he had a ray-gun which made horses bolt once it was aimed at them. Apparently one of his victims was a horse that champion jockey Greville Starkey was riding in a big race.

Although Greville Starkey was called to give evidence at the trial and confirmed Patrick's story, saying his mount had inexplicably veered off the course that day, and although the race was under scrutiny and some very large bets had been taken on the winning horse, they still found Patrick guilty of cocaine and he got the six years. It was an injustice but I think Patrick only went away because his name is Fraser.

Soon I was back on the streets and full of myself. Jackie Beatty and my good friend Dave Defreitas had kept the Hathaway club and my offices going whilst I was away so that I still had an income. While I had been away, a man named Martin Dunn had started to make a name for himself as a hard man around Manor Park. He did three men in the Star one night, then came on to the Hathaway club.

I was sitting in the main bar when he arrived. He set about an elderly chap who was taking the entrance money, as he didn't want to pay to come in. So I had to fight him. We had a tremendous battle. He was no pushover, this guy, but after ten minutes of action he dropped to the floor and lay there. His mates couldn't believe I had beaten him.

At this time I was doing a bit of training at the Atherton Suite, Romford Road in Forest Gate. One day Mark Kaylor, Frank Bruno and Sylvester Mittee were up there as well. My pal Tony Cooke was developing a spray made up from peppers to use as a dog repellant if a dog attacked you. 'This spray would make their eyes water and breathing difficult,' he said, and he gave me a spray. As I had a number of pit bulls, he thought I might need one.

Well, this day at the Atherton Suite, the northern comedian and impersonator Stanley Baxter was in the steam room. He was appearing at the Theatre Royal, Stratford. For a joke I sprayed this dog repellant into the steam room then walked out, closing the door behind me.

After about two minutes we were all watching as the door flew open and Stanley and his friend crawled out all red holding their throats. He was naked and just lay there choking and spluttering. An ambulance was called and took him to hospital, and I never saw him there again.

The police wanted me for a load of spirits stolen from Purfleet. Someone had gone to this firm with the right paperwork and just drove this 40-foot artic load away. But they had to drop the case, as the fellow who accepted the load sheets couldn't identify me as the thief. Rather unfortunate for the boys in blue, eh? They were so disappointed I could have cried for them.

So the police were still making a nuisance of themselves, but I had more weapons in my arsenal. They had me in for questioning about a load of motor engines stolen from Fords. Also some dodgy cheques. But they had to let me go after 48 hours through lack of evidence. Still, they were becoming a nightmare. They had questioned me about Del Croxson's shooting escapade in Lincoln, Barry Dalton getting killed, Peter Morris getting his head chopped off. In fact, everything that happened in Newham, they seemed to think I did or knew about.

I got my own back one day, in my own little way. I had a slug gun. It was a pistol type, a very powerful gun. Me and my young son Danny used to take it over Wanstead flats and shoot tin cans and trees. We killed many a dustbin. One day on our way home, and we got to Upton Park station and there were four mounted policemen in the middle of the road stopping traffic, as West Ham United were playing at home to Manchester United. They were directing football fans straight out of the station, down the road towards the football ground. They were using their horses to make sure the fans all moved as one. They were barging these Manchester fans with their horses.

There was one police officer on a great big grey horse being overzealous. It was beginning to annoy me – he was hurting people.

As I lined up in the traffic, I said to Danny, 'Give me the gun.' On the spur of the moment, I made sure no one could see me, then I took careful aim. I had a coat over the gun – only the end of the barrel was showing – then I fired. 'Zap' – the slug hit this grey horse right on the bum.

He reared up, the policeman lost the reins, then this great big grey horse bolted down Green Street with the policeman hanging onto his neck screaming. All the fans were laughing, cheering and clapping. Me and Danny were in hysterics. When the horse got to the Boleyn, he skidded to a halt. The mounted officer flew straight out of the saddle over the horse's head. The horse was okay and the officer was all right. He called an ambulance, went sick for months, then got retired off with a marvellous pension. At the time, though, the police were going mad.

I made myself scarce for a while until it all blew over. I reckon if they had caught me that day they would have shot me, but that is one of the biggest laughs I have ever had.

Shortly after this, my cousin Dave came to see me. He said he had a lorry load of videos he was trying to sell and did I know anybody for them? I asked a few people. Then, somehow or other, the police heard the name Woollard and took me into Dagenham police station where the serious crime squad used to be based.

I realised it was my cousin they wanted, so when they questioned me I said 'no comment'. I told my solicitor to get in touch with my home and to tell my wife I had been taken in about some videos, that it was a mistake, but to ring my cousin Dave about it if I needed bail money. Dave would realise the police were on to him and he could move the videos or whatever. I just sat it out in a cell. After one night in the cells the police realised their mistake and knew I had played them along. They chucked me out of the police station, fuming. But

I got the result I wanted. When Dave was turned over he was clean as a whistle.

My other cousin Teddy lived in Sixth Avenue, Manor Park with a girl called Pat. I had grown up with Teddy and known Pat all of my life. Her father died in the house where they lived after living there for 40 years. Then the landlord sold the house to some Pakistani speculator, part possession, very cheap. He never even gave Teddy or Pat the chance to buy it, so this Asian gentleman moved in upstairs, then straight away started to make life difficult for them, as he wanted them to move so he could have the property vacant.

First he made them get rid of their dog. Then he had all-night parties. When they still didn't move, he said to Teddy, 'You've got until Friday. Then me and my family are going to throw you out.' At this time there were seven Asians that could really have a fight. All were combat fighters, but wicked with it, all tooled up. If any Asians had been the victims of racial abuse or in any trouble at all, these seven men used to deal with it. They were called the Newham Seven, and believe me they were feared and known throughout London.

I spoke to Teddy and said, 'See if your landlord will give you a few quid to get out, and settle you in somewhere else, to avoid any arguments.'

Teddy asked the landlord but he just laughed and said, 'Woollard, Friday you're out. No money, so if your furniture and belongings are not out by then we'll throw them all in the road.'

So Friday evening, Roy O'Connor, Terry 'The Dustman' Holden, Alan Jackson, Jimmy Story, my cousin Teddy, his brother Brian and myself waited round Teddy's house, to stop his landlord from throwing him and his belongings out. We never expected any trouble. We thought when the landlord saw us he would come to some monetary arrangement with Teddy. We were wrong.

DANNY WOOLARD

We were sitting in the front room playing cards, when three car loads of Asians pulled up outside. They opened their boots and were getting baseball bats, bits of wood, iron bars and all sorts of weapons out. Someone had obviously told them we were in the house or they were intending to beat Teddy and Pat.

All of a sudden, 'Bang bang' at the door. We had one baseball bat between us. Teddy opened the door. 'You've been warned. Out,' screamed his landlord, and hit Teddy in the face with his fist. We were all in the front room, so we all ran out into the passage. Jimmy Story was the first man out of the door. He hit Teddy's landlord across the mouth with the bat, knocking him senseless. I picked up a brass ornament from Teddy's front room and hit the biggest one in the face with it. He almost did a somersault.

As he went to get up, Terry kicked him in the nose, splattering it all over his face. Then they turned to run. We ran after them. Although they were tooled up and there were more of them than us, we had done all of them, about 12 of them in all. There were bodies lying everywhere. All of a sudden a white transit van pulled up. It was the Newham Seven. Well, they were used to everyone running away from them, but we picked up the tools that the others had dropped and we ran straight at them.

There was a fierce battle – short but fierce. They were all tooled and so were we. But at the end of it, they were all lying on the floor unconscious or semi-conscious: broken noses, fractured skulls, the lot. We were all covered in cuts and bruises and blood but we had done them as well. We wrecked their mini-bus also. We set it alight. What happened next was unbelievable.

There was a club at the corner of Romford Road and Sixth Avenue. It was called The Little Eye Club. It was a black man's club, full of West Indians and Jamaicans. Well, I thought black people and

128

Asians didn't get on well. I was wrong. All these black people ran out of the club, picked up bricks and bits of scaffold tubes, anything they could find from a nearby building site, and came running down the road and joined in the fight against us. Also all the coloured people in the surrounding houses came out and joined in.

We did a few of them but there were just too many, so we got back into Teddy's house and locked ourselves in. Just before the door closed, I dragged one of the black people in with us. I thought, 'If he's with us they'll be more reluctant to smash Teddy's front door down, or his windows, as their brother might get hurt.' There were literally hundred of blacks outside Teddy's house.

Behind was a school. I looked over the back wall and there was about a hundred blacks just waiting for us to try to get away that way, so we now had a real battle on our hands – a battle we just could not win. Then I heard sirens coming. I chucked the hostage out of the front door, and for the first time in my life I was pleased to see the police appear.

There were loads of them: ambulances, response groups, you name it they were there. The ambulancemen took the injured people to hospital, then the police cleared the area. It took ages. Then they came into Teddy's house. I thought, 'We're all nicked here,' but the police only nicked Teddy. They arrested not one Indian. They played it all down as they did not want any racial tension in Newham. The local paper would not report it. Although Teddy and Pat were not on the council housing list, Newham Council offered them four different council places to live – all this to maintain racial harmony. Teddy got a small fine in court, so what he did then was he went to see his landlord and drew a few thousand off of him and moved into the council flat he had been offered. I knew from that day on that Newham belonged to the

Asians and blacks, and it was only a matter of time before all the white people would be ushered out.

ROUND 10

SPOOKY, SINISTER COINCIDENCES

A fellow from Canning Town – we'll just call him Tom to save him getting in trouble if any of his pals read this story – came into the Hathaway one night. 'I'm ruined,' he said. 'I know you don't agree with drugs but I have put all my money into getting drugs smuggled into this country. I have had one or two successes and built my money up, and in any case its only cannabis. Well, the last shipment is over here, but the police are watching it.'

I asked where it was. 'In a factory estate,' he told me. 'We've hired one unit, our stuff's been delivered there already, but the owner of the estate is my pal and he said the customs people have been following the lorry that delivered the cannabis there, and the police were waiting for us to pick it up and nick us all.'

'Let's have a look,' I said.

So he took me to this estate. His stuff was in the second from last unit in the end block. The undercover surveillance unit were in the

131

opposite unit. But behind Tom's block was a railway line. 'Take me back to the club and leave me,' I said to Tom.

When he dropped me off I asked him how much of the cannabis was in the unit. He told me 100 kilos, and 20 kilos were his share. He said, 'It's bagged up in 1-kilo packages.'

'Okay, leave it to me,' I said. I had an idea which could get Tom his money back and earn us a few quid as well. I phoned three of my pals. They came straight over. I explained my idea: we would get a convertible car and pull it in the roadway between Tom's unit and the undercover unit, with a nice-looking girl in it with a fellow. They would distract the police by enjoying themselves in front of the police surveillance post window. I would need one car parked near the entrance to the units in case it came on top, and me and one of the others would go over the railway and get the stuff out of the unit via the back door. Then we would go back across the railway lines, where our van would be parked.

'Twenty kilos goes to the bloke that stuck the bit of work up; whatever else is there is cut up five ways. We all get equal shares, including the woman.' Everyone agreed.

There was a woman who used to go in the Hathaway. I knew I could trust her. I had grown up with her family. She was married with a child. She was a real beautiful girl, about 5ft 6in with long, blonde hair hanging down her back. Her husband was a long-distance truck driver who often worked abroad. She was almost 28.

I told her what I wanted to do. At first she went crazy – 'I'm a decent married woman.' Then after a few drinks she asked how much she would get. I told her the same as all of us. So after some umming and erring and a few more drinks, she agreed.

Next night, I put a walkie-talkie in the car with the girl, who I'll call Tina, and John was in. We had put dodgy plates on a stolen

BMW convertible. I gave Henry a walkie-talkie to sit with near the entrance to the units, and me and Tony had one on us, so if anything happened we'd be warned and could get away back across the railway lines. First Henry got into position and then we drove around the back, parked the van, and Tina and John pulled up in front of the police unit.

Tony sicked up outside the van before we went. When we got across the railway, the door was in front of us. We lifted it off of its hinges and let ourselves in. We couldn't find the stuff at first; it was difficult as we couldn't shine a torch in case the police opposite saw the light. Then we saw it.

There were four sports bags. We carried them across the railway, then got Tina, John and Henry on the radio and told them to meet us back at the office in Berkeley Road. We were the first vehicle back, and had the stuff unloaded by the time the others got there. We had 80 kilos, so 20 went to Tom and the other 60 was ours. By Tom's calculations that worked out to be £120,000. That worked out at £24,000 each.

I phoned Tom. He said he would take the lot and sell it and return our money within the week. He was overjoyed.

We all sat in the office laughing and drinking.

John said he was going and drove off in the BMW, which he dumped on the way home. Henry said, 'Come on, Tony. I'll give you a lift home.' I said I'd finish this drink and drop Tina off. When they had gone, Tina asked where the toilet was. I showed her, thinking we'd leave in a minute, but Tina had other ideas. She walked in the room naked except for her high heels. 'I know what you want,' she said. 'Come on.'

Human nature being what it is, we both walked to my flat just down the hall from my office. When we got into bed, she said that since her husband was away so often she felt lonely. John had awakened desire in her which she thought she had long ago lost. So we had a wonderful night of love-making. She really was beautiful.

When we woke up it was 7 am. The sun was playing on her golden hair. I got up and had a shower, then woke her with a cup of tea. She had a shower and I could not resist it. I got back in the shower with her and we made love again.

I dropped her off near her home at 12.30 pm. I was exhausted.

Within a week I got our money. I gave John £24,000, Henry £24,000 and Tony £24,000. I only went near Tina one more time though, as I knew our feelings weren't just lust and I would never live with myself if I had taken her away from Harold. We both knew what we meant to each other, but it was too late in Tina's life for us to have any future.

I knocked at Tina's house and she smiled broadly. 'Come in,' she said, talking quietly as Harold was asleep in the other room. 'It's good to see you, Dan.'

'You too, mate,' I said, and we kissed.

'Come upstairs. My husband is tired and asleep downstairs,' she said.

I didn't want to, but I was too weak to say no. So I made love to her while her husband lay downstairs. When we finished, I said, 'Tina, I done much better from them drugs than I thought I would. Here's your money.' Then I kissed her goodbye. When she opened the briefcase there was £48,000 in it.

Call it conscience money if you like but I had given her and Harold, her husband, my share. I know that money helped Tina and Harold to go and get their little dream house and although many times I have been tempted to pay them a visit I never will. So the police lost their drugs and the villains they were waiting for. Tom got his money back and never again dealt in drugs and the dealers lost their drugs. But they can all rest in peace as they done Tina and Harold a good deed.

They do say that the truth is stranger than fiction. Well, the best man at my wedding was Billy Taylor. He was my brother-in-law, but he was much more than that. He had been a friend to me before he married my sister, Joyce. They had two sons, Billy and Barry, and were blissfully happy. One day, Joyce had gone down to their caravan and Bill was calling home to feed their dog on his way back from work, before setting off to meet her.

He got on to the A13 road near to the corner of Gascoigne Road. Suddenly, a mobile crane fell from a trailer and knocked his back wheel off. Then it bounced across the dual carriageway and, in one of those million-to-one freak accidents, hit the central reservation, bounced up into the air and smashed into his car, killing him instantly.

My cousin Dennis Holland was one of six. He lived two doors away from me when I was growing up and was the same age as me. His mum, Aunt Ollie, was my dad's sister and her husband was Joe. Dennis was short – about 5ft 6in – but very broad. A real powerful fellow. He was married with four children but unbeknown to him his wife was having an affair with his best friend. He was powerful but he wouldn't hurt a fly. He lived for his wife and children. He could see no harm in anyone. Dennis loved country and western music. This particular night, there was a country and western concert on. He asked his best friend if he would like to look after the children so he could take his wife. His pal agreed.

When they got back from the concert, Dennis said, 'Don't walk home. I'll drive you.' Dennis' wife said, 'I'll come with you, we'll only be a few minutes. I can get us a bit of supper on the way back.' So their 14-year-old daughter was left with the other three children. When they got into the car, Dennis got in the driver's seat with his wife next to him and his pal in the back. As Dennis put his safety belt on, his pal hit him on the head with an iron bar and kept beating him. Dennis couldn't get out of the car or avoid the blows as the safety belt was holding him in.

Then Dennis' wife got out of the car and got into the back seat. Her boyfriend pushed Dennis into the passenger's seat with some difficulty. Then he drove the car down the A13 into Jenkins Lane. He stopped at a secluded place and got into the back of the car with Dennis' wife and had sex with her, while Dennis lay dying and moaning in the front seat. It was a terrible thing to do to a dying man, but it turned them pair of nutters on. It was like the scene in the Jack Nicholson film *The Postman Always Rings Twice*.

When they were finished, Dennis was dragged from the car and finished off with blows to the head. He was put back into the car on the back seat, where his wife and best friend had just made love. Then the car was dumped near the A13. So that Saturday night my brother-in-law Billy Taylor and my cousin Dennis Holland both lay dead in cars on different sides of the same bridge, not a quarter of a mile apart.

Dennis' wife reported him missing next day, but the murder squad soon broke her story down and arrested her for murder. Her boyfriend seemed to have vanished into thin air. Dennis' two brothers, George and Stephen, were looking for him, as well as the police. The reason the police could not find him was he was walking about dressed up like a woman.

Eventually the police got him, and Dennis' wife and her boyfriend both blamed each other. He said she'd got him to do it with a promise to go away with him, and he loved her so he'd done it for her. He said she had told him Dennis had abused her and her daughter, and he was always beating both of them. She had said when Dennis got into the car she didn't know what was about to happen and was too frightened to help Dennis or to tell the police as soon as she could. Anyhow they both deservedly got life imprisonment.

Another incident when truth was stranger than fiction was when Buster Edwards died. There were two brothers from Dagenham who were getting hold of trailer loads of different goods. They approached me and my partner to buy the gear off of them, and we bought two or three loads. There was nothing of real value – we earned peanuts once the stuff was resold – but we kept buying off of them in the hope they would get a valuable load sometime. We didn't want them to go anywhere else.

One day they came to us with 30 tonnes of coffee granules. I tried to sell it, but couldn't. My partner tried also. He had two likely buyers who said they would buy it for £30,000, but they needed three weeks to get the money together. So me and my partner paid the brothers £15,000 for this coffee and parked it in a farm in Essex, putting the farmer in the deal. Well, the buyers backed out, so we had to try and sell it. We never had much success.

Anyhow, one day, a fellow from south London whose nickname was Big E phoned me. 'Would you like to buy 30 tonnes of coffee for £60,000?' he said.

'E, would you like to buy it for £30,000?' I said.

'It can't be done.'

'It can be done, because I own it.'

'I'll have to talk to someone first,' he said. 'Then I'll come over.'

He came over with two other guys. They said they would have the load but it had to be delivered to Liverpool by 1 pm Friday and we would have to deliver it. I said okay, as we were getting desperate to sell this coffee, but added, 'You do know once it's in Liverpool you own it all?' They agreed.

So I went to see my pal Roy Hunt from Manor Park, as he'd always dealt in lorries. I told him I needed a driver and a unit to go to Liverpool on Thursday night. Roy said he could lend me a unit but couldn't supply a driver.

'That's okay, Roy,' I said. 'I'll get a driver. We'll pick the lorry up at 4 pm Thursday.'

I phoned the farm where the trailer was parked. He said he'd sort out a driver.

So at 3 pm the farmer and the driver turned up at my house. I didn't like the driver at first, but first impressions can be wrong. So we went to Hathaway Crescent. Roy was waiting with the unit and the driver got into it. We followed in a car. At the farm, the brakes had seized up on the trailer, so we had a bit of a job, but eventually we were all set to go. I gave the driver £250. 'Fill right up with diesel,' I said, then gave him the address and added, 'When you come back I'll give you £500. If need be you can leave the trailer there. We don't really want it back.'

As far as we knew everything was fine, but the driver tried to save money on the diesel and didn't fill the lorry right up. Consequently he ran out of fuel on the motorway. He phoned up, we got help to him, but he got to Liverpool three hours too late.

Big E phoned me. 'I told you 1 pm,' he said. 'They won't unload the coffee until Monday morning now, but we'll leave the trailer in this firm's yard and they will pull it in and unload it Monday.'

'Okay,' I said. 'Tell the driver to drop the trailer and come back to

London. We'll just leave the trailer there.' This stupid driver unhooked the trailer but left the number plate from the unit still on it. Then he made his way home and ran out of diesel again.

When he rang, he left a message on my answering machine. He said he was poxed off with this job – the lorry had broken down again. Then he said exactly where the lorry was, and informed us he had abandoned it and was getting a lift home.

I arranged to have the lorry picked up and dropped at Hathaway Crescent by a heavy-duty breakdown firm. Before the breakdown lorry arrived back, Big E's wife phoned. 'Dan, the police found that coffee. They're all nicked with it. And they're looking for the lorry as they have the number plate, which was left on the trailer.'

I was in a state of shock, but the breakdown firm got the lorry back safely and I paid cash. Then me and Roy Hunt got the lorry going and drove it to my mate's breaker's yard in Romford. It was 10.30 pm but I got him to open up.

'It's important; cut this lorry up for me,' I said.

'When?'

'Jim, now. You can have it plus I'll give you £1,000.'

'It's as good as done.'

Roy phoned up Jock. 'Sorry it's late, mate,' he said. 'I've got some bad news for you. I left your lorry in the club yard opposite my flats and someone nicked it.'

'When did you leave it there?' said Jock.

'Eleven this morning, but I have been out all day. I was going to fetch it back tomorrow.'

'Okay,' said Jock. 'I'll report it stolen to the police.'

'Jock, don't say I had it, as I'm disqualified from driving. Leave me out.'

'Okay, Roy, but you'll have to give me a drink. I want £500 to leave you out.'

'All right, mate. See you tomorrow.'

So Saturday morning I gave Roy £500, which he gave to Jock. On the Monday Big E and two of his mates came to my office telling me about what had happened, and how they got nicked. 'Yes,' I said, 'but I made it clear once the lorry was at Liverpool, you owned it.' To cut a long story short, they said they didn't have the money, they were working for Peter Power. 'Give me his number,' I said. Then I phoned Mr Power and made a meet.

Down he comes to my office, but he had no money either. 'Well, who's going to pay me then?' I said

'The man who we were working for is Buster Edwards,' he said. 'Me and Big E are just middle-men, selling it for Buster.'

I knew Buster Edwards quite well. 'Right,' I said and phoned Buster. 'Hello, mate, Danny here. I've got Power here. I know they've lost the coffee but, Buster, I'll tell you the truth. Really the deal was once it was delivered in Liverpool you own it. Still, I'll tell you what I'll do. I don't expect you to pay £30,000 but the load cost £15,000. It cost £2,000 to get it up there and other expenses. Just give me £8,500 and we'll both lose a bit.'

'Dan, that's fair,' he said, 'but I haven't got the money yet.'

'Buster, don't worry,' I said. 'Give it to me when you get it.' he said

'Dan, you're a gentleman,' he said. And I put the phone down.

The next morning I heard on the news that Buster had hung himself. I was shocked and sad. I heard he had been drinking heavily, had lost a load of mountain bikes which he had paid for. He was skint, the council was going to close his flower stall and he really needed the money. The coffee was going to earn him, but instead he owed even more money to us. I didn't know it was Buster Edwards we were carting the coffee for to start with, and Jock Edwards is Buster's brother, so his lorry was pulling his brother's goods, unbeknown to both of them.

The incompetent driver who caused all the problems by not filling up the lorry with diesel in the first place was Bernard O'Mahoney. I phoned O'Mahoney up on his mobile phone and asked him to come down my office, as I wanted to see him, but he never turned up. When I rang again he had had his phone cut off. I have never seen him since, but he wrote a book as he was big into selling ecstasy tablets in Essex and was head doorman at the club where Leah Betts bought ecstasy pills and died.

O'Mahoney's book, *So This Is Ecstasy*, gives an entirely different version of the story of the load of coffee he lost, which indirectly caused poor Buster Edwards to commit suicide. Me and my partner never got a penny back off anyone. Big E and his pals got off in court, as the driver and lorry were never found, and they said they believed the coffee to be of honest origin. Incidentally, O'Mahoney retitled his book *Essex Boys* and the fool's done quite well out of it. They even made a film out of it starring Sean Bean.

ROUND 11

DEALING WITH BULLIES

At this time I still had the Hathaway and my office block running. Jackie Beatty and Dave DeFreitas were helping me all the time. Jackie was a very good worker but her husband Bob was a proper bully. Jackie had a girl from her previous marriage called Lisa, who could not do anything right in Bob's eyes. One day in the club Lisa was playing up like children do and Bob smacked her face really hard.

Jackie started to row with him and they left the club, but Bob was a big man who looked after country and western stars such as Johnny Cash and Tammy Wynette. He worked for Mervyn Conn, who ran all the big country and western shows in England, arranging all their security. He thought no one would or could say anything to him, but he obviously he didn't know me very well.

The next day Jackie was in hospital – Bob had broken her nose. That same night in the Hathaway club young Johnny Stockwell said to Bob, 'You couldn't hit a man like that.'

'No?' said Bob. 'Come outside with me then.'

Johnny was only about 11 stone, but he was 11 stone of guts. 'Come on then,' he said.

I went outside with them. Bob took his coat off. 'Stockwell,' he said, 'I'm going to give you the hiding of your life.'

'Bob, I don't think so,' I said to him, pushing Johnny out of the way. 'Bob, it's me and you.'

'John, when I have done Danny, you're next,' said Bob. 'So watch this. This is just a sample of what you'll be getting.' He rushed into me and got me round the neck in a wrestler's hold. He was squeezing me so hard I thought my head would explode. I couldn't get away he was so strong. He was trying to break my neck. I was struggling like mad to get away, but it was impossible, so I stopped trying and conserved my strength.

As I was bent over, he started to punch me in the face with his other hand. I was an easy target. I let him hit me twice, then all at once I made a grab at his private parts. I grabbed a big handful and twisted them as hard as I could. He gave a high-pitched scream and immediately let go.

Now he was the one bent in half, holding his crotch. I pummeled his face 'til he was a complete mess. He fell to the floor unconscious. Everyone was pleased to see that bully get a hiding.

Shortly after this, Jackie got a divorce and moved to Dagenham. It was the best thing she ever did.

At this time of my life I was earning money from the Hathaway club and my offices were doing well, so money wasn't a problem. My pit bulls were earning good money from fighting and breeding, but I always seemed to be in some sort of trouble.

One day me and Dave DeFreitas sat in the office talking when my old school pal Billy McCrudden came in. Billy said he had bought a truck off of a Scotsman in Canning Town in good faith. He thought the truck was perfectly straight. It was a Ford Transit. Then the police had stopped him with it and it turned out it was a ringer – a stolen vehicle with different numbers on the engine and chassis, and a different registration plate to what it should have been.

Bill never grassed the Scotsman. He said he had bought it out of the paper in an advertisement, and got nicked for handling a stolen vehicle. When he went to see the Scotsman Tommy, he said he was sorry, he didn't know the truck was stolen, but he would give Bill a replacement truck. But the truck he was given was a wreck: it was winter and it had no mudguards, so the mud and dirt was chucking up everywhere.

Bill, who had just got over a heart attack, asked Tommy to put these mudguards on. Bluntly, in front of Bill's wife Tracy and his children, Tommy told him to fuck off, and pushed him in the chest.

'Bill, don't get yourself excited,' I said when he told me. 'I'll go and have a talk with him. I'm sure I'll get him to put the mudguards on for you.'

So me and Dave went to Victoria Dock Road, Canning Town. When we got to Tommy's yard I went in and asked for him. A big black fellow said that he was not there.

'Tell him I will see him tomorrow at 10 am,' I said. 'It's about Bill's motor.'

'Okay, mate.'

The next morning, me and Dave drove down to Tommy's yard. I saw this man talking to a customer. He had a checked shirt on. He was very broad, and to say he looked tough was an understatement – he looked mean. His nose was flat, he had a big square jaw and I could see his muscles as he had his shirt rolled up.

When he'd finished talking, I said, 'Excuse me, Tommy.'

'Yes?'

'I called yesterday night about Bill's truck. Well, he's not involved you with the police at all, but he can't drive the replacement truck you've given him. If I paid you, to avoid any arguments, would you put the mudguards on?'

He sneered at me. 'I ain't doing fuck all,' he said.

'I'm not asking you to do anything for nothing. I'll pay you.'

'Listen, you arsehole, are you fucking deaf? I am not doing fuck all so piss off.'

I felt my temper rising, as I knew he had pushed Billy around in front of his family as well.

Dave said to him, 'Mate, you have got the wrong attitude.'

He turned to Dave. 'Listen, you Paki ...'

That was as far as he got. I smashed him in the mouth. His head hit the wall behind him. I pulled him forwards and punched him right in the back of the head, splitting his head open. (I later learned that would need 24 stitches.) His mouth and the back of his head were pissing blood. He fell face down. Then about ten men ran from his yard. They expected to see me down, but to their amazement it was Tommy on the floor.

Dave immediately went into his inside pocket to pull out a tool. They thought it was a gun, but in fact it was a small jiffy bottle with ammonia in it. But it stopped them in their tracks. Then this big fat bloke said, 'What, does it take two of you?'

'I haven't hit him,' said Dave.

Tommy was up by now. He looked at me. 'Just me and you, right?' he said.

I was amazed at him getting up at all. 'That's fine by me,' I said and turned to Dave. 'Dave, no matter what happens, keep out of it.'

'Right-oh.'

So Tommy took his shirt off just like an old-fashioned prizefighter. His pal, this big fat bloke, had a bit to say. His name was Paul. He got a bowl of water and washed Tom's face and head, and then said, 'Tom, you ready to send this cunt to hospital?'

'We'll see,' I said. 'We'll see.'

Then Tommy's pals and David stood in a circle outside the scrapyard, down a dead-end street. Me and Tom were in the middle. I had this gut feeling that Tom could really have a fight.

He crouched low and rushed into me, punishing my body with hooks, left and right. He had power in both hands. He was punching my stomach, kidneys and private parts. He hurt me with his first rush.

I managed to push him back as he went to tear into me again. I punched about six perfect punches into his head and face over the top of his guard. His eye opened up. This man was a real tough fighter, but where he had been in so many battles there was loads of scar tissue on his face, and every time I punched his face I was opening it up.

We fought in this manner for about 15 minutes. He was really hurting my body, but his face was a mess. Now we were involved in a real battle. I was finding it difficult to move as my private parts were swollen right up. Tom rushed me again. This man, I was beginning to think, was not human. But this time I hit him with a perfect uppercut right through his guard. He didn't expect that and he went down as though he'd been pole-axed.

Then, to my amazement, he quickly got up again, but then it was my turn to go on the attack instead of fighting on the defensive. I was beating him at will. Again he went down. He tried to get up but he was finished. His mates carried him into his yard.'

'Great,' said Dave. We waited about ten minutes, then we walked into the yard. I was aching all over. Tom was in a right state.

'Anyone else?' I said. It was a right bluff. I could hardly stand, let alone fight. But I said, 'How about you?' to this Paul.

He ducked his nut and shook his head like a coward. I later found out who he was.

'You're dead,' said Tom.

'Any time, Tom,' I said. 'Now you,' pointing to his mate fat Paul, 'take him to the hospital.' He had a face and head full of stitches. Me, I was pissing blood for two weeks, and Bill got his mudguards fixed by his brother-in-law for nothing.

About a year after this, that Paul and his brother got hold of an inoffensive man called Billy Jones. Everyone liked Bill. He had made a remark about Paul's girlfriend sleeping with a black man, which was true anyhow. They tied him to a chair in a disused factory in Dersingham Avenue, Manor Park, not 200 yards from where I live. Then the dirty cowards went back every day and gave him a fearful beating until he died. They put the body into a van and burned the van. Paul got life imprisonment, which he richly deserved, and his brother went Queen's evidence and virtually got off. So cowardice runs in the family to the last. Tom is a bully and a pig of a man but he is a courageous fighter. I admire him for that.

About two weeks after I fought Tommy, I was indoors feeling sorry for myself. I still ached all over. All of a sudden there was a banging on my front door. It was about 8.30 am. I was just sitting down to egg and bacon.

I went to the door. It was Micky, he was home and he looked great. He cheered me right up. When he left, he said, 'I'll see you later.' I saw him about a month later. He was coming out of the

Pigeons in Stratford with June – he was back with her. I felt Micky was making a terrible mistake, but Micky always was an obstinate fellow, you could not tell him anything. It's what makes Micky Micky. But June was a bad lot.

When Micky first met her she was a barmaid. Micky got talking to her in the pub and it developed from there. At the time her husband was in prison – he had tried to kill her and her son Peter, and a while earlier, when her husband came out of prison, he said he was going to kill both June and Peter. Micky moved straight in with her when he heard her husband was being released, as June was terrified but he never ever made it back to London. And he's now serving a life sentence for murder. So June was right to be frightened of him.

Micky thought a lot of June, but she was a drug addict and was very moody. One night in a fit of depression she slashed her arms and legs. Micky got a private doctor to attend to her wounds but she was driving Micky crazy, and her son Peter really resented Micky. He always wanted to sleep with June every night in the big bed, so Micky had to sleep in the spare room most nights, and the nights Micky slept with June, Peter would show off, run away and that sort of thing. Micky searched for him one night and found him in the arcades at Kings Cross. Another time he was at the arcades in Piccadilly, where all the one-arm bandits are.

So now Micky was out of prison and back living with her full time. A very bad move, I thought. Her drugs and drink had soon taken all Micky's money so, as the corner game was quiet, Micky started prizefighting again.

Roy Shaw wouldn't fight him a second time. Lennie Mclean sidestepped him. Again it was virtually impossible to get a decent fight for Micky. But there was one other man whom none of the prizefighters wanted to go in with – Terry Sharpe, who had been a very good professional boxer, a real pro. So a match was made at the Cat's Whiskers in south London, for him to fight Micky. The whole show was filmed by the BBC again.

Nosher Powell was the MC. His call of 'Fetch on the lions' was heard, and Terry and Micky went into battle. It was a war: they were cuffing, nutting, using their elbows, they hit each other with everything except the kitchen sink. After eight brutal, bloody rounds, Sharpe was judged the winner on points.

Micky went mad. He wanted to carry it on in the ring or on the cobbles. Lennie Mclean was in the audience. Micky challenged him from the ring. Mclean stormed out of the club. Eventually the promoter calmed Micky down with the promise of a return match with Sharpe, which never happened. The BBC cut the Gluckstead v Sharpe fight out of their television programme. They said it was too violent and vicious.

A week after this fight I had to meet Micky at the British Lion pub in Stratford. He'd had a debt we could pick up. Micky was there before me. As I walked in he was talking to this blonde barmaid. They were getting along like a house on fire. She wasn't young, about 36, but she spoke very posh, something you rarely hear in the East End of London. I reckon she thought Micky was just a bit of rough. She called herself Janine.

'Mick we have got to go,' I said.

'Just a minute.'

When we got outside Micky had her phone number. He phoned her within the week and started to knock about with this Janine. He was going all over the place with her. Then one day, out of the blue, Micky was crossing the Silvertown Way when a car started up and drove straight at him. But Micky was too fast – he dived out of the way and rolled over. The car stopped up the road, about to do a U-turn. Micky picked up a brick, got in the middle of the road and shouted, 'Come on then.' The car just roared off.

The next night Micky told Janine this story. She went white. 'Micky, I have got a confession to make,' she said. 'I have been going with a guy for about four years before I knew you and I have been seeing him all the time as well as you.'

'That was nice of you.'

'Micky, Jeff's a violent man,' Janine said. 'He must have found out about us. He'll kill us.'

'If he gets lucky,' said Micky, and started laughing.

About a week after this, me, Paul Foley and Micky were having a quiet drink in the West Ham footballer Frank Lampard's East End pub the Brittania, in Plaistow. We were all having a good time when the door opened and in walked a very well-known actor who we'll call 'Jeff'. He had two other blokes with him. I recognised him straight away from his films.

'Mick, I think we're in a bit of trouble,' I said.

Jeff walked straight up to Micky. 'Your name's Micky Gluckstead, right?' he said.

'You should have been a policeman, not a fucking actor,' said Micky.

'You know what all this is about,' Jeff continued. 'Let's settle it outside.'

'Oh, all right, if we must,' said Micky. 'Just let me finish my drink first.'

Jeff was fuming. Micky drained his glass and said, 'Come on, then.'

Micky walked in front with Jeff following him. As we got outside, I saw Jeff pull a knife. 'Look out, Mick,' I said.

As I shouted, Jeff lunged at Micky. Micky spun round and cracked Jeff straight on the jaw, one perfect punch. He knocked him right out. The other blokes didn't want to know. They said 'leave us out of this', as they put the unconscious Jeff in the back of the black Mercedes and roared off.

'That was close, Mick. You were lucky there.'

'Yes, I was, wasn't I?' Then he showed me a big bloodstain on his side, just above his hip. We got him to hospital straight away. He had to have 38 stitches. It was a bad wound. Micky told the police who came to the hospital he had been mugged. They knew different but they weren't bothered if Micky lived or died.

Micky carried on seeing Janine for some time. Then one day June got a phone call from a man – Micky always said it was Jeff – telling her all about Janine and Mick. She took an overdose of pills. Micky got her to hospital just in time.

When she came round, she said, 'If you leave me, I'll kill myself.' *Exactly* the same words Maureen had said to Micky years previously.

He broke down. 'No, please,' he said. 'I'll do anything. Not that.' So he packed Janine up and the relationship was over – Jeff had eventually got his way.

But life goes on and Micky got a challenge to fight Harry Starbuck, the gypsy fighter whom they all called The Buck, so it took his mind off Janine. Micky was going to fight him at the Downham Tavern, south London, on a winner-takes-all basis. There was also Colombo Steve Richards, Brian Hall and Brian Ford on the show. It was a marvellous bill and tickets were selling like hot cakes. Micky took a hundred tickets, sold them, and drew the money and spent it on June. He thought he'd pay it back with his winnings. Then, two weeks before the fight, The Buck pulled out. No reason was given.

'What are you going to do about the ticket money?' I said to Mick.
'I'll show you tomorrow,' he said.

The next day I met Micky in the Swan pub in Stratford. He was carrying a briefcase. 'What's in the case, Mick?' I said. He opened it up. There, newly printed, were 1,000 tickets for Micky Gluckstead v Harry Starbuck. 'Dan, you might as well get hung for a sheep as a lamb,' he said. 'Now we've got a lot of work to do.' I drove Micky everywhere and in ten days we'd sold the lot. Come fight night, there were coaches pulling up, thousands of people, but no boxers. Micky just got out of the way for a little while. We had a few fights over them tickets, but no one got any of their money back, so it was a good earner for us.

ROUND 12

DANGER BREWING

The murder squad was still making a nuisance of itself over Barry Dalton's death, so I said to them one day, 'Look, I have spoken to you twenty-one times about Mr Dalton. I have given you all the assistance I can. So if you want to speak to me again, speak through my solicitor.'

A police informer went to Stringfellow's night club and told one of the doormen that I had told the police he was involved with Barry's death. I hadn't been, of course. But luckily enough, a fellow who worked on the door at Stringfellow's phoned me and told me the story.

So the next day my good friend Micky Daltrey phoned the boss of the doormen up, who he knew well, and made a meet at the Blakesely Arms in Manor Park. I wanted to make the meet as soon as possible as I knew two Irishmen were on their way over. Apparently they had been paid £30,000 to shoot me, so I had to carry a gun as well. If the police caught me with a gun I would be put away; but if I never had a gun I would be helpless.

As I walked into the Blakesely, there were two big fellows standing up at the bar. Micky introduced me then walked away. 'What's all this about?' I said. Then immediately the biggest one out of the two said, 'Dan, it's all been a mistake. We were told you'd said to the murder squad you'd seen our man shoot Barry Dalton and that you were prepared to give evidence. We thought you were trying to fit him up.'

'What? Why should I want to fit that mug up?'

'Hold on a minute, Dan. Please let me finish,' the big man said. 'When this meet was called, I got hold of the fellow that gave us this information and beat the truth out of him. Everyone knows you're sound now.'

'That's all right,' I said, 'but I could have been killed for something I never did. Otherwise if I hadn't confronted you two I would have been known for ever more as a grass. Why didn't you phone me and ask me?'

'I can only apologise,' the big man said, 'but I will tell everyone about the mix-up and also how you met us on you own and sorted it out.' We shook hands and parted the best of pals, but I know I owe my life to the doorman who phoned me and warned me to be careful.

I will never give the names of the people I met in the Blakesely, but they were gentlemen and they listened to the truth. To be honest, I was half expecting to be met by two Irishmen. I'm glad it turned out like it did. If I hadn't been warned, two complete strangers would have walked up to me and shot me for something I never did, and I would have been helpless. Their had almost been the biggest underworld war London had ever seen. I know there would have been loads of casualties. No doubt some innocent parties would have been hurt or even killed as well.

Incidentally, the fellow who stirred up all this trouble up was named Brinmore. The week before I was released from prison he got shot dead in the street. I can't say I felt sorry for him.

Dave DeFreitas fetched a pal of his down the office one day. His name was Shaffi Ahmed, a Turkish fellow, and his mate was called Boag. I knew him through the pit bulls. Shaffi is a lovely fellow and him and Savva started knocking about together. What a combination: one half Greek, half Jew and the other Turkish. They were always together, they went on holiday together and were also taking plenty of drugs.

Shaffi came to my flat one night and said, 'Dan, I have had £30,000 worth of cocaine on credit. I already owe these same people a fortune for the drugs me and Savva have taken. I can't pay them back, so I'm going to sell the coke they have given me and bolt back to Turkey. I have got a family there. I have got a crooked passport, so no one will know where I have gone. I am just leaving everyone behind here. There is nothing between me and my wife anyhow.'

He shook my hand and left, and that was the last I saw of him. Well, rumours started circulating around the East End that Shaffi had been killed and robbed of the drugs. I don't know who started this rumour – Shaffi, I suppose, to cover his tracks. The murder squad came to see me. I told them I had not seen him and I did not know where he was, which was the truth. He could have just said to me he was going to Turkey and gone anywhere. In any case, if I had known for certain where he was, I wouldn't have told the police, because the people Shaffi knocked for the drug money would have given a fortune to know where he was. They would have killed him as an example to anyone else thinking of knocking them.

For some unknown reason Savva started telling people, mainly women, that he had shot Shaffi for his drugs. He seemed to think he was impressing people. It was the cocaine talking, making Savva feel like a gangster. He even started calling himself Tony Montana after the character in the film *Scarface*. He did look just like him. I got hold of Savva and explained that if the drug dealers whom Shaffi owed the money to heard Savva was responsible for Shaffi's disappearance they would want their money from him. So Savva stopped talking rubbish and the rumours died down – or so I thought.

The Hathaway was a bit quiet so we were looking to earn a bit of extra money somewhere else.

ROUND 13

JUDASES WIN.
WE LOSE

Micky was a having a drink in the Norseman club in Canning Town, when a fellow started to try and chat up the girl Micky was having a drink with. Micky politely asked him to leave them alone, when this fellow broke a glass and lunged at Mick. Micky was lightning fast. He moved his head a few inches so the glass missed his face and Micky hit this left, right, left, leaving the bully unconscious with a broken jaw.

This fellow who Micky had done was a pal of Nicky Gerard's, who was fast making a name for himself as an enforcer. His father was the infamous Alf Gerard who, with his partner Freddie Foreman, was feared all over London.

When Micky had knocked this guy out, he didn't know it was Nicky's friend, not that it would have made any difference. There was bad blood already between them, as Micky had bedded Nicky's girlfriend one night when he wasn't there, and it would only take the slightest thing for them both to go to war. They hated each other.

Nicky knew he would have no chance in a straight-up fight with Micky. A strong rumour started to circulate in the East End that Nicky was going to shoot Micky dead. I told Micky what I had heard. He laughed and said, 'You don't want to believe all you hear.'

On the Saturday night, Micky was drinking in the Britannia when someone told him Nicky was in the Norseman at Canning Town, mouthing off at what he was going to do to him. 'I suppose I'd better go and see him then,' said Micky. He caught a cab to the Norseman on his own. As he walked into the bar area he saw Nicky with two other fellows. As Micky started to walk towards Nicky, he said, 'Do you want to see me?'

Nicky pulled out a .38 gun and shot Mick point blank in the stomach before Micky could get to him. But it never stopped him. Micky rushed Nicky and knocked the gun from his hand. One of Micky's pals pulled another gun, and a bullet grazed Micky's head. Another shot was fired, which hit Micky in the ankle, but they couldn't stop him. He span around and knocked the second gunman to the floor with his fist. Then the third man hit Micky across the face with a meat cleaver. Micky smacked him straight in the face knocking him down as well. As Micky bent down to pick up the meat cleaver up to defend himself, Nicky hit him several times on the back of the head with his gun. Micky was beaten to the floor but he was still fighting.

Unbelievably he got up and went for them again. The three of them turned tail and ran out of the club as fast as their feet would carry them. No one offered Micky any help at all, they were all too frightened of the Gerrards – more of Alf than Nicky, I suspect. Then Micky heard a female voice say, 'Micky, you're losing a terrible amount of blood. You need help, fast.' It was an old girlfriend named Gloria. 'Come on,' she said, 'I'll come with you.'

Micky had no time to waste. He walked out as the police walked in. In fact, Micky shoved the police out of the way. Micky and Gloria ran into the road and stopped the first car they saw. They both jumped in and Micky said, 'Sorry, mate, but I'm bleeding to death. Can you get me to a hospital?' The driver was only too pleased to help. He broke all the speed limits to get there.

They got to the Queen Mary's Hospital, Stratford, in five minutes flat. The hospital could see it was an emergency and started working on Micky instantly. They put 20 stitches across his face and 25 in his head. They took the bullet from his ankle, but it had smashed the ankle bone completely. The doctor said, 'I'm sorry, Mr Gluckstead, but you'll never walk on that foot again, and the bullet in your stomach is too near to your spine to operate. Its better to leave it there.'

Micky thanked the doctor. 'You're wrong about one thing,' he said. 'I will walk again.'

'Sorry son, you won't.'

But the doctor didn't know the willpower Micky had. It took Micky five days to stand, as he not only had a pain from his ankle, but also excruciating pain in his stomach to contend with.

Gloria visited him every day in the hospital. She was a real pal, offering Micky encouragement all the time. The doctor couldn't believe his eyes, and in six weeks Micky walked with the aid of crutches out of hospital. All the doctors and nurses applauded him as he walked out with Gloria. Micky spent the next few months resting and improving his walking. He used to struggle going to blocks of flats walking up and down the stairs, but he made a good recovery. Not perfect but good enough.

By this time Nicky and George and Alan Dixon's step-brother, Billy Knight, had been arrested for the shooting at the Norseman, plus a third man. The police had 72 witnesses so people weren't so frightened of the Gerrards after all. Alfie Gerrard, Nicky's father, went to Patsy Cahill Yard in New Barn Street, as Pat knew Micky, and said, 'Tell Gluckstead to leave England. We don't want him here to be able to testify or I'll kill him.'

'What, do them people think I am a grass or something?' Micky said. 'I am staying here. Fuck them.' And obstinate Micky stayed in Canning Town. Micky feared no one and no one told him what to do. He was lucky. One night a petrol bomb was hurled through his window, but Micky was out. Needless to say the debt was repaid.

Micky went to see Patsy Cahill and said to him to tell the others to call a halt, as he wasn't going to grass anyone and in any case if it came to it they would lose. So Gerrard and his pal Foreman decided to just leave matters alone.

Micky avoided talking to the police, but eventually they picked him up and subpoenaed him to appear at court as a witness against Gerrard and his mates. If he didn't attend court he was automatically fined on the spot £3,000. At the Old Bailey, on oath, Micky said, 'You've got the wrong men. These men are my friends. They're innocent. They were trying to help me.'

The judge said, 'Mr Gluckstead, stand at the back of the court. There will be a perjury charge pressed against you later.' Well, during the trial Micky slipped out. Billy Knight found not guilty, Gerrard was found guilty and got seven years. The other one never attended court, he disappeared. Nothing's ever been seen or heard of him since. Alfie Gerrard, Nicky's father, died in Brighton. Apparently he died eating a lobster; he was supposed to have choked on it, but who knows?

Nicky went on trial for killing Tony Zomparelli in revenge for killing Ronnie Knight's brother. Nicky was acquitted. Ronnie

Knight's wife Barbara Windsor gave evidence in this highly publicised trail. The police forensic department had wanted to take Micky to the hospital to remove the bullet from his body, to compare it with the one that killed Zamparelli. Of course, Micky refused this, and wouldn't let them have it. So although he got no thanks for it, Micky went a long way to getting Gerrard cleared.

Nicky Gerrard later had his head blown off in Stratford. A man named Tommy Hole was charged with this killing, but he was later acquitted. The police investigating Nicky Gerrard's killing said they had interviewed hundreds of people in the East End of London and they couldn't find one person who said one good thing about him. He was a real bully.

Well, life goes on and we still had to get a living. But the police wanted Micky badly now. They charged him with taking protection money from pubs. He spent 13 months on remand, then got off at the Old Bailey. They wouldn't let him alone and no one would work with him as he was red hot. They were determined to get him. Then one day, out of the blue, Micky bumped into Janine. They went for a drink, and she told Micky she was going to Barbados to write a book. They wished each other good luck and parted the best of friends.

When Micky got home, June was smoking a mixture of cannabis and cocaine. She had seen a friend of hers who had told her she had seen Micky with a big blonde bird. Micky tried to explain but it was useless. She was going mad. Micky walked out of the house. As he was leaving, June said, 'I will see you rot in hell.'

Micky took no notice. However, in a few days Micky was eventually picked up for an offence that was so out of character that all his friends had no problem accepting his protestations of innocence. Nonetheless, when the jury convicted him, the judge gave him nine years.

I knew the flat where June spent clandestine nights with her police lover. I knew the bedroom was at the front of the house, as a pal of mine rented the flat to June and he had told me the layout. So one night I spotted the officer's car outside the flat. I went and bought six rats – my pal always kept a few rats to sharpen his terriers up on. He used to catch a good few, then take bets on how long it would take his Jack Russell to kill them all after they were all released in a dog pit. He never lost one bet.

Anyhow, he put these six rats in a sack, plus I also asked him to put a house brick in there as well. Then, at 2.30 am I drove near to the flat, got out of my car and quietly walked to June's flat. I undid the top of the sack, then screwed the end round. Then I swung the bag, and it smashed right through their window. I learned later the sack had landed on their bed with all the rats running and squeaking everywhere. I don't think June ever saw any more of the police officer after that – all rats together. The last I heard of June, she was having an affair with another officer.

I missed Micky a lot, but life goes on and the police were hounding me too. Every little thing that happened, they pulled me in. Looking back I should have moved away from the East End but it's always easier to look back in hindsight.

Paul Foley had a flower stall at Mile End station. I often used to spend a bit of time with him. One day we were talking and a big black Mercedes pulled up. It was the actor 'Jeff' and two of his pals.

He let his window down and sneered, 'How's the nonce getting on?'

'That nonce made short work of you,' said Paul.

'I was ill at the time that mug done me,' said Jeff.

'Are you ill now?' Paul said. 'Because Micky's a better fighter than me and I'll accommodate you now.'

'Micky reckons your bird Janine is no good in bed,' I butted in. 'Can I have a go? I might improve her.'

Jeff went potty, and all three jumped out of the car. That was what they pulled up for anyhow. I ran at Jeff. He pulled a knife and cut me over the top of my eye. Then I caught him with a terrific right hook. The knife fell from his hand as he reeled back.

I hit him four more times, then he fell down unconscious. I turned around and Paul had knocked the other two spark out. Paul had a tremendous punch. Two big hits and two big men spark out. I later learned these two gorillas were supposed to be Jeff's minders. So Paul and me drove off with these three mugs laying in front of Mile End station unconscious. A while after this bit of trouble with Jeff he died of AIDS.

I was sitting in my office feeling sorry for Micky one morning, when a knock came at my door. It was my old friend Tony Nichols, a lovely man who I had known for years. He came in and put a deal to me. The deal was, his friend Mr Eugene Puyatt had been left a half-share in a flat in Iverna Mansions, Kensington. The other half had been left to his father's mistress.

Well, he needed the money, but she wouldn't sell the property. He had no money to take her to court to force her to sell, so he asked if I would take her to court on his behalf and get the flat sold. Then I could have half of his share. 'Okay,' I said. 'I'll see what I can do.'

So I got hold of Bill who is good at paperwork and, foolishly, I trusted him and John, who knows a bit about the law, and we started working on the case.

It was a complicated deal and Mr Puyatt had to come all the way up from Redditch to sign different papers, so he gave Bill full power of attorney to deal with the property. We all trusted Bill implicitly.

It took us a year. We went to the High Court in the Strand about six times, but eventually we won the day. We sold the flat and we had £250,000 to come, as we had proved that Mr Puyatt had exclusive right to the flat, not 50 per cent. Mr Puyatt's father had settled his mistress up with her 50 per cent of the flat before he died.

When I first approached Bill, he was penniless. I told him I would stick up all the finances for the deal. If I lost it? That was a chance I was prepared to take. Mr Nicholls lent Mr Puyatt £20,000. It was to be paid back on completion of the sale. It cost me £15,000 in court fees etc. And I was giving Bill money to help him out. At long last we were in the money. But it had been hard work.

I had £52,000 to come, Bill and John had £36,500 each to come, and Mr Puyatt had £12,500 to come. Then, right out of the blue, Bill played the most dirty trick he's ever going to play on anyone. He ran off with all the money, including Mr Puyatt's. We looked everywhere for him, but he stole all the money and disappeared. Poor Tony Nicholls lost his pub. It bankrupted him. I had known Bill for a number of years and I had always found him an honourable man, up to this point. But he almost ruined me as well. I would love to see Bill now. He was a real Judas. I bet that money will do him no good.

He also hid a gun in my barn. Two days later the police searched my house and went straight to the gun. I'm sure he must have told the police where he left that gun, to give himself more time to get away. But life has a way of evening itself out. One day I will see him. You never know, it may be in prison. That man destroyed all my trust in my fellow man. He really is the lowest of the low.

Jackie did all the paperwork and he didn't even pay her. He's a jackal. I wish him nothing but bad luck and I hope he rots in hell. Jackie started to do some work for a crooked accountant, just to make ends meet. She was doing all his typing and computer work. She made a room upstairs in her house into an office they could use.

JUDASES WIN. WE LOSE

Then one morning, out of nowhere, the police searched Jackie's house, looking for fraudulent paperwork. They found lots of the accountant's papers and got all the paperwork together and she was arrested. She was allowed home on police bail. Apparently the crooked accountant had also been arrested.

ROUND 14

THE SNOWHILL ROBBERY

The very same week, Angelo and his associates, began doing their homework for the most daring and potentially lucrative job of their careers: the Snowhill Robbery. Millions and millions of pounds were there for the taking. They planned it in painstaking detail.

It was 5 March 1995. They were in the East End heading for the centre of London. They had good information that their fortune was to be shipped in an armoured Omega security van.

Right outside a police station, as the van came into view, Angelo got out of our vehicle. Alone and with a road map he waved the driver down as though he was lost.

As the driver slowed down and stopped, Angelo pulled out a sawn-off 12-bore shotgun and forced the driver, a Mr Roy Adams, to let him in the passenger's side.

Angelo then forced Adams to drive to some arches. Their van followed. At the arches, Angelo tied Adams' wrists to the Omega van's steering wheel.

But there was one thing nobody could have planned for. Just the day before, the whole locking system for the van had been changed. This meant all our homework was useless — there was no way the van could be unlocked.

They'd come all this way, though. They couldn't give up now. It was time for plan B: smash a hole in the van's solid steel roof with jack handles and send in the smallest member of the gang.

'X' said it was so dark inside you couldn't see anything. Still he managed to get a haul of 48 bags out before they started hearing sirens. Then it was time for them to make their exit.

They had obtained £400,000 worth of diamonds and £7,000,000 worth of bearer bonds. But the job had taken too long and they had left £4 million in cash in the van.

The robbery was headline news in all the national newspapers and there was loads of TV coverage. They stashed what they had for a few weeks until things had quietened down a bit. Then they started making moves to cash it up. I was also getting Jackie to forge the bonds so we could sell them twice over. This was pure greed as the bonds were worth £7 million anyhow.

I phoned Peter Power who understands all about bearer bonds, who in turn got in touch with Kenny Wilmott. Eventually Wilmott found a buyer from Sheffield, but the bonds had to be delivered to Liverpool Street station. So me, Jackie and Peter Power delivered them. Apparently, when the buyer left us, he got himself nicked with these bonds. I thought it was just a con to avoid paying us for them – 'Hello,' I thought. 'We've been took to the cleaners twice.' But much worse was to follow.

What we didn't know was that we were all bugged up to high heaven – the office, the yard, the lot – because the police still thought I was something to do with the death of Shaffi. We never had a clue. We were like lambs to the slaughter.

THE SNOWHILL ROBBERY

At 6 am one morning the police arrived on my doorstep. They charged me with conspiracy to kill Shaffi Ahmed, disposing of the body, altering police evidence by disposing of the body, possession of a shotgun and a second firearms charge. So now I had to face two firearms charges and conspiracy to handle stolen bearer bonds.

The police was all dressed up like aliens, all heavily armed. They also nicked Angelo, Jackie, Peter Power, Bob Orly, Kenny Wilmot and Angelo's brother John Hayman. I went with Peter Power and Kenny Wilmott to Brixton prison; everyone else got bail. Apparently the surveillance people had put listening devices in my office to try to catch Steven Savva. As I predicted, the police had heard that he'd been telling all and sundry that he'd killed Shaffi.

Savva had been arrested with us at first, but the police had let him go through lack of evidence. So Savva, the big mouth who had started all this trouble was the only one walking about scott free – but a fool full of cocaine saying stupid things can do plenty of damage. Because Savva had no real home he used to stay at my office quite regularly. The police obviously got wind of this and that was how my property got bugged.

It took us ten months to get a committal hearing – the last old-style committal hearing in the country, incidentally – and at that I was cleared of any involvement with the Shaffi disappearance and we got bail. Then we had to go to committal proceedings concerning the other charges. Power, Wilmot, Orley, Hayman and Angelo all got bail. Jelly and Reeves opposed my and Jackie's bail. It was a degrading and terrible experience for her. The following week a judge granted her bail, but the police still objected to my bail so I had to go back to Brixton prison on these charges.

In Brixton prison around 75 per cent of the people were black and 25 per cent white. I was put on the induction wing to start with. The induction wing in Brixton is where the Cat A prisoners used to be housed before the new unit was built. And in any case most Cat A prisoner now go to Belmarsh Prison.

Well, that induction unit is a daunting place. You go into a wing, then up some stairs in the middle of the building to the top floor. So in fact, it's a prison within a prison. There are no windows at all. I did a few weeks in there, and then I was moved out onto a wing. The first day on the wing, an enormous black chap with a shaven head came up to me with two other blokes. You could tell he'd spent endless hours in the gym. He had muscles everywhere. The big fellow was obviously the Guv'nor. 'Don't forget to get me my phone card in your canteen this week,' he said.

'What phone card?' I said.

'Everyone gives me a phone card a week,' he said. 'In case I decide to clean their cell out for them.' And then he laughed. Serious again, he pointed to me and said, 'So don't forget.' Obviously these three were running the wing. No one answered them back at all. I thought I'd give them a phone card to stop any bother.

There was a young white boy next door to me. He didn't look old enough to be in prison. He was a slight lad, very quiet. Well, on the Wednesday he had a visit. His visitor passed him some cannabis, which he bottled – pushed up his arse – on the visit. One of these bullies saw him do it.

That night the three of them went to his cell and asked him about the cannabis. He denied having any. Then the big fellow put his hand down the lad's tracksuit trousers and got the cannabis out of this bottom. It was so degrading for the young boy, but what could he do against three big blokes? When they left, I heard him sobbing in his cell, but no one helps you in prison.

Thursday was canteen day. That means you could spend your

meagre bit of money in the canteen, another name for the prison store. I got my goods plus a pp9 battery for my radio. As I left, the big black fellow shouted out from upstairs, 'You got my card?'

'I'll fetch it along in a minute,' I said.

'As long as you do,' he said.

But I had changed my mind. He wasn't getting no fucking card off of me. I went to my cell and I was banged up. I got the pp9 battery and put it in a sock. At 6 pm I was let out. I walked along the landing till I got to the big fellow's cell. I looked at his name on the cell card: it was Dilliway. I looked in and the three of them were playing kalooki. They had a table in the middle of the cell, between a cabinet and two bunk beds. Dilliway had his back to the door as I opened it.

'I've got your card here,' I said.

'Just put it on the cabinet,' he said.

As he looked away, I slid the sock and battery out of my pocket and swung it at the side of Dilliway's head as hard as I could. He looked at me, and screamed at the last possible moment as the battery smashed into his eye socket, smashing it to bits. He rolled off his chair onto his bed, blood pumping out of his face. As if in one movement, my hand swung around, like I was doing a backhand shot in tennis, but this wasn't tennis.

The second swing shattered Dilliway's mate's jaw and teeth. He was immediately unconscious. The third bloke jumped on the top bunk, huddled in a corner, screaming, 'No no.' I just let him stay there. But Dilliway wasn't getting away so light. He was half lying, half sitting on the bottom bunk. I set about his legs with my battery: one smash on each leg. Then I quietly let myself out and went back to my cell.

Within ten minutes alarm bells were ringing. Screws were running everywhere and the two black men were taken to the hospital wing.

The rest of the wing was banged up. Next morning at 7.30, two screws came for me. They took me to the segregation unit – 'the block'. At about 11 am they took me into the governor. 'Woollard, what do you know about Dilliway and Osborne's injuries?' he said.

I didn't even know the second one's name was Osborne.

'Nothing,' I said.

'Dilliway and Osborne are saying nothing also,' he said. 'I can't nick you. But I know you're responsible. I just cant prove it.' So obviously some little grass had informed on me. 'Woollard,' he said. 'I don't want you or the likes of you in my prison causing trouble.' Then he said to the two screws standing each side of me, 'Go and pack Woollard's kit. He's leaving us.'

That night I was housed in Pentonville prison E wing. The governor of Brixton had got me out of there as quick as he could, I think to avoid a racial dispute. I didn't care. I liked it better in the 'Ville anyhow and had taught Dilliway and company some manners.

Jelly and Reeves was still opposing my bail, so I went backwards and forwards to Pentonville jail. I was banged up 23 hours a day. After five months, we had to go to the Guildhall Magistrates' court for a 'pleas and directions' hearing. Jackie sat near me. She looked really well and I really didn't think we had too much to worry about. I told Jackie's brief Mr Vidler that Jackie only ever took orders from me or the accountant. She had nothing to do with anything illegal and the paperwork they had found at her house belonged to me. Of course, it was all lies, but I made a statement to that effect, as I knew it would get Jackie off. I hate to see any woman in court.

We all got committed, but the evidence was flimsy, and Mr Vidler said with my statement Jackie would have no case to answer to. The next morning, a screw opened me up at 7 am. 'Woollard,' he said, 'you've got to phone this number.' I looked blearily at the number. I didn't recognise it. I phoned and a young lady answered the phone. It was Debbie, Jackie's youngest daughter. 'Dan, are you all right?' she said.

'Yes. Why?'

'Mum died last night.'

I was dumbstruck. She said she had a cerebral haemorrhage. I went back to my cell. I couldn't believe it. I phoned my solicitor, Colin Nott, and I told him what had happened. I had a court appearance in two days' time anyhow, the application for bail. Colin laid it on thick about Jackie dying on top of everything else. But I got no bail, so after the 20 years of friendship I'd enjoyed with Jackie, I couldn't even attend her funeral. The day of the funeral I just sat in my cell alone with my private thoughts. Apparently Jackie had a good send-off. I was pleased about that.

Angelo had to go to Snaresbrook. First they nicked him for stealing these bonds (armed robbery). So Angelo, unbelievably, got a guilty verdict. Angelo's barrister said, 'Mr Hayman, you could get eight years for this.' Judge Medaware gave him 15 years with another 5 years concurrent. Next, Judge Medaware asked for our trial, as he wanted to try us as well. He gave us the same treatment as Angelo. Me, Kenny Willmott, Bob Orley, John Hayman and Peter Power were appearing at Snaresbrooke Crown Court for conspiracy to handle stolen bearers bonds. We all pleaded 'not guilty' but John Hayman, after talking to his barrister, unbelievably went 'guilty'.

Judge Medaway was very tough. I was in the box for four and a half days giving evidence – me and the CPS, a Mr Lett, had a right old battle. Anyhow, like Angelo, we got guilty. My barrister said this judge might give me a four. If we can get it under that, you only do half. Kenny Wilmott got off. I don't know how he managed that.

As we stood up, Judge Medaware looked at me. He said,

'Woollard eight years, Power seven, Orly six years, Hayman five years.' As he read out the sentences a gasp went around the court. It was outrageous. I said to Medaware, 'Is that all? Thank you very much.' Then I said, 'Thank you,' to a few jury members who had come back to court just to see us sentenced. I said 'Have a nice Christmas,' I said. 'Think of me.' It was 17 December.

It put me in mind of the song 'I Fought the Law and the Law Won'. For now. I personally think they've just won the battle, not the war …

What really hurt was that Wilmott's man, who had got caught with the bonds, Mr Saka Kham, grassed us all up, giving evidence behind a screen in court – very dramatic – but got only two years. And he was caught in possession of the bonds. As he walked past the dock after giving evidence, I started to sing the old Vera Lynne record 'We'll Meet Again'. The Judge went potty. He said any more veiled threats and he'd charge me with trying to intimidate witnesses and altering the course of justice.

Although the sentences were ridiculous, we were all guilty except one man, Bob Orley. Bob was totally innocent of all charges levelled against him. All he was doing was acting as a chauffeur for Kenny Willmott, driving him all over the place for a few quid. Yet Ken got acquitted and Bob got found guilty of conspiracy to handle stolen bearer bonds and got a sentence of six years. It was a complete travesty of justice. How could John Hayman, who not only got the deal started but acted as the middle-man, get only five years and Bob, a totally innocent man, get six?

ROUND 15

NAMES IN
THE NICK

So they shipped us back to Pentonville to start our unfair sentence. I made some good friends in the Ville: Bugsy Maloney, Benny Stafford, Richie Faulkner, Lennie Smith, Robert Fox – all good men. After a month I was shipped out to Wayland. My solicitor, Colin Nott, has not stopped working for me. I owe him a huge debt of thanks. I am proud to call Colin not only my solicitor but my friend. He has always been there when I need him and his advice has been invaluable. He's a good man.

My pals in Wayland were John Waites, Peter Spelling, Danny Hinton, Brian Darby, Sauce, Jason Hooper and, of course, Reg Kray. All lovely people. I felt sorry for Reggie: he spent 32 years in prison. Its difficult to imagine anyone surviving that sentence, but he never moaned or groaned at all. He was a real man who I was proud to call a friend.

As I sat at my window looking at fields, I had two more gun charges to come courtesy of a lying grass, then my appeal. So I just had to wait and see how long I had to serve. I opened my mail – a card from Micky Gluckstead. He was home, so one was in and two out. Paul was still on his farm. Since I had been in prison I had heard many stories about Micky that even I didn't know. It was the general opinion that Micky was one of the hardest people in the prison system and every prison he'd been in he'd been top dog.

Me and John Waites left Pentonville together. First we had to call into High Point prison near Newmarket, where Lester Piggott had done his time, as four other prisoners from the 'Ville were going there. We had dinner there. As the ruddy-faced screw served out dinner, I said, 'Guv'nor, I've got a serious question to ask you.'

'Go on,' he said.

'I know this is racehorse territory,' I said, 'so answer me this question if you can – When is the only time a twenty-stone black man has ridden a Derby winner?'

'You've got me there,' said this country yokel, scratching his head. 'Who's that then?'

'Piggot's cellmate.'

This screw went potty. 'What?' he said. 'Lester's a living legend round these parts.' And he stormed off. Me and John creased up laughing.

Then onto Wayland. Wayland prison is the end of the line. If any other prison won't accept a prisoner, he gets shipped out to Wayland. It's miles from anywhere, in the heart of Norfolk. It's a C-Cat prison, with A-Cat security in force. The first day out in the yard, a barrel-chested fellow came up to us. John knew him. It was Peter Spelling. He gave me and John two phone cards each and said, 'Here you are. Ring home.'

On the same day, Reg Kray did the same thing – and phone cards are gold dust. I hadn't seen Reg for years. He still looked well though. After a six-week induction period, both me and John went to C wing where both Peter and Reg were housed. That wing's mainly for long-term prisoners, so you do get some sensible people in there, not your little housebreakers or car thieves. People like Ray Gilbert, a real tough gentleman of a man; Richie Reynolds from Harlow, a man whom I respect. I know he's always been loyal.

Reg Kray may have been in prison for 32 years, but people still hadn't forgotten him. One day, I said, 'I've got a good idea for the lottery, Reg. If I knew Richard Branson, I'd tell him.' Well, in a matter of minutes Reg had Richard Branson on the phone. He was talking from his holiday home in Italy. I spoke to Mr Branson and agreed to send my idea to him by post. I don't know anyone else who could have got hold of Richard Branson just like that. Me, Jake, Reg and Gary Hallberg, a real good fellow from Southampton, all saw the millennium in together.

Reg should have got a D-Cat in the beginning of 2000, but his old pal Freddie Foreman went on a documentary show on the television and said he had killed Frank 'The Mad Axeman' Mitchell for the twins. That stopped Reg from getting his D-Cat. Reg was very, very disappointed in Fred Foreman. Not angry, just disappointed.

We might have only been drinking prison hooch on millennium night, but I would sooner drink hooch with people like Reg, Gary and Jake than the best champagne in the world with the likes of Foreman and co. What the outside world didn't know was that Reg tried to keep fit, but suffered terribly with what we first thought was Irritable Bowel Syndrome. At least we hoped that was all it was. The man went through hell, and he never complained. I could write a book about Reg alone.

Another pal of mine Ian Gullefer – Gully – got himself into a fair bit of bother when he was first in Wayland. Gully, an armed robber from Dagenham, was doing ten years. He'd had trouble in Belmarsh and Maidstone prison before he came to Wayland, and the trouble followed him. Here's his account of what happened.

On Wednesday, 17 November 1999, in Wayland Prison at around 4.10 pm in the afternoon, I walked to my friend's cell on spur D, C wing, to have a cup of tea and a chat with him. His name is John Waites. I sat in his cell for about 15 minutes in all, talking to him mainly about the D-Cat which he had got. I then left his cell to return to my own.

On leaving Mr Waites' cell, I walked to the end of D spur's corridor on my way back to my own cell, when two black inmates approached me. One grabbed me by the throat and started shouting racial abuse at me, whilst the other closed in on me from the right, making it impossible for me to move. By this time, a few more black inmates joined the two that were picking on me. Then I was pushed and dragged into the dining hall. Altogether there must have been about ten of them; a lot of them were screaming racial remarks to me.

I said, 'I have done nothing. Why are you picking on me?' A black inmate screamed at me, 'Don't tell lies. We have been told by two officers that you're one racist bastard, that you hate blacks and in Belmarsh Prison you went out of your way to get black men nicked.'

I replied, 'It's all lies what these officers are telling you.' I then noticed that with all the noise we were making the dining hall was getting quite packed. There must have been about 40 people in there in total. The vast majority were black men, and lots of them were calling me all sorts of names and throwing racial insults at me. I was scared to death, as I noticed that by this time, both the entry and exit doors had been closed and barricaded to stop anyone coming in or out, with at least ten black inmates on each door. Therefore it was impossible for me to escape this mob.

The inmates who had first attacked me punched me several times in the face. I tried to get away. Then I was attacked from the side. About five punches hit me. I turned to face this black man who had hit me. I was just fighting on instinct and survival but I started to get the better of this black inmate. There was a circle of black inmates around me, all screaming racial abuse all the time. As the one I was fighting backed up, I received blows to the back of my head from the black men behind me. On turning to see who had hit me, the black inmate who was fighting me grabbed this opportunity to attack me from behind. He punched me a few times to the back of my head, and I received several blows from the crowd hitting me in the face and body. In fact, they beat me to the floor. I really thought I was about to die.

Then a big fellow stepped in to protect me. I now know his name is Danny Woollard. He grabbed the black inmate whom I had been fighting with, as he was lashing blows to my unprotected head now. I was defenceless on my knees trying to get up. He broke his arm; he just snapped it like a twig. Woollard then dragged me to my feet, and with the help of another inmate, Mr Eddie Stampton, they pushed and dragged me through the black crowds, and somehow managed to get me back to my cell.

They sat me on my bed, and both of them stood guard at my door. There must have been about 20 black inmates gathered outside the cell door, all shouting and hollering abuse. But I felt pretty safe as Woollard and Stampton were there with me. About three or four minutes later a lady officer, Miss Jackson, walked down the landing and stopped outside my cell and used words to the effect of 'You're a popular lad today, Gully. What have you been up to?' whilst laughing and smiling. I was then banged up behind my door for one hour, till I was opened up again for tea.

I find it most alarming that with at least 40 inmates making all that noise in the dining hall, not one officer heard a thing, or if they did, they didn't investigate to see what was happening, when the main office is directly above the dining hall. I feel I owe my life to Mr Woollard and my thanks to Mr Stampton. I am indebted to both of these men.

Further to this incident, Mr Woollard was jumped in the shower by two black inmates. The two black inmates went into the shower room armed with pool balls in a sock to bash him up for protecting me. In the process of Mr Woollard defending himself and giving the two black inmates more than they had bargained for, he was caught in the right eye and he had broken blood vessels in the eye. The next morning he reported sick to the health centre in Wayland jail. He just said that he had slipped over in the shower. SO Burton said, 'Funny thing, that shower. Must be very slippery, as two other inmates were found in there very badly injured. Both of them were unconscious. They both said that they slipped over as well.' Woollard was blind in the eye for over a week, and his jaw had been badly damaged, but it was all hushed up, true to prison life, and the two black inmates were shipped out of Wayland as soon as they could leave the health care.

This concludes the incident that happened on the two dates.

After this trouble, Gully got in touch with every organisation you could think of – including the Prisoners' Advice Service, his MP, his solicitors and the newspapers. He had already got a big court case going against six screws in Belmarsh for a serious assault on him, and every day for two months he made out a request and complaint form to see the governor, not only telling her about his treatment but about every single other thing wrong in Wayland. As the six screws in Belmarsh had been suspended from duty pending these investigations, the screws in Wayland just steered clear of Gully, just let him do his time and go his own way.

One day I was training down the gym with Garry Langstone from Harold Hill, Romford, when the phone shrilled. The phone in the gym is extra loud so that the gym orderlies can here it. To my amazement it was for me. The burly gym orderly shouted out, 'Woollard, you're wanted on a legal visit.' My mind was racing at 100mph. What was this?

I soon found out. Two members of the murder squad were waiting for me. 'Hello, Danny,' they said, and we exchanged niceties.

'Well, what can I do for you?' I said.

One of them pulled out a picture of Jill Dando. 'Do you know this woman?' he said.

'Not personally,' I said, 'but I do know it's Jill Dando.' Her photo had been everywhere since she had been shot dead in London.

He then produced a photofit picture. 'Could this be Stephen Savva?' he said.

'It could be Al Pacino as far as I can tell.'

'Well, we know you got nicked with Savva concerning a murder. Do you think he's capable of killing anybody?'

'All Savva is,' I said, 'is a little car thief who gets on cocaine and tries to make out he's a gangster.'

'Well, he is fancied strong for killing Miss Dando,' the police officer continued. 'He's even been heard bragging about it.'

I just couldn't stop laughing. Savva with his big mouth again. He had been bragging about killing Jill Dando this time. The murder squad had spent over £500,000 investigating him, only to nick him for housebreaking and stealing cars – hardly murder, is it? It was poetic justice. Finally Savva's big mouth had put him away for a long stretch. You've got to laugh, haven't you? Ha ha ha. Anyhow, these two murder squad officers asked me my opinion about the Jill Dando case. 'Your appeal's coming up,' they said. 'If you scratch our back we'll scratch yours.'

'Interview terminated,' I replied.

Just after this incident I had to attend the appeal court in London. That appeal court in the Strand is a very daunting place. It has eight miles of corridors. It's also got its own museum, including Guy Fawkes' original charge sheet. When you go into the dock, you go up a spiral staircase, so when you walk into the court you're about 30 foot above the barristers and public. You're level with the judges. Three of them sit there with microphones in front of them; three old fools deciding your future. All them judges just take notice of what the police or your trial judge says. They just won't go against them. It's like playing dice when your opponent's dice are loaded. It's really so unfair. Unless you've been in the position we were in, it's difficult to imagine.

Most of them judges are far too old for the job. They've lost contact with the real world. In fact, in one case, Cliff Richard was mentioned and the judge said, 'Who's Cliff Richard?'

At the exercise period in Wayland prison, a group of us used to go onto the back field and spar with each other. There would be Reg Kray, me, John Waites, John 'Sauce' Smith and his cousin Paul Smith, plus a few others. Paul and Sauce are travelling people, both very tough lads, but a real likeable, honest pair. I palled up with Sauce when I first came to Wayland. He was always playing jokes on Paul and likewise Paul was always messing about with Sauce. Sauce had done lots of boxing, whereas Paul was just a toughnut. Reg Kray taught us all how to turn a man and slide a punch properly. He was far and away the best boxer among us. Although he was in his 60s, he was so fast and skilful. Even now it makes the mind boggle to think how good he could have been.

My relative John Jones got sent to Wayland. He never used to join in on our sparring, but I knew John to be a very tough man. He's not a liberty taker, but he wouldn't stand for any liberties from anyone. We were all situated in C wing. Now, on A wing was a group of travellers, always together, always taking liberties: robbing people, knocking people about and taxing the weak. This group was led by Mushy Lee. He's done a lot of boxing. In fact, all his family are well-known fighters. His two pals were John McDonald, a big grey-haired young fellow from the caravan site in Stratford, and Eamon Davies, the biggest one of them all with his shaven head. The others just followed these three about and obeyed orders.

Well, they made a very bad mistake. They robbed Sauce and Paul's relation, who was on A wing, and gave him a fearful beating as well. They had taken a diabolical liberty. They had made it clear they weren't bothered about Sauce or Paul or any of us. So the next day at the exercise period, Sauce and Paul went to meet Mushy and his pals to sort it out. Myself, John Waites, Jason Hooper, Lee Desbiens, Jason Campbell and Eddie Stampton went with them to make sure that if it came to a fight, Sauce and Paul would get fair play.

Mushy told them both to fuck off. So Sauce challenged John McDonald to a fight, as he was the one who had done the robbery. 'Okay,' said John, 'round the back of B wing.' As they squared up, Sauce caught John with a tremendous right hook, knocking him down. Sauce stood back to let him get up. Big Eamon rushed through the crowd to get to Sauce, but I managed to get to Eamon first and smashed him a perfect punch into his chest: a heart punch. As he staggered back, gasping for breath, holding his chest, I followed it up but he was finished. 'I don't want to know,' he said as he dropped to his knees.

John McDonald staggered up and Sauce put him straight back down again. Then the rest of the traveller's gang all started fighting. Mushy took a cheap shot at Paul. Paul squared up to him and Mushy had a real battle. Mushy could really fight, he's an England representative boxer, and he'd got the all-important first blow in. But Paul stuck to him. Reg's coaching had really paid off. Paul started to get on top. Mushy went down after about five minutes.

Lee Desbeins knocked a big, rough traveller unconscious with one blow when he had tried to get involved. A half-caste fellow ran at Lee before he could get anywhere near him. Lee's mate Eddie Stampton pulled him down and gave him a fearful beating. Mushy got up and carried on fighting but Paul had his measure now. After about another minute he was down again. This time as he got up he looked round for some help, and called out.

Three Irish tinkers ran out from B wing with pieces of wood to help Mushy and co. Well, John Waites, Jason Hooper and Eddie Stampton ran to meet them, and they really made short work of them. Although unarmed, they knocked these three tinkers to pieces, leaving them on the floor, covered in blood, moaning and groaning,

All of a sudden, the cry 'Kangas' went up (kangaroos – screws). So everyone packed up fighting and just walked away. But all in all there had been eight fights that day, and Mushy's lot didn't win any. Later, as we walked around the exercise field, there was me, Sauce, John Waites, Lee Desbiens, John Jones, Babyface and Eddie Stampton all together. All of a sudden, John Waites said, 'Just look behind us now.'

It was Mushy with about ten black fellows, all from the gym. We slowed down, and Sauce said to Mushy, 'I want my relation's stuff back.'

'You ain't getting it,' said Mushy.

Then this enormous black fellow, the biggest one out of the lot, said, 'Don't worry, Mushy. I'll look after you if any one of these start.'

John Jones' temper just snapped. He ran at Mushy and they were having a real toe-to-toe battle, when all of a sudden Mushy stopped punching and grabbed hold of John around the neck. He was trying to gouge his eye out. It was a bad mistake by Mushy, as John is a very good close-quarters fighter. He bit Mushy right through the lip and chin.

Mushy went straight into shock and packed up fighting immediately. The pain was too much for him. He was bleeding like a pig. When Mushy's black pals tried to set about John we started to bash them all right up. The big muscly fellow was the first to run. Then, again, the cry went up: 'Kangas'. Almost immediately, another shout went up, 'Fuck the screws.' But this time we all stood firm to tackle the hated screws. We were ready to do them all. Even though they had large wooden truncheons they just couldn't have beaten us.

All of a sudden, a voice called out, 'Don't be mugs, boys. That's just what the screws want. Pack it up now.' It was Reg Kray shouting. It was uncanny. Everyone in that yard did what Reg told them immediately. The man commanded that much respect in prison. We just disbanded and walked way. Have no doubt, Reg Kray stopped a major riot that day. Mushy and John MacDonald plus four others were kept in the hospital. John Jones, Sauce and Paul got shipped out to Norwich. Me, Lee, John Waites, Eddie and Jason all got shirts taken away to be tested for blood, and had our hands looked at. Obviously we had destroyed the shirts we had been wearing at the time of the fight by that time. The two lasting memories I have of that fight are John spitting a lump of flesh out of his mouth when he broke away from Mushy, and that unnerving silence when Reg ordered us all to pack up.

After the battle with the travellers, the screws really had the needle with us. They knew who had been fighting, but they just couldn't prove it. The prison had a complete shutdown that afternoon. We all got a security spin. First they body searched us, then they took our cells apart. None of us was stupid enough to have anything in our cells, or so I thought, but at bang-up time that evening, officer Baxtram (the security screw) presented me with a nicking sheet. They had found an unauthorised object in my cell: a knife.

I was shocked, to put it mildly, as I never knew anything about any knife. My first reaction was that the screws had planted it there, because once they body search you they make you leave the cell and search it on their own. This is not right but it's prison procedure. Next morning I had to go down the block and in front of the governor. I knew it would be about 28 days' loss of remission, but I was completely innocent. I was fuming.

As I left my cell to go to the block, Babyface Hooper came up to me. 'Dan,' he said, 'I have got something to tell you.'

'Go on,' I said, 'I'm in a hurry.'

'I know you leave your cell unlocked,' he went on, 'so when you went to work last Tuesday me and four other fellows cut an ounce of puff up in there. We used your cell because the kangas were making themselves busy spinning all our spur, looking for the gear. We were in a hurry to do it and we accidentally left the knife behind.'

'Thanks, Jay,' I said. 'Who're the other blokes?'

'I won't grass on them,' he said, 'but I have already told the SO it was me.' I wouldn't have asked Babyface to own up even if I had known it was him, but he did. None of the others even told me.

Well, I got off and Jason – who's doing 12 years for armed robbery – got 28 days, but it proved to me he was a real man. The governor insinuated I had paid Jason to speak up and cover for me, which of course I had not.

That was on Thursday morning. Thursday afternoon is when we get all our goods from the canteen, and if you are owed anything or you owe something to a fellow inmate it's paid on canteen day. The kangas know this. So this Thursday I bought eight phone cards and I had five cards owing me which I had lent out. So Thursday night I had 13 cards in my pocket. We were only allowed eight cards. If you were caught with more than that in your possession they would take all your cards and nick you.

Well, I was playing pool with Johnny Waites when these two mug screws walked up to me and said, 'Woollard, cell spin.'

'Leave off,' I said.

'Come on.'

I had these cards in my pocket, but they were watching me very closely. I walked closed to Danny Reese to pass them to him, but they were on us, so I just went with them. As I got halfway down the spur I saw Ronnie Hillier coming down the stairs. I dropped suddenly and ran back to the foot of the stairs. 'Hold on a minute,' I said to the startled screws. One of them ran after me, but they were too slow. I passed my cards to Ronnie. Quick as a flash he passed them to Eddie who passed them to Terry. They finished up with Jason Sharpe.

'What did you pass to him?' said the kanga.

'A phone card,' I said. 'I owe it to him. He's been asking me all day. I have only just seen him to return it and he wants to make a call tonight.' So they took me and Ronnie into my cell and body searched us. All they found was one card that Ron luckily had in his possession. Again they could do nothing, but I had some homemade weights in my cell. They couldn't nick me for them, but they took them off of me as they had the right needle. So in one day, Babyface, Ron, Eddie, Terry and Jason Sharpe all saved me from a nicking – but that's how inmates are with each other, the proper ones. I didn't even know young Terry Dowman from Tilbury or Jason Sharpe, a coloured man from Camberwell, but I hold them in the highest esteem, as I do all my friends in prison.

Especially Babyface Hooper. Unbeknown to him, when I came back from my nicking at the block, I was determined to find out who the other people were who had taken the liberty of using my cell when I wasn't there. A few phone cards and a bit of tobacco can work wonders in prison.

I soon found out that Jason hadn't even been in my cell. But he had seen four other fellows in there and told them they were taking liberties and he chucked them out for me. When he heard I had been nicked for the knife he was in a dilemma. He knew a nicking for me would ruin my chances of a D-Cat prison and take away all my hard-earned privileges, also making visits very awkward for me, but under no circumstances would he grass these four parasites up, so he sacrificed himself and took the nicking.

Babyface knew he had nothing to lose, only the 28 days, because he'd already lost his enhancement and any chance of a D-Cat when he had been nicked for knocking out a peter thief – someone who robs fellow inmates' cells. Jason only did what anyone else would have done, but unfortunately the peter thief grassed Jason up and he lost everything – all his privileges in fact.

This time, these other four scumbags had just left Jason to take the nicking. Jason didn't even know I knew the true story, but on the next Thursday, as soon as the canteen was delivered, I paid all four scumbags a visit, one by one, on my own and took all their canteen off of them: phone cards, tobacco the lot. Two of them put up a bit of a fight, but they quickly realised the error of their ways. I gave it all to Babyface. I just said I had some money sent in. It was my way of thanking him. I never did tell him the truth. But Babyface is a true friend to me, who sacrificed a month of his life to give me a chance. I admire him greatly.

I should explain Babyface's nickname: when he wakes up in the morning or from an afternoon nap, his face and eyes are all puffed up, just like a young baby's, so everyone calls him Babyface. Britain had got its answer to America's notorious Babyface Nelson – we have Babyface Hooper.

It's funny in prison. Someone will call someone something, then everyone in the prison knows them by that name. There is no nastiness in it all. Dave Courtney's cousin was in the cell above me when he first arrived – in the flashiest jacket you've ever seen: sequins, velvet, the lot. So everyone knows him as Jacket. Lee Desbiens looks like a young Charles Bronson – same physique, only Lee's tougher. consequently he's known as Bronson. My great pal Peter Spelling is always grumpy in the morning. He can't be spoken to until at least one hour after he gets up. Peter is an outspoken, tough man and single-minded, but he's so grumpy and miserable in the mornings that he's earned the nickname of Vic, after Victor Meldrew in the television show *One Foot in the Grave*.

Jason Isaacs has a terrible habit of coughing and making a funny sound at the same time. It sounds like he's saying 'Hello'. It's where his nerves are shot to pieces. Nevertheless, he's known as Hello. John Waites is a lovely fellow, but when he passes wind it's a really terrible smell. On one occasion he was bodily lifted from his chair and thrown out of the TV room. I swear John could empty the Albert Hall with just one fart. He passed wind one day in his cell and a big bloke by the name of Jason was on the phone at least 40 yards away – when the aroma hit him, Jason started to vomit. So John is known as Fartpants, after the comic-strip hero Johnny Fartpants.

Johnny Bryan is called Sawn-off, because he's so short, only 5 foot tall, but he has all the bounce of a 6-foot muscleman and his voice should belong to Arnold Schwarzenneger. He might be short but he's got all the answers. He named Reg 'Fruit' (Fruit and Veg – Reg). Reg Kray wrote a book about rhyming slang.

Gary Langdon is covered in scars. I always wondered where he got them as Gary doesn't argue with anyone. Then one day he had a drop of hooch and he was the biggest nuisance in the prison. He managed to upset everyone. The next day, he told me he had got all them scars fighting in pubs after drinking. In fact, on his manor he's known as The Nutter. So now everyone calls him Bread, short for bread and butter – nutter.

Another fellow had alopecia – all his hair fell out in patches. Though it's all grown back now, everyone still calls him Patch. We all used to call Lennie Mclean Pig's Head, owing to the size of his head. Nicknames sometimes stick on the outside. Jack Comer was known as Jack Spot, because Jack always seemed to be on the spot when any trouble happened. There's Mad Frankie Frasier, which is self-explanatory. Albert Dimes was called Italian Albert, owing to his Italian ancestry. Even the biggest gangster and mobster the world has ever seen, Al Capone, was known as Scarface.

One of the worst aspects of going to prison when you first get convicted is waiting to find out who you're going to have to share a cell with. First, after conviction, you get sent to a prison such as Brixton, Pentonville, Wormwood Scrubs or Wandsworth. They're known as 'locals', and they hold you for a while. Then, after a time, you get categorised and moved to the appropriate prison to serve your sentence.

So on each wing in the local you get a very mixed selection of convicted people waiting to be moved on, so everyone is together. In fact, a joyrider can be banged up with a murderer or a very violent criminal. Also the system infiltrates rapists, nonces, all sorts of perverts into the main prison, so no one knows who is who.

In Wandsworth prison there was a fresh-faced young inmate of 21, a first-time offender. He had got caught driving over the limit. In his panic he had driven off, knocking the police officer over. He got sentenced to two years in prison. The daunting atmosphere of Wandsworth prison must have terrified him anyway – then they banged him up with a tall, muscular black fellow by the name of Ishaki. Unbeknown to the other inmates, this Ishaki character was a pervert of the worst kind.

On the first night this young fellow was locked up, this Ishaki said to him, 'Listen, I'm breaking out tonight. I don't want you to get into any trouble, as you're supposed to press the bell and report me. So what I will do is I will tie you up and gag you before I make my escape.' This young lad was so terrified of Ishaki he readily agreed.

So at 9.30, after the screw on duty had made his rounds and checked everyone for the night, Ishaki ties and gags this young fellow up, after cutting his bed sheets into strips. When he was securely bound and gagged, Ishaki raped him not once but several times and physically abused him all through the night.

When the cell door was eventually opened in the morning, after what must have seemed an eternity for the young man, he was in a terrible state. This Ishaki had not only repeatedly raped him, he had beaten him black and blue and had bitten him all over. He was in such a state of shock he could not even talk.

Of course, the other inmates gave Ishaki a terrible beating and cut him to pieces. The prison authorities took both Ishaki and the young lad to an outside hospital. I never saw either one of them again, but what an ordeal that poor youngster went through. He suffered just because the system forced him to bang up with Ishaki.

I have purposely avoided the young inmate's name as I have no wish to cause his family any embarrassment or to darken this youngster's name at all. It wasn't his fault. He was entirely blameless. Why did the screws put that tender young man in with that animal Ishaki? Was that their idea of a joke?

The lad never got through his sentence. I heard through the prison network that this tormented young man, who had done nothing to be ashamed of, hung himself before his sentence was finished. In his tortured young brain he just could not face his family. I hope the screws enjoyed their joke.

After I was in Wayland for about six months, John Bryan told us his pal Jason Hooper was on his way, as he'd been chucked out of Blantyre House. Jason fitted in straight away with everyone. He was always laughing and joking. A pleasure to have around you. But he often said longingly, 'If I was in Blantyre House now, I would be getting home leave.'

Anyhow, one day he told us he'd seen Lawrence Woods, who he thought he had to settle a score with, get off of the sweatbox. He had come to our nick. So at exercise time, when I was on the phone, Andy Mills walked up to me. 'Quickly,' he said. 'Jason's going out to see that Woods.' I put the phone down and walked out. As I walked outside this Woods and his pal walked up to Jason.

As Woods put his hand out to shake Jason's, Jason smacked him right in the mouth. He hit him twice more and Woods went down. Woods' mate ran away immediately. He got up, and him and Jason were grappling with each other. Then Jason caught him again, but this time as he went down Jason kicked him straight in the mouth, smashing his teeth and nose and breaking his jaw. There was blood everywhere.

Woods was immediately shipped out of Wayland.

Another neighbour at Wayland was Stuart Blackstock, the man who shot PC Olds in Hayes, Middlesex. They put a tiny computer in the policeman's spine, which enabled him to walk and move like a doll. He had the operation done in California. The newspapers all called him 'Robo Cop', which gave filmwriters the idea for the

RoboCop films. PC Olds committed suicide after five years of this existence. Stuart got life. He's done 18 years already.

Stuart is one of these people who does an awful lot of reading. He is a very knowledgeable man and anything he's doing, he goes right into it. Well, he was taking a course in pottery. He must have read every book in the library on different clays, different glazing methods, different kilns, the lot.

Reg Kray had a cup with his old pal Bradley and his wife Donna's photograph on it. Reg broke the handle off, so he fetched it to Stuart to see if he could fix a new handle on. Stuart said, 'Don't worry, Reg. Leave it to me.'

'Stu,' I said, 'if I was you I would just make a new handle and superglue it on.' As I know you can't glaze new things twice.

'No, I know what I am doing,' he said. 'I will make a handle for the cup, fit it on, and glaze it and the cup all in one.'

'I don't think you'll be able to.'

'Just wait and see.'

So the next day in the pottery workshop Stu's messing about with the kiln for a good hour. Then he put some wax chippings in the kiln, which he made up himself. I don't know where he'd got them from. He put the cup and handle already fixed onto it into the kiln, and switched it on.

'I have increased the temperature,' he said, 'and coupled with the wax chippings, the increased heat and pressure will glaze the cup and handle just perfect.'

After ten minutes, the increased heat and pressure blew the inspection cover right off the top of the kiln and flames of about 12 feet shot into the air. Then the front of the kiln exploded, blowing the door right off, and blasting white clay and wax everywhere. The whole workshop was covered in dust. Stuart had wrecked it with his good ideas.

Stuart is a bald man with glasses, and he was covered in white dust, clay and wax and poor Bradley got cremated along with Reg's cup. Me and John Waites was creasing up laughing. Stu was immediately sacked. As we got back on the wing, who should come shuffling along the landing but Reg. Now, Reg has got a habit of greeting everybody by saying, 'Lovely day, eh?' As he got close to us and said this, Stu said, 'Lovely day! Fucked if it ain't.' What made it so funny was that Stu never swears. Reg never had his deaf aid in so he didn't hear him properly. I was killing myself laughing.

Reg stops and turns around and says, 'Stu, that cup you're mending, could you make six more for me, please? And Stu, you look in a right mess. Go and have a shower and change your shoes. You're making a terrible mess on the floor.' Then he shuffled off. Stu just walked away shaking his head.

In prison you pick up certain characteristics with people. Reg Kray had 'Lovely day, eh?' Even if it was raining or snowing. The gypsy fellow Ted Perfect always remarked as soon as you saw him, 'Ere's a life, bruv,' and Big Mick Johnson's greeting was, 'I'm fed right up. Have I got the pox of this or what?'

That night, Stu walked into my cell armed with his pottery book. He went, 'Look here. That kiln should work like this and that. It's not my fault the fucking thing's too old. Anyhow, it was Reggie's fault asking me to do the impossible: making a fucking cup for Bradley.' Needless to say no one else ever asked Stu to do anything for them and Stuart's clay-modelling career was over.

Unless a person has been in prison, locked up in small cell for endless hours, it's hard to imagine how your brain works. If a con receives a phone call and their girlfriend or wife doesn't speak in the right tone to them or tell them that they love him, or makes some chance remark, that person goes back to his cell and turns the words over and over in his head until a molehill has turned into a mountain. And sometimes coincidences happen that can drive a man crazy. A prize example of this was when my old pal Danny O'Leary died.

John Waites, my next door cell-mate and best pal, also knew Danny very well. In fact, Danny was more like an uncle to him. Danny was very seriously ill in hospital and me and John made regular phone calls to the hospital, as John's family were constant visitors to his bedside. One day me and my good friend Sauce had a cup of tea in John's cell. John never had one. He didn't fancy it.

John kept two jugs: one for making tea, the other for his descaling liquid, for cleaning his toilet out. Well, this day he'd made a mistake and made us tea in the wrong jug. When we were banged up for dinner, John realised his mistake and could do nothing about it. But he knew the descaling liquid was very poisonous. He had his dinner, then fell fast asleep,

After about an hour, a screw opened his door and said, 'Waites, you're wanted upstairs.' As he walked bleary eyed into the office, the prison chaplain sat there said, 'Waites, we have some bad news for you. Danny's dead.'

'Oh, no. What have I done?' he said. 'When did he die?'

'Half an hour ago.'

'How about Sauce?' He was panicking by now. All he could see in front of his eyes was 'PRISONER GETS 25 YEARS FOR DOUBLE KILLING.'

'I don't know anyone by that name,' the chaplain said, 'but Mr O'Leary passed away peacefully in his sleep. He didn't suffer at all.'

'O'Leary?' said John. 'So Woollard's okay?'

'Well, he was when we banged him up,' said the screw.

'Thank fuck it's Danny O'Leary.'

'That's not a very Christian reaction,' said the chaplain. 'Take him away.' John was led away full of smiles.

In fact, your mind plays all sorts of tricks on you with long periods of confinement. I remember once I had a terrible night when the name Chris, short for Christine, got mixed up. As soon as I was opened up in the morning one phone call sorted it out, or if you arrange to phone someone and they're not there, you think the worst. Then afterwards you think, wasn't I stupid?

It's also funny how fate and the unexplained can play such a big part in your life. When I first came to Wayland, Jason Isaacs and his Turkish mate Mimi put my name forward to do a first aid course, just for a laugh. So two weeks later I was not the slightest bit interested. I found myself doing this course. Jason and Mimi thought it was a great joke. I passed the course quite easily, getting my certificate, which I put in my drawer and thought no more of it.

Most mornings when were not working me and Johnny Waites would walk over to the next spur and call on our great pal Peter Spelling, then go out to exercise, just the three of us. Well, this particular morning I felt tired, and was still laying in bed at exercise time.

John came to my cell, and said, 'Come on, let's go over Peter's.'

'Leave off, John,' I said, 'I don't feel like it today.'

John pulled all the bed clothes off of me, then threw a cup of cold water over me, so eventually I said, 'Okay, John. Let me get ready and we'll go over to Peter's.'

When we got to Peter's cell, Peter said, 'Let's go upstairs and give little John Bryan a shout,' as John was also a pal our ours. On every single other occasion, us three would just meet John on the yard.

'Leave off, Peter,' I said. 'Right up them stairs? We'll see him in the yard, anyhow.' Johnny Waites echoed my opinion.

'Come on. Let's go up for him,' he insisted, more or less ordering us up the stairs. I was moaning like hell, walking up all them stairs.

The sight that greeted us was quite horrific. John had taken an overdose of pills and was dying. He was almost paralysed, the sweat was pouring off of him, and his eyes were just staring, not even blinking. He could not talk. His limbs were all bent up. As we walked into the cell he saw Peter and his eyes lit up. I looked at John. I knew we had to act quickly. It was like my brain went into automatic pilot. I knew exactly what to do. I had learned it all at the first aid course and it all came flooding back.

Between the three of us we managed to save John, and within a week he was back with us, as right as ninepence. He came up to me and said, 'Thanks for saving my life, Dan.' But had Jason and Mimi saved his life by jokingly putting my name forward for the first aid course? Had Johnny Waites saved him by forcing me to go to Peter's cell? Or had Peter saved him by making us go up to John? Why was Peter so insistent that we went for John? We never had before. I think the mind is a very powerful tool and I believe John was calling for his good pal Peter and Peter got the message.

In the two years I spent at Wayland with Reg, we became very close friends and we used to confide in each other on almost every subject. If something was bothering me I would tell him, or ask his opinion, as he did with me. And I do know that during the last year of his life one or two of his pals did upset him badly. There was Fred Foreman's book and then his appearance on TV. Roy 'Pretty Boy' Shaw did the same thing with his book. Then Dave Courtney came to visit Reg in Wayland and then went on TV and said that him and a pal had visited Reg in Wayland and had a secret camera concealed in a watch on them and took lots of photos.

I saw Reg's papers for his review to get a categorisation to a D-Cat. Then it's about 18 months to freedom. His reports said they felt Reg should stay in a C-Cat prison as he'd denied being involved in Mitchell's death. But in reality it mentioned Foreman and Albert Donahue in particular, saying Reg and Ron had ordered Mitchell's killing and police were looking into it with a view to charging Reg. It also mentioned Dave Courtney coming to the prison taking photos. Reg's close pal Joey Pyle and also his dear friend Wilf Pyne tried to smooth it over with Dave Courtney, as did Mark Epstein, our pal in Wayland, but Reg didn't want it smoothed over. He just wanted to blank Dave completely.

It wasn't all bad, though. Frank Fraser Reg held in the highest esteem. He knew Frank would always tell him the truth, if he liked it or not. Billy Curbishley was also very good to Reg. He really did respect Billy. I won't say here for fear of embarrassing Mr Curbishley but I do know some of the good things he did for Reg and I consider him a gentleman of the highest honour. Also a fellow from Uxbridge called Chris Brooks always played square with Reg. Reg respected Chris greatly but once he had lost his D-Cat possibility, and the chance to get out with his beloved Roberta, he succumbed very quickly to his illness. Those papers had taken all his hopes and aspirations away from him, poor Reg.

When I first read that Reg Kray was getting married, I thought, 'Oh, that's just another ruse to influence the powers that be to get Reg to a D-Cat prison and then to let him out.' How wrong I was. I lived very close to Reg for about two years, and believe me Reg and Roberta thought the world of each other. When we were unlocked first thing in the morning, sometimes I was still in bed, but I would overhear Reg saying, 'Good morning, Rob,' all sprightly. He was always the first person on the phone in the morning and the last person on the phone at night, saying good night to his beloved Roberta. It really was a crime to keep them two apart.

On the visits, Rob visited him on every available occasion, and I watched them. They had only eyes for each other. They sat there holding hands like two newlyweds, planning their future. Before each visit, Reg was a bundle of nerves. I bet he cleaned his teeth ten times and went to the toilet continuously, just till his beloved Rob turned up. Likewise, Rob just lived her life for Reg. Reg must have phoned her hundred of times unexpectedly and not once was Rob out. Yes, these two lovely people had definitely found true love. They were so close it was unbelievable. Reg was the worst writer I had ever seen – it looked like Chinese. Yet Rob understood it straight away unbelievably, and typed all Reggie's answers to his colossal mail bag every week. All from the scribbles he wrote that no one else in the world could understand.

When I first came to Wayland and I got talking to Reg, I found out he had lost contact with Georgie Woods, so I gave him George's phone number and I arranged a visit with George and Micky. Reg had a visit with his wife Roberta the same day. When Reg saw Georgie they just hugged one another as old friends do, and they had a lovely visit. From then on Reg phoned George at least once a week, and when the lifers had a special visit out on the back field, Reg invited George. Reg said that in his 32 years in prison it was the best visit he had ever had.

In February 2000, I received the sad news that George had died. I spoke to Micky Daltrey on the phone. 'What music shall we play at the funeral, Dan?' he said.

'Mick,' I said, 'there's only one song – "Maybe".' And that's what they played. I only wished I could have attended the funeral. So did Reg, but we both sent wreaths and I sent a few people to represent me. I'll really miss George. He was 77 but he was never out of place with teenagers or old folk alike. I respected him greatly. I'm only glad I was able to put George and Reg together again. It made them both happy.

Reggie Kray did a lot of yoga exercise. He was very supple and could bend his body all ways. One day, as we were waiting to go out on exercise, the biggest fellow in the nick sparred up to Reg. He wasn't serious but you don't always feel like messing around. Anyhow, quick as lightning, Reg's foot hit this giant in his private parts. He gasped and had to hold onto the wall to save going down. Reg just walked away as though nothing had happened. Later on that day this big fellow came up and apologised to Reg for being so heavy handed. Reg had stomach ache, and when this giant framed up he'd caught Reg quite hard in the stomach, accidentally on purpose I thought.

Reg Kray got mail from all over the country. One day I saw a picture of Peter Sharpe amongst his letters. Coincidentally, I had met Peter Sharpe years before. He got a life sentence for shooting his wife, who was tormenting him. Then another time I saw a photo of my cousin George Holland, whom I found out is doing life in Kingston jail. It really is a very small world in the prison system.

My co-defendant Bob Orly was housed right near Charlie Kray in Pentonville, so when Bob sent me a letter saying how ill Charlie was I was able to tell Reg straight away, so Reg had already put in to see Charlie before he got really ill. I knew Charlie outside. I was sad when he died. He didn't deserve that long sentence he got. He was only a middle-man. I felt his barrister made a bad mistake calling Mad Frankie Fraser as character witness for Charlie.

Reg did an amazing job for Charlie's funeral. He arranged it all personally on the phone from inside Wayland prison. Every single detail, which was a feat in itself. It was a real strain on him but he did it all single-handedly. Still, it took an awful lot out of Reg. Later, when Reg went to the Chapel of Rest to visit Charlie, his

Aunt Charlotte was also in there. Reg didn't even know she'd passed away.

As for poor Reg himself, the stomach pains were starting to get unbearable. He had a lump in his stomach, which was worrying him as well. Reg went to the health care nearly every day, but all they would give him was milk of magnesia. For almost two years I had to witness poor Reggie suffering like you could never believe. In one day Reg used up five toilet rolls. It shows you the state he was in.

He also had a job to pass water. The doctor stuck an instrument right up his penis into his bladder, but this only made matters worse. Every time Reg passed water, he was in terrible pain. One night, he was in so much pain he called out to me, as I was the listener on the wing. The screws just left him and wouldn't get me out.

On top of all of this the old boy opposite Reg's cell had somehow contracted TB, so Reg had to got to the hospital to have all sorts of tests and injections. The dentist who was treating Reg also had a patient who had HIV, so Reg, plus five other inmates, all had to go to Norwich hospital for treatment and yet more injections. Reg finished up with jaundice over that episode. He couldn't hold his water; he was more terrified of wanting to go to the toilet on the van than of anything else.

When Fred Foreman went on the TV and said that Ronnie and Reg had got him to kill The Mad Axeman, there was talk in the papers of the Crown Prosecution Service charging Reg with this offence. Reg was so worried that he would have to keep leaving the court and go to the toilet. In fact, that was the only thing he was worried about.

I could see that Reg was deteriorating badly, so I went to see PO Burton, PO Heighton and SO Mcleary, who hated Reg, and I told them the bad state Reg was in. They all said, 'It's the health care's responsibility.' I also wrote a letter to Jack Straw, the then Home Secretary. He never even bothered to reply to me. I went and saw the doctor in the health care. All he said was, 'We're doing all we can.' So I had to sit and watch my very good friend Reg suffer. Whatever he had done in his life, he didn't deserve to be treated like this. I tried to get help everywhere, but every avenue it seemed was blocked to him.

He saw a private doctor but good old Wayland wouldn't let him have the medication this private doctor had prescribed, even though Rob, Reg's wife, had already paid for it in full. I have never felt so frustrated in my life, just watching Reg fade away and die. It was criminal. Reg didn't die, he was executed by the state.

They wouldn't let him have any letter heading or photos sent in as he used to send them to people who had written to him. I have had my fair share of stress and frustration. I have seen people hang themselves; I saw one man get murdered; I have also had many personal problems; but compared to Reg I have had it easy. When I first went away, Reg told me it was best to break my ties outside. I think it was good advice but at the time I didn't understand it. Unfortunately I do now.

A more suitable nickname for John Santry than Jacket would have been Fagan. In prison everyone tries to help each other in their own little way. Everyone except Jacket, that is – he's all take. He was the most disliked fellow in Wayland. If a fellow inmate's relative died and they wanted to phone home and never had a phone card, Jacket would lend them one and charge double back.

He took one or two hidings over his graspy, slimy ways, but that still didn't stop his greedy attitude. When he worked on the hotplate dishing out food he short-changed some of his fellow prisoners on their meagre bit of feed, regularly. Then he sold it back to them for tobacco or phone cards a bit later on. Also, when he was doing the washing, if someone had a few more dirty clothes to wash then was allowed and they didn't pay Jacket, they never got their clothes washed. He would definitely win the award for being the most unpopular person in Wayland.

During my first year there, I went back to Snaresbrooke and got all my outstanding charges sorted out. It was good to see Angelo again. The judge sentenced me to another two years nine months. My heart nearly stopped until the judge said that magical word 'concurrent'. So at least now I had a clean slate. Then at my appeal I got one year off, so now my sentence was down to seven years

One of the most disappointing things about my appeal was that my barrister said I should get at least three years' reduction in my sentence, yet all I got was one year off. Poor Bob Orly only got a year off as well. Peter Power and John Hayman never showed up, but they got the same as us in their absence. But that was not the most disappointing thing to me.

When John Hayman's barrister got up and said John had been helping the police with their inquiries all along, that's what really disappointed both me and Bob Orly. It completely gutted us. No wonder John never came to court. To hear that in open court was a body blow indeed.

When I got back to the prison, I heard the sad news that Tommy Hole had been shot dead in Canning Town at the Beckton Alps. Poor Tom had previously found his son, young Tom, hanging dead in Parkhurst prison. It was an open secret in the East End of London that Tom had shot Nicky Gerrard to death, so perhaps it was something to do with that. Who knows?

An old pal of mine in Wayland, John Bates, is doing a life sentence for stabbing a fellow to death in a pub fight. He's done 18 years already. He's a very nice, unassuming fellow, but in 1995 at Little Hey prison in Cambridgeshire, there was a screw who rubbed John up the wrong way. John was trying to get his D-Cat, so he stood it for as long as he could. This screw was a born-again Christian, always quoting the bible and talking about Jesus, saying, 'An eye for an eye,' and that sort of thing. He used to wear his peak cap right over his eyes and just growl all the time at John. John stood it, and stood it, then one day, John just snapped.

He went to his cell and got his blue Thermos flask with a yellow cup on top. He unscrewed the bottom of the flask and pulled out the glass container inside. Then he pissed and shit in it, then went along the spur and got other people to do the same. When he'd finished, he just screwed the top on this shitbomb and calmly walked to the office. There were four screws sitting in there, drinking tea. The hated screw was one of them. 'Oi! Screw! Share this out amongst you,' he shouted, and launched the bomb straight at him.

He ducked, but the bomb exploded on the wall just above his head. There was mess and urine everywhere. All over the screws. You'd have to see a bomb made up out of a thermos flask go off to fully appreciate how it explodes, spreading its contents and glass everywhere.

John was taken to the block and was shipped out. When I saw John in Wayland he said, 'Okay, I lost my chance of a D-Cat, but it was worth it just to see his face all covered in shit.' It cost John at least three years on his sentence, which I thought was very unjust.

There's two things you always see in the cell of an inmate who knows the ropes: one is a Thermos flask, the other is a bottle of Encona hot pepper sauce. The sauce bottle is made out of very thick glass and is an ideal cosh – and if the screws do spin you, what can they nick you for? A bottle of sauce or a Thermos flask. That screw was very lucky John Bates chose the Thermos flask to attack him with and not the sauce bottle.

In August 2000, Reg Kray was taken to Norwich hospital for an operation. I was down the block at the time so I missed him going I was upset about that. Reg's neighbour, Ken Churchman, who was into his 27th year in prison, got Reg a card, and we all signed it for him, which I thought was a very nice gesture. Ken is an avid boxing fan. He said he had the Scots ex-world champion Ken Buchancan's phone number and that he was going to give him a call. 'Oh, I know him, Ken,' I said.

The next day as I was walking down the spur, Ken Churchman was on the phone. 'Danny, Ken Buchancan on the phone,' he said. I think deep down he suspected I didn't even know Ken.

I got on the phone and Ken had just been elected to the boxing hall of fame. It was a real pleasure talking to him and he asked how we all were. He remembered all the names around Manor Park and Dagenham from when he was there. I believe Ken to be the best boxer Britain ever produced. But above all this, the man is a real gentleman, and there's one quote that really applies to Ken: 'It's nice to be important; but its much more important to be nice.' And Ken even sent Reg a card wishing him well. A great man: a boxing legend who still hasn't lost the common touch. Ken could mix with royalty or beggars and treat them just the same.

The card Ken Churchman had done for Reg had been signed by ten of Reg's neighbours, myself included. Out of curiosity, I added up how much bird the people who signed their names on that card had done. It added up to 220 years. After all the adversity these men had faced in their lives, they all remained cheerful and hopeful for the future.

On Friday 11 August 2000, we all officially got the sad news that we secretly feared: Reg had definitely got cancer. Poor Reg had suffered so much over the time I had been in Wayland.

NAMES IN THE NICK

One of the most harrowing experiences in prison and one I will never forget didn't even concern a human being at all, but of all things a seagull. Let me explain. Seagulls come inland for the winter months and literally hundreds of them descend on Wayland Prison looking for food. It's amazing really. They arrive at about 7am in time for breakfast scraps and what's thrown out of the kitchen; then again at about 1.30 pm, dinner time; then at 6 pm, tea time. Everyone moans about the noise they make, but most prisoners are very soft-hearted round animals, and nearly everyone threw them their scraps to eat. Hardly anyone threw their food in the bins provided. So the gulls got plenty of food.

Sometimes we got nicked for throwing food out of the windows, but most people still did it. One day at about 2.15 pm I heard this gull making a hell of a noise, squawking and screeching. It was a very bright day. I looked out of my window. About 150 yards away is the perimeter fence – very high with razor wire on top of it. Razor wire is illegal in this country, incidentally. The prisons pay a fine every year to the court of human rights in Europe to keep it up. It looks like Colditz.

Well, this gull had flown too low and got caught in it. All the other gulls had flown off in panic, except one that was flying high above the one in trouble. That one was squawking as well. Myself and loads of other prisoners got on our bells, making a hell of a racket. A screw came to my door. 'What's wrong?' he said. I told him about the gull. 'Well, there're loads more,' he said.

'Take me to the fence,' I said. 'I'll get it untangled.' He just banged my door and walked away.

That gull took 20 minutes to die. He was cutting himself to pieces, struggling to get away. We were all so helpless. When he died, I saw a screw casually walk up to the fence with a long pole and unhook the poor creature. It crashed to the ground, a grotesque mess of red and white. I hated them screws for not trying to help that poor gull. As the bird crashed to the floor, all our wing yelled all sorts of obscenities to the screw. He just stuck his finger up. As I looked up above, the other gull flew away. The memory of that poor bird squawking and screeching in fear and panic will live with me for ever.

Another violent image sticks in my mind. As usual it revolved around drugs. A big scouse fellow was selling some heroin for a couple of Irish lads who had smuggled it into the prison. This Scouser told the two Irishmen that he'd had a spin and thrown their stuff out of the window, just to get rid of it. Obviously that area was thoroughly checked out, and guess what? No heroin was ever found.

The Irish lad just said to the Scouser, 'Don't worry, mate, we understand. Anything is better than getting nicked.' But I saw a momentarily glance pass between the two of them. I knew the Scouser was in trouble. Well, on Sundays the Scouser always slept in till at least dinner time. He was heavy into heroin, so after Saturday night's session, he was unconscious. Saturday night the Irish lads tore two sheets from their beds into strips. Then on Sunday morning, as soon as we were unbolted, they walked straight up to the Scouser's cell. Two other men also made there way to his cell, slipping in unnoticed by anyone as it was breakfast time, and everyone was scurrying about, going about their business.

Once in the Scouser's cell, they gave him what they call an apple turnover, where a man gets either side of the bed and pulls the bedclothes really tight, so it's impossible for the person in bed to move. Then the Irish lads produced the strips of sheet from underneath their tracksuit tops and proceeded to wrap them round and round the bed, making it physically impossible for Scouser to move. He was screaming and shouting. So paddy smacked him straight in the mouth and growled, 'Shut up,' and then gagged him. He was totally helpless.

Then he got a bottle of liquid from one of the other men. It was a descaling fluid which had been stolen from the outside works department. It is a very corrosive liquid, some sort of acid. Then one of them started to laugh and proceeded to put the liquid all over Scouser's bedclothes, where his lower body was positioned. I'll never forget the look of fear and horror in the Scouser's eyes as his bedclothes started to smoke and smoulder and the liquid started burning his legs and private parts. All the time, all the paddies were laughing hysterically. Then as quick as it all began, one of them said, 'Come on, let's fuck off and leave this cunt to cook.'

I was the last one out of the cell, but I couldn't just leave this man to die an agonising death. So I pressed Scouser's button inside his cell to call a screw to his assistance. We were all back in the paddies' cell before the hue and cry went up. Everyone knew who had done the Scouser, but life just goes on in prison, no one said a word, including Scouser.

After his stay in Norwich hospital, which is where he was taken to treat his burns, he was shipped out to Stocken prison in Leicestershire, and life just carried on in Wayland as usual. I was glad I had not turned into a complete animal like the others, and had helped that poor man. I know he had done wrong, but he didn't deserve the punishment that was intended for him.

It's funny in prison how a small thing makes you really laugh. Next door to me in Wayland was a right aggressive Pakistani gentleman. His cell stank. I never once saw him in the shower. Every night, I fetched back loads of bread when I was working on the hot plate, and threw it all outside his window. Then every morning at 7 am sharp outside his cell would be invaded by squawking seagulls making a hell of a racket. Every morning he'd be up at his window screaming, 'Bloody fucking birds. Shoo shoo.'

He got hold of the wing officer one day and said, 'Please, sir, why do them birds always just go outside my cell?'

The screw couldn't work it out. Of course, me, Reg, Jake, Johnny Waites and Peter Spelling all knew the reason and it kept us laughing for months, till Mr Patel went home. Everyone in the nick called him Burt after Burt Lancaster in the film *The Birdman of Alcatraz*. Mr Patel was the Birdman of Wayland.

One day in May 2000, as I walked out onto the exercise yard at Wayland, I heard someone call, 'Oi, mush.' It was Sammy Gumble, a travelling man from Harlow in Essex. He had got six years for an armed robbery. I got on well with Sam from day one. Reg Kray also thought he was a likeable, well-mannered young man. As we sat in Reg's cell telling each other our stories and having a joke, it suddenly struck me – all those years ago at Barnet Horse Fair, when Reg and Ron Kray made sure we got a fair go with Don Adams, Kenza Gumble, Sammy's grandfather, was the referee. Now about 35 years down the line, there's Reg, me and Kenza's grandson all banged up together in Norfolk, enjoying each other's company. It's funny how people's lives cross over.

On our spur at Wayland was all long-term prisoners. Lifers Johnny Bates from south London and Sean Wallace from the same area are two fellows I got on particularly well with. They both gave respect to people and expected it in return. Young Sammy fitted in well with everyone. His grandfather would have been proud.

One of the worst things about prison life is that, unless you knew an inmate on the outside before you came to prison, or one of your friends in prison recommends a fellow con to you, you don't trust anyone. You get perhaps 150–200 men on a wing and you don't know what they're inside for.

Nowadays they put people that cons hate the most – bacons (nonces, grasses, child molesters, rapists) – on the wing with everyone else. The screws use them as informers. They keep quiet about their convictions as long as they receive information back from them. They're only moved to the segregation wing if someone recognises them. Consequently, anyone not from London is asked to show their court depositions. If they won't, they're quite quickly dealt with, although sometimes their depositions are forged.

A fellow by the name of Johnny Smith came to Pentonville from Romford, a big gypsy fellow. He said he was inside for fighting in a pub, badly injuring the publican. He showed us his deps. He seemed all right to me, but my pal Bugsy didn't like John from the start. There was something about him, he said.

Bugsy was right. When I got to Wayland, another gypsy fellow called Levi knew John. 'Yes, he's nicked for smashing the governor of the Beacon up in Dagenham,' Levi said, 'but I bet he never told you what he's already done eleven years for.' It turned out John broke into a big house in the country one day. He knocked at the door at first, but when there was no answer he broke in. But the woman of the house had been in the toilet and hadn't heard John knocking at the door.

She was about 45, a rather large, well-to-do lady, very well dressed. As John was ransacking the front room she walked in on him. She screamed, 'Get out of my house.' John slapped her about a bit, took her watch and rings off of her and made her sit down on the settee. Then he just carried on looking through her drawers. He then went into the bedroom to continue his search for her valuables, after pulling the phone out of the wall. The lady, thinking this was her chance to escape, ran to the window and tried to clamber out, but being a bit portly she got stuck tight half in and half out of the window. The more she struggled, the tighter she got wedged.

John, meanwhile, had walked back into the room. 'Who's been a silly girl, then?' he said. The woman was terrified, screaming at the top of her voice by now, but no one could hear her. 'Be quiet now,' said John. Then he pulled her dress up to her waist and took her knickers off. She was completely helpless. Then he raped and buggered this terrified woman. Can you imagine the terror and humiliation this poor helpless woman must have felt? Then he calmly collected his swag and walked out the door, leaving this whimpering woman, still half naked, for someone else to find her. He never even bothered to save her modesty and cover her up.

I got word back to the 'Ville, but John had already been moved up north. He got a life sentence for the fight in Dagenham with a recommendation he serve at least 25 years, so that was one good thing.

When I was first on remand in the 'Ville, three co-defendants were on G wing together. Anyhow, someone recognised them; they were three scruffy heroin addicts that were always poncing. I never ever saw any of them in the shower. They all had brown rotting teeth and greasy, lank hair, full of tattoos. What they had done, they had broken into a big house in Woodford late at night. When they were searching the house, they realised this house belonged to a judge.

The house was empty but upstairs the judge's young daughter was sound asleep. These three animals woke up this terrified, utterly defenceless young girl of 15, gave her an injection of heroin, then the three of them raped her and humiliated her every way possible. Eventually they left the girl alone and hurriedly made their escape. By this time she was unconscious and in a bad way.

NAMES IN THE NICK

The judge got home at 2.30 am. He had been held up at a legal meeting in Birmingham. On finding his daughter in this state, he called an ambulance and the police. These three animals in their rush had left fingerprints everywhere, so they were soon arrested.

When they were recognised in the 'Ville, it went around the landing like wildfire who they were. The same night, one of them went to get his tea and he was jugged – an inmate had made a mixture of boiling water and sugar to make a hot, sticky syrup, and then threw it over No1. As he was screaming, someone came behind him and put over 100 stitches in the back of his neck and face. No one saw a thing.

No2 was watching television when someone sat behind him and poured boiling cooking oil over his head, which they had got from the hotplate. His skin just melted. No one saw a thing.

No3 somehow or other injected himself with an overdose of pure heroin on the same night. They took him to hospital but he didn't survive. So the bacons play a dangerous game. The two animals who survived got ten years each. I got eight years for conspiracy to handle stolen goods, not even handling – just two years less then those bits of filth. Where's the justice in that? Swift justice was handed out to the three animals in the 'Ville, even though the victim was a judge's daughter and that same judge had most probably sentenced some of the men who avenged the men's crimes, but that did not matter. Most criminals realise that children cannot be held responsible for their parents' actions.

Later on it came out they had given this innocent young girl a venereal disease, and that she had finished up a heroin addict. They had ruined her life completely. She died of a heroin overdose at the tender age of 20. When she had been attacked she was a virgin and she finished up selling her body in Kings Cross just to feed her habit.

It was a very sad end for her.

Prisoners can be compassionate, but of course they can be heartless too. As you walk onto a wing in Wayland prison you shout, 'One on, Guv', and as you leave the wing you shout, 'One off, Guv.' This keeps the prisoners count right. When David Colley got killed over a £2 phone card, someone shouted, 'One off, Guv,' for a joke. Then at tea time another fellow said, 'David is dead. Can I have his tea then?' The screw on the hotplate said no. This inmate then argued the point till at last the screw gave it to him, just to keep him quiet. 'Too right,' the fellow said. 'David don't need it now.' You get no pity or sympathy in prison, I'm afraid to say. And the humour can be dark.

In May 2000, Governor Phillips called me to the office and told me at long last I had got my D-Cat. Obviously I was overjoyed at this news, as it meant I would soon be going to a less secure prison than Wayland. The only condition Governor Phillips stipulated was that I had to work on the outside gardens for a month before I could make any more progress, as the outside gardens is a position of trust.

I didn't mind, as I was in no hurry to leave Reg Kray anyway and, as his review regarding his categorisation was due at the beginning of July, it could work out we'd be shipped out to a D-Cat prison together. I duly left my job on the hotplate and reported to the outside garden party on the Monday morning.

The man who was running the garden party workers was a tall, heavily built man. As well as maintaining the outside garden area, this character used to look after a herd of prize winning sheep in Wayland. One day he said to me, 'Oi, can you walk the sheep, one at a time, like you would walk a dog, with a bit of rope tied round their neck, to get them used to people for when they enter shows?' So each morning I had to walk right past the offices. Everyone in that building thought they were comedians – screws, officers, girls, the lot, shouting out remarks and laughing out of the windows, generally taking the piss. I just ignored them, as I didn't want to get into any trouble. Then a security screw said to me, 'See that big ram in the field? Don't get anywhere near him, he'll cripple you. He's left on his own because he attacks all the other rams, as well as people.'

The very next day, this cowboy said to me, 'Today, Mr Woollard, you can exercise our prize ram. That one in the field on its own.'

'Okay, I'll do that,' I said, 'but first I'll have to put my prison boots on, as my trainers will get ruined with all the mud on that field.'

'Okay, Woollard.'

He made a bad mistake. After dealing with pit bull terriers for years, I wasn't scared of a sheep. I was ready for anything. Anyhow, I walked onto the field on my own. He was standing outside the gate, leaning over it with just his arms and half a bucket of food dangling in the danger zone. He was rattling this bucket of food to attract the ram over.

All of a sudden, the ram's seen me and heard the bucket rattling and come running at us at full pelt. When he was almost upon me, he stopped abruptly, looked at me, then the bucket of food. He didn't know what to attack first. Then all at once, his head was in the bucket gobbling the food. Immediately I grabbed him by his horn. He went potty, bucking and struggling frantically but I managed to pull him over on his side.

'Give me that rope you want me to use as a lead,' I said. Then I made a halter out of it, as I used to so many years before with my dad's horses. This gave me more control over the ram's movements than just a rope round his neck. Then I pulled the ram to his feet.

As he tried to butt me, I kicked him in the ribs. This ram was really trying to do me some serious harm. But eventually he knew every time he reared up or tried to butt my legs I kicked him hard in the ribs with the steel-toecap boots which I had put on specially for this animal.

Within a short time, the killer ram was walking on a lead like a poodle. The guy was gutted – an old London boy had tamed his pride and joy.

One dinner time, we were having a laugh in our shed at this cowboy's expense. He overheard us laughing about him from his office next door. He came rushing into our shed all red. I was really sick of him and his gardens, and the fucking sheep, so I said, 'You're a big man. It's obvious you don't like me, and I can't stand you, so be a man for once in your life and prove it. Make your mum proud of you. Let's me and you go in to the field behind the shed and sort out our differences man to man.'

He looked on the floor and said, 'I can't.'

So I said, 'Well, you coward, fuck off.' As he turned round I kicked him up the arse, completely humiliating him.

I lost my D-Cat after that and all I worked for as a result of this incident but I was glad of what I had said and done.

I told Reg Kray about it the day it happened. He said, 'Dan, you want to watch they don't ship you out.' Poor Reg was so ill at the time I didn't want to leave Wayland as I knew Reg liked talking to me and I did watch out for him. So perhaps losing my D-Cat had done me a favour. But 27 July 2000 was to be Reg Kray's last day in a prison.

When we woke up that fateful Thursday morning, little did we know what the day had in store for us both. I had my breakfast at 8.30 am, then I went to Reg's cell. Yunis Bhad, another lifer, and

John Bates joined us. We were all laughing and joking. Then, as we were all on the wing, we all went down on the pool table for a while. At 10 o'clock a screw told us the mail was in, so both me and Reg collected our mail from the office and went back to our cells to read our letters. Then I thought I would go back up for Reg and go out to the exercise yard, as it was about 11.15 am.

As I was going up to Reg's cell, a screw said to me, ' You're wanted down the health care to see a chiropodist.'

'I'll go a bit later on,' I said.

'No, go now as they're expecting you,' he said.

I saw Reg walking down the stairs. I called out, 'Reg,' but as he's a bit deaf he never heard me. I ran to the stairs but he had gone out into the yard. All of a sudden, I got the strangest feeling. I can't explain it. I know Reg had psychic powers and I also knew, deep in my heart, I would never see Reg again. I told myself, 'Don't be silly, I'll see him when I come back from health care,' but really I knew I would never see Reg again.

As I got to the health care, six security screws came out of the segregation unit and said, 'Woollard, come here.' As I got to them they all got round me and said, 'Come into the block.'

'What for?' I said.

'Tomorrow you're being shipped out to Blunderstone,' one of them said.

So into the block I goes. The bloke in the next cell told me Blunderstone was right up near Lowestoft. 'I don't think I'll go,' I thought. So I rings the bell and tell this screw 'I'm not going.'

He just laughed and said, 'Oh yes you are.'

'Governor,' I said, 'you'll have to take me out of here kicking and screaming and I know a few of yous will be going to hospital if you try.'

Next morning they opened my door with breakfast. I chucked it straight at the screws and screamed, 'Go and fetch your mates now.' At about 11.30 this door opens. It was Kate Crawley, the No1 Governor in Wayland. 'Woollard, just go back on the wing,' she said. 'You haven't got to go anywhere.' So unbelievably I was sent back to the wing. Everyone was shocked to see me, as once you go to the block in Wayland you're gone.

When Reg had heard I had been 'shanghied', he went around the office causing a right row, threatening to put my story in the newspaper. He had made such a fuss about it all that the prison authorities thought it prudent to let me stay at Wayland. That afternoon, Reg had been taken to hospital in Norwich so we'd both been taken off the wing on the same day.

A week after all this happened, ten security screws came to my cell and took me to the block for the second time. I kicked right off in there, and then once again Kate Crawley came down, this time with Governor Phillips, and sent me back on the wing to get ready to be moved to Rochester prison. This time Roberta Kray took my part.

As I walked past Reg's cell, I saw someone had put a notice on his door. It read, 'Long live the legend; Let the legend live on. Reg Kray. God bless.' That was how I found out that my good pal Reg had died. The screws tore that notice down six times and each time it was replaced with another. I took Reg's prison card down from outside his cell. I still have that card. That was the last prison card Reg ever had.

Poor Reg had finally succumbed to his illness in August. Whilst I had been down the block, Reg had phoned my house and left a message for me. He said, 'It's been a pleasure to know you.'

That message upset me more than losing my D-Cat or

anything. Poor Reg had just days to live but he still thought about me and phoned up. He was a real gentleman and a proper soldier. I also owe his lovely wife Roberta a real big debt for sticking up for me once she knew I was down the block the second time. She's a real lady, who I owe a lot to. I learned so much from the real Guv'nor, Reg Kray. And I know I'll be a much better man for knowing him so well.

ROUND 16

FINISHING OFF IN ROCHESTER

So I was off to Rochester. As the sweatbox pulled up, I looked out of the window. I could see Cookham Wood ladies' prison on the left hand side. This was the prison that the notorious Myra Hindley spent so many years in. Then the barrier was lifted and about 300 yards away stood Rochester men's jail. It's a very daunting old place to look at from the outside. It's a converted old borstal. In fact, it stands in the village of Borstal, as it was the first borstal in existence.

The driver tooted the horn, a pair of big old gates opened and in we went. In reception I was allocated to A wing. It's a big old building with three dormitories in it, 16 men to a dorm. I was put in No. 1 dorm. I saw a good friend Tyfen Sakir ('Tony') straight away. I knew him to be a really genuine fellow, so that was a good start. Also there were Bob Woolley and Stevie Walford, basically straight men who had been duped into letting cannabis be loaded on their respective lorries. They never knew what was on their vehicles but Bob got six years and Stevie seven. Still, no one ever heard them moaning. Tony Humphreys, an animal rights activist, and Chris Gaynor, an armed robber, were also there. They'd both been transferred from Swaleside, where they had been friends with Angelo. Chris was doing 11 years and Tony 7.

Rochester is a working prison, and the first week I was allocated to work on the farm. As soon as the screw walked me out on the farm, I could smell the pigs. It stank putrid, but I thought I'd give it a go. As I got near the sties, I heard a deep voice bellow out, 'What you doing here, you cunt?'

I spun round aggressively, ready to give an answer back or whatever else it took, but the sight that greeted me was a sight for sore eyes. It was my old pal Big Mick 'I'm fed right up. Have I got the pox of this or what?' Johnson: a real giant of a man – at least 6ft 8in and as wide as a lorry. I went back many years with Mick, who is Del Croxson's cousin. I used to see Mick regularly on the outside. He is Joe Longthorn's minder, as well as being related to him.

I personally think Joe is the most talented entertainer alive today. I remember when I first saw him in Harry 'The Buck' Starbuck's pub in Abbey Wood. Mick said, 'Just listen to my relative, Dan.' He was unknown in those days. I genuinely thought Joe was miming to tapes, but he was impersonating all these superstars singing. I knew from that night on Joe was a megastar, and a real nice down-to-earth fellow as well. Obviously I took notice as his career blossomed, but by a cruel twist of fate he got cancer. He fought it with all the courage in the world but finally it beat him.

Mick also takes care of George Michael and Tom Jones and many more stars. I also used to bump into Mick at the trotting races. He used to usually go with Tommy Taylor, who was a very handy bare-knuckle fighter in his day. The only times I can remember Tom getting beaten was when he used to take on much heavier fighters. Tom's not a big man, but he's got the heart of a lion. He'd fight anybody. Mick would always see fair play and make sure no one else got involved or if there was any arguments over paying out the bets at trotting races, Mick always collected the money. The thing I always liked about Mick was despite his size he's never been a bully. But when Mick was boxing he won 35 out of 37 bouts, losing the 2 on points. Obviously I was pleased to see him at Rochester, and we became constant companions.

Unfortunately my career as a farmer didn't last very long. The second day I was out there, Mick was herding these dairy cows into a paddock. Well, they were being a bit obstinate. As I was hosing the yard down with a high-powered washer, I thought I'd help Mick. So I squirted one of these cows on her udders.

She took off like a bat out of hell, straight into the paddock. 'This is a good idea,' I thought, so I started squirting them all to make them run into the paddock. It was like a stampede. Unfortunately they carried on running and smashed right through the paddock and took off. So now there were about 50 cows all running wild through these fields near the prison. Mick collapsed in laughter; the farm manager went apeshit.

It took eight men six hours to catch the cows and half of them stopped yielding milk with the trauma. So in two days I'd seriously depleted Rochester farm's milk yield. John the farm manager sacked, or rather 'transferred' me and Mick to the pigs side of the farm. Well Jock, the Scots foreman in charge of the pigs, put both me and Mick clearing out what they call the fattening house. There's roughly 500 pigs in there, getting fattened up for market.

In this fattening house, there are two alleys either side of the pigpens. What you do, you close a gate in the pig's pen then, after pushing all the mess from the pen to the alley, you clean that portion of the alley. You do a pen at a time. Anyhow, I thought for speed I'd do four pens at once. How was I supposed to know pigs from different litters fight each other?

I opened the four pens, each with a dozen piglets and a sow in, and mixed up about 50 pigs. As soon as they got together, they started squealing and taking lumps out of each other. There was murders. The noise was unbearable and Jock came running in. He went potty, as not only were all the pigs going crazy but unbeknown to me they shouldn't have been mixed up, as they were bred differently. Anyhow, in his panic Jock slipped over in all the pigs' shit. It was a proper pantomime. When Jock went down, me and Mick both started laughing. Needless to say we both got the sack straight away. So my farming career came to an abrupt end, I'm sorry to say, after three days. Mick went to work helping an electrician and I got sent to Kent Life, a farm museum, with Tony Sakir.

Being in a dormitory brought with it some amusing incidents. In the summer, the temperature was well over 100 degrees. It was so humid, the 16 men in the dormitory were all bathed in sweat. At 3 am, Stuart Munday – an armed robber who had robbed an armoured van in Dunmow, Essex, and a guard was shot – got up to go the toilet. Well, the practical joker of the dorm, Frank Edgar, a short, very well-built black fellow from Upton Park, who was doing six years for drug smuggling, heard him. He was laying awake as all the dorm was in the intense heat. Frank waited for Stuart to get in the toilet, then he stripped himself naked. As the dorm was in total darkness, no one could see him, and he crept on his hands and knees and got into Stuart's bed.

When Stuart returned from the toilet, he laid down straight on top of Frank's naked body. Well, Stuart hollered in fear and surprise, jumping up like a rocket. Everyone just broke up laughing. The funny thing was, Stuart had glanced at the bed, and couldn't see Frank in the dark as Frank laid deadly still. It was talked about in the prison for days.

It wasn't all fun and games though. In our dormitory was a big, white South African gym orderly, who thought he was really something. He always seemed to be in the bath or shower, and was always posing. I didn't like him at all. I saw him tell a couple of people off and they didn't answer him back. Well, this night, Old Jimmy, a really nice elderly Turkish fellow, and some other old boy was sitting talking to me in my bed space, when this bully South African came up clad only in a bath towel.

He stood there and said to Old Jimmy, 'I bet you're a right raver, taking smack and ecstasy.' Jimmy just looked on the floor, then this mug said to the other old boy, 'I see you've got your Roberts Rambler. [An old radio which all the old boys had in prison.] Proper sounds, man. I bet you're always out clubbing.' Again he got no answer. Then he looked at me. 'I'm sure I've seen you in clubs round Soho as well,' he said.

'No, you couldn't have seen me in the clubs you frequent,' I said. 'I don't go to homosexual bars.'

Now to call a South African macho man a homosexual is the ultimate insult. He glared at me. 'Right, you,' he said. 'In the showers.'

'I thought you'd never ask,' I said. 'I'd love to,' and picked up an Encona sauce bottle as he walked in front. As soon as he was in the shower room, he spun round – just as the bottle smashed into the front of his head. I hit him twice more as he went down. He was unconscious for nearly 15 minutes. Two or three of the blokes got him round, then they banged on the door for health care service, saying he'd slipped over in the shower.

He came back to the wing three days afterwards. I went straight up to him. 'Do you want a return?'

He glared at me. 'Not just yet, I don't,' he said.

I forgot all about him as I went about my business. I just thought he'd swallowed it. I should have known better really. Rochester is situated with stairs at both ends of a big passage with three dormitories off the main passageway. About five weeks after this, I walked out on the passage to go down the washing area, to pick some clothes up. It was on a Sunday, so most people were on town visits. The place was completely deserted.

As I got to the passage I had a sixth sense of foreboding. I heard the big door slam at one end of the passage. I turned round and looked. It was three of the South African's gym buddies. I just carried on walking. As I got near to the other end, the South African and a massive black man came through the door. 'I'm in for it now,' I thought.

All of a sudden a giant appeared behind these two. It was Big Mick. I have never been so pleased to see anyone in my life. Mick had overheard them talking about how they were going to hurt me badly. Mick punched this big black man behind the ear. He fell flat on this face, as though he'd been pole-axed. The South African hit Mick on the jaw with a tremendous right hand but it had no effect. Mick smashed him on the jaw and, with one blow of his mighty fist, smashed his jaw in three places.

In the meantime, the other three members of the ambush ran up to us, but now it was only three against two. Then me and Mick smashed the three mugs all around the passage. There was blood everywhere: all up the walls, some even splashed on the ceiling. When the five of them were all spark out, me and Mick both made ourselves scarce. Within five minutes, there was an alarm bell going off. Screws were running everywhere. All dorms were locked off and the outside police were called in, but full marks to our opponents, they didn't say who did the damage. So we got away with it. Still Mick Salmon, the SO (Superior Officer) got hold of me and Mick in the office. 'I can't prove it but I know you two did them five blokes,' he said. 'No one else in the prison is capable of doing that amount of damage.' Then he said, 'Just get out of my sight.'

As we got up to leave, Salmon said, 'Woollard, I got you out of Wayland. We know all about you. Since you've been here, we've had six hospital cases. Before you arrived everything was running nice – that's how I like to keep it. If I *do* catch you or your sidekick you'll both be shipped out.'

It went very quiet for a while. Then, one morning, Obie and Henry Eastwood and Teddy Perfect, three gypsy fellows, came up to me. 'There's a fellow on your dorm,' they said, 'who said last night all gypsies should be drowned at birth, as some gypsies had stolen his lorry. When Ginger Cormack said, "Well, I've got two gypsy children," he said, "Well they should be six feet under as well."'

I never said anything at first, but I brooded on it. My Danny and Sharon are half gypsy. Then I caught this guy in the TV room and told him not to be so stupid as there's good and bad in everyone.

For three days this fellow just ignored me. Then, on the fourth day, he came into my space and said, 'I didn't mean that for you, but I just hate all gypsies.' So I just clumped him. I didn't catch him quite right, but he hit the wall and started screaming, 'No, please don't hit me.' As I thought – a proper coward. Tony Sakir was sitting there. 'Dan, don't hit him no more,' he said. 'He's not worth it.' So Tony saved this guy's bacon.

Three other blokes, typical grasses, were watching. I told them to mind their own business, or else I would do them. Amazingly I never heard anymore about this incident, but I was the hero of the 'Travellers' Rest' – the dormitory where all the gypsies were. I had done their dirty work for them. They wanted me to move in, but I was happy in the dorm with Big Mick and Tony. My good pal Spencer Taylor – the nephew of Tommy Taylor or 'Boxer Tom' – was in the Travellers' Rest. Me and Mick wanted him to move into our dorm, but he liked it with his own kind. I didn't blame him at all. Incidentally, his brother Wayne Taylor got arrested for that attempted diamond robbery at the Dome in London. Long before that, in 1977, their uncle Boxer Tom had fought John Stanley for 2 hours 15 minutes in a field at Watford with John proving victorious. That's the longest fight I can remember with gypsies fighting bare knuckles.

Opposite A wing at Rochester was B wing – the young offenders' unit. All night you could hear them shouting out of their windows. They called themselves window warriors. They'd call insults all night to each other but if one called out, 'Go and suck your mother,' it meant he was challenging whoever he called out to to a fight, and this insult had to be answered. One morning, as I was going over to the gym, I saw two young boys about 16 or 17 years old arguing with each other. This black lad said, 'Go and suck your mother.' This young white lad pulled a fire extinguisher off the wall and smashed it straight into the black lad's mouth. There was teeth and blood and gore everywhere.

The prison had an immediate lockdown. An ambulance was called, the black lad went to hospital, and the outside police took the white boy away to be charged. I thought it was so sad, two young men starting out on their lives like that. That young offenders' wing was really bad. Four young boys even broke the fluorescent lights, ground the glass down and ate it one night, in a futile attempt to kill themselves because they were being terrorised by bullies on the wing.

FINISHING OFF IN ROCHESTER

They were all in hospital for ages. They were too frightened to say who was terrorising them, but in reality the screws knew, anyhow. Still these four terrified boys were sent straight back to Rochester to live in fear. So sad for them and their families.

After the incident with the South African and his mates, me and Big Mick weren't very popular with the inmates in Rochester, as with no orderlies there was no gym. I knew everyone was moaning behind our backs, but no one said anything to our faces. Rochester is full of grasses, nonces and YPs (young prisoners) – so not the kind of people I had been used to. Really, me and Big Mick just stayed on our own, with one exception – Jason Cormack. He was like us, he'd done a bit of bird with Reg Kray in Maidstone, and Reg had mentioned him to me before, saying he was okay. He'd looked after Reg's pal Bradley Allardyce and took his part a good few times. Its funny in prison, people always find their own level. So Jay palled up with us. He was doing six years for armed robbery. I used to like Jay's sense of humour.

There was a big Irishman who thought he was a bit of a chap. A proper bully. Anyhow, he had a budgie in his cell. One day Jay walked into his cell, and the budgie was dead. So he takes the budgie into his own cell and very gently cuts its head off, then wraps it very thickly in cling film. Then he said to this Irishman, 'Paddy, I think it's on top for me. I'm expecting a spin. Can you bottle [push up your bum] this bit of heroin for me? I'll give you half of it …'

So Paddy goes, 'Right-oh, Jay. You're on.' So he sticks his budgie's head up his arse. Meanwhile, Jay's told everyone. And Paddy's walking round all day with this budgie's head bottled. Anyhow, at bang-up, just as Jay thought, Paddy's got the parcel out to rob a bit of it. It was only ten minutes after bang-up when Paddy screamed out, 'You cunts. I'll kill you all in the morning.'

Everyone was laughing their heads off. In the morning, Jay was in his cell like a rocket. Paddy didn't want to know. Just a bully as we all thought.

There were only a few cells in Rochester on different landings to us. A right queen lived next door to Paddy. We all called him Linda. Jay found a dead mouse one day, so he cut the head off, put the mouse's body in an envelope and tacked it to Linda's door. He laid the head on Linda's pillow. It was a joke imitating the Mafia in *The Godfather*, who put the horse's head on a pillow. Linda just fainted. It caused quite a stir at the time.

After the turnout with the gym boys we never got into much more trouble. I just went my own way. I passed the time of day with the screws. If they spoke at all to me, it was just a nod of my head, that type of thing. Unlike a lot of cons I don't speak to screws unless I have to. Mick Salmon put himself out a few times for me. I respect the man greatly.

I had a good bit of news one week. Big Mick had been slung off works and came to Kent Life with me.

Me and Big Mick were doing very well in Kent Life, but then our lives were turned upside down once again. After a few months, the foot and mouth epidemic broke out and being as they kept livestock at Kent Life and also at Rochester prison farm we couldn't go to either, as the prison governor thought we might carry the virus either to or from the farm. So me, Big Mick and all the others were sent onto a new project that had no animals. It was a huge old fort in Chatham called Fort Amherst. Another pal of mine, Jason Place, came with us too.

Jason is one of the cleverest people I have ever come across in prison. He got five years for a massive computer fraud. The police were so lucky to catch him, it was unreal. They were keeping observation on his pal Barry Sales. Barry paid a few visits to Jason's massive house in Walderslade village, and fetched the attention of the National Crime Squad with him. If it hadn't been for Barry's visits, Jason would have got away with millions of pounds. As well as being a computer wizard, Jason is a master locksmith. He can open almost any safe or lock with ease.

We had it sorted right out within days of being at Amherst. First we got a few hundred pounds' worth of shopping dropped off. Big Mick done all the cooking. We had steak, fish, bottles of drink – in fact, anything we wanted. We were living like kings. Jason sorted all the staffs' computers out for them, as they didn't seem to know what they were doing. While he was in the office, he knocked a hole in the floor, found some spare phone wire and connected us our own phone up, free of charge. Me, Jason and Big Mick didn't do any work at all, we just used to sit round telling the foreman gangster stories, which the old boy used to love hearing. He never gave us one job to do all the time we were there.

Little Stevie Desmonds also worked at the fort. He was about one year from the end of his ten-year sentence for drug running, so obviously he didn't want any trouble at all. He just wanted to do his bird and get out as quickly as possible. The one thing he didn't need was a nicking.

Well, one day Jason fetched a mobile phone to the fort for us to use when we was working away from our own personal line. As Jason was showing us the phone, Steve came into our building and said, all helpful like, 'I've got my own locker here. It's got a pick-proof lock on it. You can leave your phone in there if you like. No one will ever find it.'

'Okay, Steve,' said Jason. 'Thanks very much, mate.'

The next morning we got to the fort a bit early and Steve's pick-proof lock was no challenge at all to Jason. He opened it in about ten seconds flat. Then we hid the phone up, and told the foreman to tell Steve that we'd had a security spin.

As Steve came in, Mick said, with a face as straight as you like, 'Them bastard security screws have taken all our food.'

After about ten minutes, Jason said, 'Steve, give us my mobile. I've got to go into Rochester.'

When Steve opened his burglar-proof locker and found the phone gone, he went pure white. 'It's not here,' he said.

Bert, our Foreman, gave me a knowing wink. 'Oh, them screws went into the office and got the keys to all these lockers,' he said.

'Fucking hell, this ones down to me,' Steve said. 'They'll nick me for it.' We all sat there, solemn faced. As soon as poor Steve left we all broke up laughing. That's all we heard all day from Steve, except for one remark he made: 'Fuck yous, cunts,' he said. 'That's my parole out of the window. That's the last time I mix with yous. You're all fucking gangsters.'

Anyhow, when the bus came to pick us up to take us back to the prison, Mick put the driver in the joke. 'Desmonds, you're not going back to A wing,' he said. 'I have to take you straight to the block.' Poor Steve just kept laughing; obviously his nerves had got the better of him. Then, as we got right near to the prison, Jason said to Steve, 'Steve, did I ever tell you I was a master locksmith? Your unpickable lock was just child's play to me.'

'Oh yeah?' went Steve, miles away in thought. Then all of a sudden the penny dropped. 'You cunts,' he said, but good old Steve took it all in good par. It was one of the best jokes I've seen played in prison.

It's funny inside. Unless you've experienced being there, it's difficult to explain. You can be right pals with someone, then one day, mostly over a trivial thing, you finish up fighting. This happened to

Jason and me. Jason is about 5ft 10in tall and weighs 18 stone and he's an extremely powerful man. What with his broken nose, he looks a real handful and he's also got eyes similar to Roy Shaw's – sort of staring with a puffiness round them and scars over the two of them.

One day were all sitting in our office and something had tickled Jason. He kept on laughing. 'What are your laughing at?' I asked him. He said, 'Nothing,' but just kept on laughing. He was really annoying me, so I walked outside and went into the other building just to cool off. After about half an hour I looked up and Jason's standing in the doorway. 'What's the matter with you?' he said, smiling, but with what I thought was an air of menace. Obviously I'd thought he'd come round to find me and sort matters out, so I grabbed him and nutted him straight in the face. He reeled back, his nose pouring with blood, but to my surprise he didn't try to defend himself at all. He just went, 'No, I won't fight you. You're my friend.' I didn't hit him any more. I was gutted at his reaction. I just sat him down and put a cold flannel on his nose.

When it stopped bleeding, he said, 'Dan, I am no fighter. I never have been. A proper bully done my nose and eyes. I only came round to explain why I was laughing. It was Big Mick. He put a strong laxative into old Bert's coffee and Bert shit himself in the main office before he could get to the toilet. I couldn't tell you in our office as Bert was sitting there.

I felt about as big as a flea. I had taken a proper liberty, but Jason was okay about it. He went on to say, 'Dan, this building's all videoed as they've lost some tools and bits and pieces out of it. So we'll have to destroy the tape otherwise they will just ship you out to another prison.' I had no clue the place was videoed, but Jason soon found the recording machine in another building about half a mile away. The camera was in the place where I had nutted Jason, in an electric socket. I couldn't even tell it was a camera, even after Jason had told me. He destroyed the tape and put a replacement one in, and messed about with the machine, so no one could tell it had ever been interfered with.

No doubt about it, Jason made me feel worse than anyone ever has in any bit of trouble I've ever been in. In reality he's a very inoffensive gentle man of the first order. From that day on, if anyone argued with Jason Place, they argued with me.

There was also a proper mouthy screw in Rochester who I will call 'Swill'. He was always talking to everyone like they were a pig. This Swill was all bluster. One day, Big Mick, who had an enlarged heart, had severe chest pains. He was waiting to go to the health care as he needed his heart pills straight away. 'Okay, I'll phone in a minute,' said Swill. 'When they're ready I'll give you a call and you can go and collect them.'

After about an hour, Mick's chest pains were getting much worse, so he went back into the office with me. 'Swill,' he said, 'did you arrange for me to pick my pills up yet?' This Swill looked at Big Mick and he sneered. 'I told you once. When I'm good and ready I'll phone healthcare, then I'll give you a shout.' Then he waved his hand dismissing Mick as you would a little child, adding, 'Go and sit in your little kennel, like a good little boy, and when I'm good and ready I'll give you a call.'

He spoke to Mick as though he was just a proper mug. Mick glared at him and started to shake. 'What are you looking at?' said Swill. 'Scoot away, boy.'

'Come on, Mick,' I said. 'That mug's not worth the effort.' I knew this Swill wouldn't fight you. He would just get you nicked. I'd met his type of screw in other prisons – proper cowards. He heard me say this to Mick about him being a mug, so he did everything he could to belittle me after that. Remarks, smart answers, the lot. He also made sure that Mick went back to Kent Life working while he left me at Fort Amherst on my own. He made the life of Dave Stacey, another pal, such a complete misery that he escaped.

In my mind I thought, 'If I bash this fool up, I'll get no parole and another nicking,' so I thought of another way of completely belittling him, just so he knew how it feels. I wrote half a phoney letter. In this letter, I wrote that this Swill was a real mouthy screw, who's a known homosexual, and that an inmate was having sex with his wife on a regular basis. In fact, I wrote anything I could think of to insult this fool, I hated him so much. I also wrote that I'd like to oblige this Swill with a man-to-man turnout with no comebacks. But as he's such a coward, I added, this would never happen. Then when I went to work, I made sure Mick Salmon saw my letter, which I carried in my kit bag on purpose.

'What's this?' he said.

'Oh, its only a letter I'm in the middle of writing,' I replied. 'I want to finish it off at work.' I knew Mick Salmon would confiscate the letter, which he did.

'Pick it up in the office later on,' he said.

Anyhow, when I got back from work, Mick Salmon called me straight into the office. He had a face like thunder. There was three other screws in there, including Swill. 'Woollard, this letter,' he said.

'No, Mr Salmon,' I insisted. 'That's not a letter: no stamp on the envelope, no address. It's only part of a letter I was writing ...' so he couldn't nick me for trying to get a letter out of the prison system without it going through the censor.

'I take great exception to what you've written about one of my officers,' he went on.

'Which bit don't you like?' I said.

'This bit.' He pointed to one or two paragraphs.

'In fairness to your staff, could you please read it out loudly, Mr Salmon?'

After much hesitating, Mick Salmon read this letter out. I saw one screw look to the other and grin. This Swill was getting redder and redder. Anyhow, Salmon couldn't do nothing about it. If he could he would have nicked me. All he could do was just confiscate my letter. But news travels fast in prison and within a few hours Swill was the laughing stock of the entire nick. It was very satisfying, but this Swill was always on my case afterwards. Fuck him. I still think he's a 22-carat mug, anyhow.

After I'd been to Fort Amherst for a while, I got to know Bert the foreman very well. One day a fellow who worked at the fort had a right go at old Bert in front of about ten people, over a trivial matter. Well, Bert was in his 60s – a frail, very inoffensive man, whereas this other fellow was well built. He was one of these action man types. So even though I knew I should just keep quiet and mind my own business, when I saw this bully humiliating old Bert, my instincts took over.

As he was ranting at old Bert in the visitors' centre cafeteria, playing to an audience, I stood up and said, 'Oi, action man, you're shouting at the wrong person. I'm Bert's assistant. I take all the credit plus all the complaints. In fact, I'm what you might call in charge of the complaints department.' If any prisoner gets caught fighting on a project they're immediately shipped out of the prison back to a C-Cat nick, thus losing parole. So I was risking quiet a lot.

Anyhow, action man, afraid of losing face, says, 'Perhaps you're the right man to see then.'

'You're dead right, I am,' I said. 'And I suggest we take your

238

complaints outside to the tunnels, so we can talk in private.'

Like most bullies, he folded immediately. He ducked his nut and said, 'No need for all that.'

'Oh yes, there is,' I said, 'Now, you apologise to old Bert in front of these people, or we get it on man to man.'

'No need for that,' Bert interrupted.

'Bert, please let me deal with this,' I said.

'I'm sorry,' said action man, quietly.

'I can't quite hear you.'

So he said loudly, 'I'm sorry.'

Bert said that was okay, everyone in the café started laughing, action man strode out, and no one saw any more of him.

After that day I could do no wrong at the fort. Old Bert gave me a key to the unrestored area, right at the top of the fort, and said, 'Dan, just let yourself in and out as you like and do more or less as you please.' So I just used to pass my day sunbathing or taking one or two visitors to my private area. I just used to lock myself and my guests in.

All in all I was enjoying my days at Fort Amherst, as much as you can enjoy being away from home. I was just passing the time till I could go on outside work, which starts six months before your parole date. All was as sweet as I could possibly get it at Rochester prison. Then suddenly, on Friday, 13 July, of all days, my life took yet another twist.

I went down to the visitors' centre café at 2.15 pm as usual, just to have a quiet cup of tea whilst waiting for the bus to pick us up and take us back to the prison. In the café that day were a lot of squaddies, all dressed up in their army gear. They had been having some sort of a do at the fort. Like all squaddies, they were very loud, all mouth really, making a nuisance of themselves. One soldier in particular seemed to be real lairy and flash. A fellow about 6ft 5in tall, with short-cropped, steel-grey hair. All you could hear was his voice.

So I picked up my tea and sat on a chair outside the café, as I didn't want to be near these men. I could sense bad vibes coming from them. Also there was a girl about 19 or 20 years old serving behind the counter, and I didn't like the remarks they were making to her.

At this time I was going through a bad patch myself. I just felt so low. I don't know if it was depression or I was just down in myself generally, but I didn't feel as though I had any strength left in my entire body. I just felt so weak and lethargic all the time. It wasn't a physical problem but a mental one. I thought to myself, 'Just let me get away from these men.' I really don't know if I was frightened, or just avoiding trouble. It was the first time in my life I'd ever felt this way. I just felt as though I had no more fight left in me, as though my body was giving up on me, like a whipped puppy might feel. All my power and confidence had seemed to desert me all at once.

There were also some young children with their parents in the café, and these soldier boys were making them feel uncomfortable too. In fact, several people got their children together and left. The bus couldn't pick me up quick enough, to get me back to the prison and safety.

All of a sudden I heard aggressively raised voices. A volunteer down the fort had his children in the café with him and had asked these squaddies to keep their language down. Well this loud-mouthed grey-haired fool had made an issue of it, and slagged this volunteer right off in front of everyone. As the volunteer went to leave the café, this loud mouth had followed him onto the patio where I was sitting and continued to shout insults at him in front of his three children. This volunteer's son was about 13 years old, and had started to sob, half in temper and, I felt, half in shame, as this loud-mouthed squaddie was making his dad look a complete coward in front of everyone.

I felt my temper and aggression slowly come back to me. This squaddie half smirked, half grinned and said, 'If you were a man I'd take you down those tunnels and give you a good hiding.' This quiet family man just looked at the floor, saying nothing. All of a sudden my temper snapped. I got a quick burst of adrenaline. Once again I felt strong and powerful, nothing and no one could beat me. I was back.

I sprang out of my chair and went straight into action. I still had my steel-capped boots on. I heard a sickening crack as I kicked him just as hard as I possibly could. My boot had smashed his leg just below the kneecap. His mouth dropped open and he involuntarily screamed out, half in panic and half in pain. He doubled up, his face twisted in agony, grabbing his shattered leg with both hands. As he did, I instinctively jumped back two paces and booted him straight in the face. His head sprang back as though it was on a spring. He was unconscious. Before he hit the floor, his face was a mass of blood and gore. I went straight into the café and hollered as I tore my work jacket off, 'Right-oh! Who wants a trip down the caves with me?' The silence was deafening.

Old Bert said, 'Calm down, Danny. I'll call an ambulance for the squaddie.' Three of his mates were round him by this time. Anyhow, the ambulance arrived before my work bus picked me up. The screw driving the bus made himself busy asking questions etc., but no one would speak to him.

Everyone at the fort tried to cover up for me, as they knew I was in the right, but that night I was called into the office at Rochester prison, and the PO said to me, 'Woollard, I know exactly what went on today down the fort. I know no one will say or do anything against you, as your so well liked down there. Otherwise you'd be on a charge right here and now.

'The army's making a few inquiries and making a bit of a show of things, as one of their men's been badly beaten, but I am sure their inquiries are only a show and will not come to anything. But you must understand I have no option but to take you off that fort project for two reasons. One, although I don't expect you to admit anything, I do know you were sticking up for one of them down there, but they're normal people. They have never seen such raw violence like you showed today, and they're frightened to have you around them, just in case you turn on one of them. Also, I can't afford to let you stay there in case those squaddies seek a bit of revenge. Then a few innocent people could get hurt. So if you're not there it can't happen. This prison will be holding its own enquiry.

The SO said, 'If anyone stands up against you, you do know you'll be charged, sent to an outside court, and shipped out of this prison, don't you?'

I just nodded. As I went to leave, the SO said, 'Woollard, off the record, I know exactly what happened. Old Bert told me unofficially the full story, and I won't pursue anything unless I'm ordered to. I can't officially condone any form of violence but I am not keeping you locked up in the prison whilst the inquiries are in progress, not for what you did. I'm putting you on the best project here, Strood Yacht Club. By the way, Old Bert said if it was wartime you'd be a hero, but in peacetime, unfortunately, there's no place for men of violence like you.'

I knew the SO had a job to do, or at least to be seen to be doing, but deep down I knew he agreed with what I had done, and perhaps secretly admired it.

FINISHING OFF IN ROCHESTER

Anyhow, Monday morning, bright and early, I'm off to the yacht club for some more fun and games. I knew so far I'd been lucky. I was the only person to be slung off two projects and still be in Rochester prison. I'm sure other people who have done long sentences will know exactly how I felt and how close I came to letting the system and life beat me. I felt my spirit had almost been broken. But my two old friends, trouble and violence, had made me realise I was still a man, and still very much alive. I was officially back.

Although I didn't think I had any chance with these soldier boys, when I got that surge of power in me I knew I couldn't lose. My fear was replaced by courage, and my doubts by confidence. I thank God or the Devil, whichever one's on my side, that someone gave me strength and power when I needed it most.

ROUND 17

ROCHESTER RIOT

On Thursday, 18 October 2001, there was a funny atmosphere all over Rochester Prison. The air was electric and you could feel that something was going to happen. For no apparent reason I had nervous butterflies in my stomach all day. The feeling of expectancy was everywhere.

B wing housed 63 young offenders and feeling in that wing was running high over the lack of association time and mistakes on the canteen. Some of these lads had been shipped in from Feltham where they'd been involved in riots and some from Dover where there were also riots. Now the worst cases were under one roof, Rochester B wing. A recipe for disaster, I thought.

One young inmate was stirring all the others up, so he was taken to the block to try to avoid any confrontations. His name was Chambers.

Anyhow, at about 6.30 pm the alarm goes off – there's trouble in B wing. So the screws from all the other wings rush over there.

I saw them all running to get there. They all went into the main door at the front of the wing. Then I spotted three screws from the reception area race to the door at the other end of the building. This door was the nearest point of entry to the reception area. Just as they went into the wing, the second alarm went off to evacuate B wing, as the situation was out of control. Unfortunately the three screws from reception didn't hear the second alarm. Consequently all the other screws evacuated, leaving these three alone. So all the young offenders' attention was focused on just them. As the three screws tried to get away they were being pelted by pool balls and all sorts.

Officer Ray Smith was beaten to the floor. The other two officers made good their getaway, leaving poor Mr Smith to the mercy of this mob. As the two screws got outside they also locked the door, so there was no way for Smith to get out. So Smith was cuffed up and taken as a hostage – they cuffed him up with his own handcuffs. Then these 63 young prisoners smashed B wing to pieces. At one point they put Smith up to the window with a knife at his throat. They demanded cases of lager. Then they demanded a helicopter. They barricaded themselves in by wedging pool tables against the doors. The rest of the screws surrounded the building, but every time they either tried to get into the building, or officer Cadmore tried to negotiate a settlement, they just said, 'If you try anything, Smith gets it proper.'

So it was stalemate. All them screws just stood by helpless whilst the wing was obliterated. At about 4 am the mufti squad – riot squad – arrived, around a hundred of them in total. One of the inmates who wanted out of the situation told them which cell Smith was located in by shouting from a window.

The mufti started to beat out their message by banging their truncheons on their shields. It was a frightening sound, just like Zulus attacking. When they started to move forward, one of the inmates went to set about officer Smith with a blade.

Some of the other lads turned on the inmate and set about him, breaking his jaw and giving him a real bad beating. They realised that if officer Smith was hurt badly or even killed, they'd all get life sentences.

In the confusion the mufti threw stun grenades into B wing. The noise was horrendous and the grenades lit up the roof and sky above. There were about six loud bangs and dazzling flashes. While this was going on, battering rams had smashed both doors down, and the mufti were in.

Officer Russ Barker's job was to get officer Smith out. He dashed straight to the cell Smith was in. No resistance was offered by any inmate. Then the mufti marched all 63 inmates of B wing into the gym and held them there, and everyone there was either sent down the block or shipped off to different prisons. Six inmates had been injured. No officers were hurt at all except for Smith.

When Barker marched him out, all the mufti stood and clapped him, just like a hero. I bet he got a medal. 'Just up his street – all the odds in his favour,' I thought.

At 5.30 in the morning, in darkness, Rochester prison's B wing lay completely deserted and wrecked. Just the shell was left standing. The quietness seemed eerie, as though it was haunted by a thousand ghosts. Especially after all the noise and action that had just taken place. As for the young offenders, eight of them were charged and are now awaiting their fates.

After the riots, Rochester prison was closed down. By Christmas Day 2001 there was only eight of us left in Rochester A wing, as the closure of the nick was imminent. As you can imagine, after spending the Christmas week banged up, we were all completely poxed off. Anyhow, it was about 11 o'clock and we were all sitting in the TV room, none of us talking at all.

Stuart 'Taffy' Higginson said, 'Come on, lads. Cheer up. What we'll do is we'll have a talent contest. Each one of us has to tell a joke or sing a song. Dris, the Moroccan, will be the judge.'

Taffy started the ball rolling with the worst rendition of 'White Christmas' I have ever heard in my life, followed my good pal Ted Perfect singing 'Lonesome Valley'. I glanced around the room and thought, 'If only the outside world could see or hear us now.' Taffy was doing ten years for attempted murder. Ted Perfect was doing five years for breaking a fellows legs. Tony Humphreys was doing a seven for explosives charges, all stemming from his love for animals – he used to be an active member of the Animal Liberation Front. There was Len Bedja doing six years for firearms and attempting to kill. The wizard on the computers, Ben Emmanuel, was doing a five for conspiracy to kill his mother. The Moroccan was doing 18 years for drugs and firearms. John Watts was doing six years for armed robbery. All of us so-called villains were there, singing very badly and telling corny jokes.

I sang 'Baby Face' and was voted the winner, and Ted gave me a phone card as my prize. It's funny when you're put in a corner, the things you do to amuse yourselves. Anyhow, it did the trick, and we all went to bed on Christmas night a bit happier. I won't mention what else we did to cheer ourselves up, as one or two of the lads are still waiting for parole.

One thing I have a quiet chuckle to myself about at times is Johnny Watts singing 'Jingle Bells' all out of tune. How anyone can manage to sing jingle bells out of tune is a mystery to me, but Big John somehow managed it.

I kept myself to myself a lot at this time as my parole was about to be heard. In my cell, all alone, I had a thousand thoughts. I thought about Angelo's brother John. He only got five years and went straight to a cushy D-Cat prison, but I bet many nights he lay awake and thought about Angelo and me.

I was the last prisoner to get paroled out of the place on 8 February 2002. The authorities let me finish my time in Rochester. It was so weird when there were just two of us in the prison: me and Tony Humphreys, who no other prison would take. I don't know where he finished up, but wherever it is, good luck, Tony!

My parole board officer told me I'd been involved in 45 disturbances in my time in prison, but they were prepared to take a chance with me and let me out on licence, as I had saved two people's lives in Wayland.

One good bit of news I heard was that when John got released from Stanford Hill prison he found out that his wife Suzanne had deserted him. Then two weeks after his release, someone burned his house to the ground. All I can say is it's a pity he wasn't in it.

I also thought about the first time I met Kate Kray. I met her one night in the Royal Hotel at Victoria Park in the East End of London – the same pub that, a short time afterwards, Jimmy Moodey was shot dead in. It was at a benefit night for a fellow who used to be a second in the fight game, who was dying of cancer.

I was with my son Danny and my old pal from Essex, Nicky Cook. Nicky turned up at my house with 'Birmingham Bernie' – Bernard O'Mahoney. It was the first time I had met Bernard. Kate Kray was in the company of Joe Pyle, Alex Steine and one of the Nash Brothers. She was married to Ronnie Kray at the time.

I liked Kate. She is a very bubbly, attractive blonde woman, with a lovely personality to match. She would turn any man's head.

She has written a book called *Hard Bastards*. I know most of the people in that book are what you might call hardnuts or villains. I don't know that I agree with everything in it, but Kate's book does make interesting reading.

There's one bit in particular which I did find very intriguing. Albert Reading says he had a prizefight with Brian Hall, who a lot of people considered to be the best prizefighter of the lot. Well me and Terry Butwell staged 37 major prizefights and the ones we didn't stage we attended as spectators.

I saw Albert fight Brian, and to my mind Albert just ran out of stamina and got himself knocked out easily. Brian fought for us a good few times. He was an old professional boxer who knew his way round a boxing ring. But the only two fights I ever saw him win were against Albert and then when he fought the nonce and grass Danny Woods, later known as Reece. Again, Brian clung on and messed Woods about using his boxing experience and Danny ran out of steam, then fell over completely exhausted.

To say Brian was the best prizefighter is ludicrous.

I staged Brian's last prizefight. Peter DeFreitas bandaged his hands and acted as a second for him. Peter's a good man to have round you in a boxing ring, and he only did it as a favour. Brian fought a fellow from Hackney. Brian was game enough, but every time this fellow caught him, Brian went down. Peter gave Brian every chance but eventually I jumped up and stopped the fight, Brian had no chance at all. So in my opinion, Albert Reading had got Brian Hall's fighting abilities all wrong.

Micky May was only a middleweight, but he could really fight. This local boy fought at the prizefights – ex-champion boxers, the lot, and beat them all. Then, unfortunately they coerced him into boxing a heavyweight called Vernon Shaw – no relation to Roy – at

Dartford Football ground the same night Roy Shaw fought Harry 'The Buck' Starbuck.

Micky was winning easily, but Shaw, the much bigger opponent, threw a haymaker punch over and caught Micky – a sucker punch that knocked him spark out. Micky had got careless. He never boxed again. As Micky was being carried from the ring, one of the spectators started calling him names, as he'd lost a few quid on him. Bobby Reading – Albert's brother and, to me, the hardnut of the family – hit this fellow, knocking *him* spark out.

A mini riot ensued, but Bobby Barry Dalton, Joe Carrington plus a few others calmed it all down eventually. One thing stuck in my mind that night above all others. When Joe Carrington got home, he had a little bit of blood on him. His wife, Lil, said, 'Joe, what's that in your head?' It was someone's tooth – embedded in Joe's head where he'd nutted someone. Lil just pulled it out. But I have always imagined Joe going to the dentist and saying I've got a bad tooth that needs pulling out, and pointing to his head.

At this time I also dreamed of Paradise Row. This is a string of houses in Bethnal Green with a very colourful past. It is mentioned in the song 'Mother Kelly's Doorstep'. The old film and music hall star Arthur Lucan, more commonly known as Old Mother Riley, and his partner Kitty McShane lived there at one time. Arthur had a very sad life and died of a broken heart. Legend has it that Arthur's ghost still haunts Paradise Row to this very day. Daniel Mendoza was the very first Jewish bare-knuckle champion. He also lived in Paradise Row. When he retired from the prize ring, he toured music halls giving exhibition bouts. Mendoza died in Petticoat Lane in East London in 1836. He'd drunk all his money away and was penniless. His great grandson is Peter Sellers.

But most of all I dreamed of freedom and open space.

DANNY WOOLARD

On 8 February 2002, after all my trials and tribulations, I was finally released. As I walked to my car I heard, 'Oi!'

It was my very good pal Ted Perfect. He hadn't forgotten me. Although Ted is a very hard man, he's the most feeling person I have ever met. I love him like a brother. He took me into Rochester, bought me a real slap-up breakfast and gave me a bundle of £50 notes to start me off. Then I set off down the M2, the best road in the world. The one going back to London.

ROUND 18

MY 'HARD MEN'

I'd like to take this opportunity to list, in no particular order, one or two really hard men who you've heard little or nothing about so far.

BERT ASSIRITI

I met Bert when I was about 19. He was getting on a bit then but he was still an impressive man. He was looking after a club in the West End and I saw him throw five roughnecks out of there one night single-handedly. Even though he was getting on, he handled them like babies. Bert was reckoned to be the roughest toughest man ever to get into a wrestling ring and was undefeated against the best they could offer. He toured the USA, throwing an invincible Terrible Turk right out of the ring. He was heavyweight champion of the world, at a time when wrestling wasn't a comic show but a serious sport. He also held the world record for strength, and they reckon he used to do a wrestler's bridge in the ring that no one could ever break. Bert came from Islington. I think he was a Greek. Now there's a life story worth writing. I don't think I've ever met anyone that could have beaten Bert in a pub fight. Sadly, I learned he was blind in later life. A real lovely man, Bert.

BILLY 'THE BOMB' WILLIAMS

Billy had a good amateur boxing career. Then, when Cassius Clay came to this country, Angelo Dundee stopped Billy and took him back to the States with them to his training camp. Bill won all his fights in America. He was doing very well, coming up the ladder fast, then he paid a visit back to this country, got into a bit of trouble and finished up in prison. It was a terrible shame, because Bill had the potential to go very far in the fight game. He has got an enormous reputation in prison and in the East End of London as a one-punch KO specialist.

DAVEY HUNT

Davey Hunt is a straight businessman who owns a scrapyard. Dave looks after himself and trains regular. He takes after his uncle Teddy. Dave, like Teddy, has never been beaten in a fight, and some good men have tried to take his reputation. One night he had a straight fight with Gary Stretch who was good enough to fight Chris Eubank for the title, but Dave knocked out Gary Stretch in quick order. A good fighting man, Dave, and a thorough gentleman as well.

NICKY COOK

Nicky is a very close friend of mine and also one of the best fighters I have ever seen. Nicky runs a farm and the farm work keeps him fit. He trains as well. He once fought a giant of a rugby player for 20 minutes on the cobbles, before proving victorious. Nicky is another man everyone likes, not a liberty taker, a pleasure to have around you. But he is a Tasmanian devil in a fight – a real wolf in sheep's clothing. No man has ever beaten Nicky.

BARRY KEELEY

No list of hard men would be complete without Barry. He came up the hard way, won countless amateur championships, then his fiery temper got him into trouble. If he had kept out of trouble, Barry would have been a champion boxer. He can hit with either hand, delivering KO punches, he takes a good punch, and Barry fears no man, unlike a lot of so-called hardnuts. Barry treats them all the same. He doesn't hand pick his opponents. I've got a lot of respect for Barry. He's a first-class man.

FREDDIE BOTHAM

When I first met Fred he was running the Circus Tavern at Purfleet. Fred was as wide as he was tall, a fine figure of a man. He taught Del Croxson how to box. In later years he had been ill, but a young man went to a pub on the Thames View Estate that Fred was running and challenged Fred to a straight-up fight. This boy was the best fist fighter in Essex. Fred accepted this challenge and had a bare-knuckle fight with him in the car park. After taking the young fellow's best punches, Fred knocked him right out. Without a doubt, Freddy Botham is one of the best, if not the best fighter I have ever seen.

DANNY WOODS

Danny started prizefighting under the name of Dynamite Dan and he was dynamite. As soon as the bell rang, Danny used to rush into his opponent, throwing hard, powerful punches. I have never seen anyone punch faster. No one could stand up to him. All his fights were one-round KOs. He looked unbeatable. He beat Brian Hall, an old professional boxer in this fashion. Brian immediately asked for a return and promised he would beat Dynamite. In the return match, Dan rushed into Brian, but this time Brian was ready and held Dan at bay and boxed him. In the third round Brian hit Woods, not at all hard. He wemt down and was counted out. No one could believe it.

Danny got himself into trouble and went away for a long time. Then he refused to go on a segregation unit. He had many a fight in prison and always won them, sometimes against overwhelming odds. He remains a one off. And one of the toughest men in the prison system. He is always in the gym training and no one can beat him. Regardless of his failings, Danny Woods is a real hard street fighter, who must come into anyone's list of hard men.

PAUL SYKES

Paul Sykes is a very hard man who's spent many years in prison. Paul holds many weightlifting records and is a giant of a man whose fingers are as thick as bananas. He is one of the toughest men in the prison circuit. When he was released he won many professional fights, eventually fighting John L Gardner for the British heavyweight title. But in the heat of the battle, Sykes proved he never had a true warrior's heart. Gardner had him under pressure and Sykes did the unforgiveable act of turning away from the battle. The fight was immediately stopped, with Gardner the winner. Sykes could not take the real pressure.

He lived in Wakefield. When his boxing career was over, he came to London to fight Billy 'The Bomb' Williams, but for some reason it never happened. I think it was something legal that stopped the fight occurring but that would have been some fight. Sykes, like Danny Reece, is still one very, very tough man to fight in the street –

a difficult man to beat. He once killed a prison cat, skinned it and made a Davy Crockett hat out of it. That's Sykes.

YOLANDE POMPEY

Yolande Pompey was a Trinidadian fighter that lived in Canning Town when I knew him. Pompey was one of the hardest-hitting men I have ever seen. Heavily muscled, he fought as a middleweight, then as a light heavyweight boxer. He finished Randolph Turpin's career. Then he fought Archie Moore for the Light Heavyweight Championship of the world. Two days before the fight he slipped in the bath and cracked two ribs, but in those days if you didn't go through with a title fight you never got another chance, so Pompey fought the all-time great Archie Moore with two broken ribs. He was well winning, but Moore's body shots got to him and Yolande was stopped in the tenth round. Still, it was a heroic performance. When my pal Tony Dove fought him they had a war. Pompey won on points, but neither man ever fought again. Pompey died when he was 49. He was working for the Trinidadian embassy. Tony Dove died shortly after at the age of 51. Tony was an associate of Abbey Life. Two brave fighting men who perhaps killed each other.

JOHN MURPHY

Johnny Murphy, or 'Spud' as he was affectionately known, was a tremendous fighting man, with a KO punch in each hand. His brother Terry was also a first-class boxer. Unfortunately him and John were exactly the same weight so, as they would never fight each other, one or other of them used to stand down, allowing his brother to go through and win the titles, because no one else could stand up to either of them as an amateur. John still holds the record for the number of KOs he scored and the two brothers won many titles, but if they had been different weights the tally would have been double. Terry turned professional and John retired to avoid fighting his brother. John went into the pub business. He took the Royal Oak, Canning Town, where Frank Bruno, John Stracy, Maurice Hope, Jim Watt plus many more champions trained. But they knew Spud was the Guv'nor.

When Maurice Hope was in his prime, he got arguing with John and John knocked him down, almost out, with just one punch. There were always rumours that John was going to fight Roy Shaw, then Lennie Mclean, but these fights never happened. Neither Shaw nor Mclean fancied fighting John. He stopped three men taking protection money off of one of his pals one night – then these three cowards stabbed him to death. The first wound got John in the heart, but this didn't stop him. Then they stabbed him another 27 times before he died, before dumping his body on Wanstead Flats. In court all three blamed each other and they all got life sentences. Terry's son went into acting and is very successful, starring in *London's Burning*. John's relative Craig Fairbrother is an actor now too, playing the part of Lennie Mclean in the film *The Guv'nor*. In real life, John was the guv'nor.

ERIC HORST

Eric was a legend in his own lifetime. He was a very violent man who used to draw protection money off of the stallholders in Walthamstow market. Eric always worked alone; he never needed a gang. One stallholder started to argue with Eric one week about paying him. Eric hit him with a hatchet, taking two fingers off of his hand, as the stallholder was putting his hands up to try to defend himself. Everyone steered clear of Eric. He upset the Kray twins once. They said in one of their books they went looking for Eric but could not find him. They were 12-handed. Even so, Eric did not hide from anyone, so perhaps the twins just showed a bit of face, then decided discretion is the better part of valour.

In the Temperance Billiard Hall, Walthamstow High Road, I saw Eric play a game of snooker for £50. When this other fellow won, Eric set about him, then unbelievably lifted one end of a full-sized snooker table off its legs, then threw a snooker ball and smashed a big clock and walked out. No one liked Eric as when he'd been drinking he always wanted to fight, no matter how many men he was against. There was only one man who ever gave Eric a real fight – a gypsy called Benny Lights. He fought him outside the Prince of Wales pub in Leyton, after Eric had been insulting him all night. These two warriors fought each other to a standstill. After 20 minutes, with blood and teeth everywhere, the police broke it up, I think to the relief of both men. Needless to say they never had a return. Yes, Eric was a nuisance and a bully, especially in drink, but nevertheless a very hard man.

BERTIE COSTER

Bert was one of the finest welterweight prospects in this country. He trained and boxed for East Ham. His trainer was an old police champion by the name of Arthur Craddock. Bert got into the final of the ABA, where Brian Nancurvis beat him on the narrowest of points decisions. Brian later changed his name to Curvis and beat Dave Charnley in a British title fight and fought Emile Griffiths for the world crown, which he lost. Bert became an England representative and it took the Russian champion to beat him, as there's no professionals in Russia and the amount of people in Russia compared to England is enormous. It's no wonder Bert lost.

Bert packed up boxing and was always in trouble, getting long sentences along the way, mainly for blagging and armed robbery. The police sent in a dog to get Bert once and he killed the dog with his bare hands. He had a siege with the police at East Ham and it took an SAS-type operation to get him. He broke out of prison and was recaptured a while later at Chipping Ongar. Bert and Frankie Fraser were two of the leaders in the riots at Hull prison, and in Parkhurst prison him and Roy Shaw got nicked for murder, which they both got acquitted on. On his release he married Maggie Jenkins. Her brother Bill's young daughter, Billy Jo, got murdered in Hastings, battered to death. This left Bert a broken man and sadly him and Maggie split up. Bert was meant to be a boxer not a criminal.

FREDDIE MILLS

Freddie Mills was a very tough man who came from Bournmouth. He learned his trade the hard way, through the boxing booth. He fought Gus Lesnevich for the Light Heavyweight Championship of the world. It was a terrific battle, which Lesnevich won. Freddie's head was dislocated from his spine, so he actually had his head knocked off his shoulders. But Freddie kept on fighting and he beat Lesnevich in a return fight. Neither man was the same after the first epic battle. Freddie lost the title to Joey Maxim shortly afterwards, in what was supposed to be an easy match.

In his career, Freddie fought a lot of heavyweights. He was ultra game, but he was no match for Bruce Woodcock, Joe Baski and several others, who gave Freddie some fearful hidings. Fred retired a national celebrity and hero. He opened Freddie Mills' night spot in the West End, but I feel Freddie had been knocked stupid. He was a bisexual if not a full-blown homosexual. Michael Holliday, the singer who had a hit with 'The Story of My Life' was his boyfriend. Holliday committed suicide a year before Freddie shot himself. There was a lot of gossip – some said he was depressed over Holliday's death and took his own life.

There were other rumours. George Cornell, who Ronnie Kray shot in the Blind Begger, was bragging to everyone that he'd killed Freddie. So consequently, when Ron shot Cornell, a lot of people said that Ron had shot Cornell to avenge Freddie's death. I don't believe that story for one minute, because if Ron had wanted to kill Cornell in revenge for Freddie, I feel he'd have done it more discreetly and got away with it. But Cornell had insulted Ron publicly by calling him a fat poof, so Ron killed him publicly so everyone would know that you don't insult Ron Kray.

Also, Freddie had lent the rifle which had killed him from a fairground pal of his, so did Cornell creep up on Freddie and take the rifle off him and shoot him? I don't think so. If Cornell had wanted to shoot Freddie it would have been simpler to have taken a handgun with him and just shot him through the window of his car. Also, Fred was shot right in the eye. Cornell would have had to have been a better shot than Buffalo Bill to achieve this, as everyone knows fairground guns are interfered with to miss the target.

My belief is that Freddie was responsible for six women of easy virtue who had been tied up, tortured, then strangled to death. One woman actually had her breast bitten off. Most of these women were covered in bites, which only a disturbed person would do. When Fred died the murders stopped, although a security officer was also a suspect and he killed himself about the same time as Fred. A very high-ranking officer told me that Fred had been in for questioning, which was common knowledge, but what was not common knowledge was that the forensic people had taken impressions of Fred's teeth and they matched up with the wounds on these women. Fred knew he was about to be arrested, he could not face the shame or the inevitable life sentence he would get, so he shot himself.

Fred epitomised the British bulldog spirit in his fights. He never gave up. I personally think the punishment he took addled his brains – the police just let the British public keep their hero. I have made many enquiries and all the sensible people in the know all agree with me. Fred was too game for his own good.

CHARLES BRONSON

I first met Micky Peterson, or 'Charles Bronson' as he now calls himself, in the mid-eighties when Paul Edmonds fetched him down to the East End of London to do a bit of prizefighting. Paul called him Charles Bronson as he thought the name sounded so much harder than Micky Peterson. When I say fight, obviously Paul had sorted out an easy opponent for Micky. The same as most of the prizefighters did. Micky won easily enough. He was as strong as a horse, but a complete novice at the fighting game. You need more than just strength to win fights in the ring. In his book he says he challenged Lenny Mclean. I think Lenny could have beaten Micky very easily.

PETER OAKLEY

When I think of hard, rough, tough men, there is one man whose name always springs to mind – Peter Oakley. We've been in some very tight corners and I know Peter's never ever been found lacking in any quarter. I could tell you endless stories about Peter. For instance, one night he had a straightener with the hardest man amongst the bikers. A circle of motorbikers with there headlights on was the ring. After 25 minutes the biker was knocked unconscious. Pete is a very quiet, working, family man, who doesn't mix with many people. But believe me, I know what he can do with fists or tools. He deserves the utmost respect. He's earned it the hard way. He's got a very casual, nice way about him, but when needs be he's a proper gladiator.

BIG MICK JOHNSON AND DEL 'CROCKO' CROXSON

Two men who could have been so much more than just hardnuts were cousins Mick Johnson and Del Croxson. Mick, a giant of a man, could easily have made the grade as a boxer, he had the lot: size, power and agility. And his little cousin, 6 foot 2, 8 stone, Del Croxson, feared no man. He was known as one of the gamest and hardest men in the prison system, but as we know he died at the tender age of 32. As for Mick, he got married young and, just to please his wife, gave up his very promising boxing career, but every time I think of them two I know they were both undefeated street fighters who won many brutal battles. I wonder what might have been.

ANGELO HAYMAN

Has proved himself time and time again against some very hard men. Not only that, he's very tough mentally. What he's been through would have broken most men. I respect Angelo immensely. He is soft-hearted and will cry at a film, but upset him at your peril. He's full of scars but, against all the odds, has never been beaten by any man, or indeed the system.

GARY NELSON

Another extremely tough man in the prison system, is Gary 'Tyson' Nelson. He's acknowledged all over the country as a real prison hardnut. He's the only man I have ever heard of busting out of a restraining body belt. God knows where he got the strength and power to do that.

THE FINAL ANALYSIS

So who was or is the hardest man in Britain? There's no doubt about it, Roy Shaw was a very hard man who could have a terrible fight, but he wasn't a natural heavyweight. At the most he would be fighting as a middleweight. I think as a young man, at his correct weight, Roy would have been almost unbeatable, but he did nearly ten years in prison and put on loads of muscle, which is all surplus weight to a fighter, and consequently his stamina suffered. If a fight wasn't finished in short order, the extra weight Roy was carrying never done him any favours. Also Roy was about 40 when he came out of prison, a bit old for a fighter, and Roy had a liking for the good life and used to get very drunk, then someone would challenge him. Every time I have heard of Roy getting done outside the ring he was drunk.

Lennie Mclean was a natural heavyweight. If Lennie had started boxing when he was young, he could have gone all the way. Even so Lennie did very well against the prizefighters. I think Lennie's two greatest battles were fights in which he lost. He fought Cliff Fields, a natural heavyweight boxing champion, who had done five years in prison. On his release he came on the prizefighting scene. Roy Shaw had more sense to fight him. Lennie took him on, and after eight torrid rounds was finally knocked unconscious. In the return it went exactly the same way. In the eighth round Len was counted out. Lennie was never the same fighter. Johnny Waldron, a pumped-up middle to light heavyweight boxer, fought Lennie twice, knocking him out both times in the first round. After that Lennie started with training using steroids. He put on loads of weight, but the same as Roy Shaw got very short of breath.

They are just two of the candidates for the hardest man in Britain. Micky Gluckstead never backed down from any challenge and has never been beaten in a street fight. He fought the best of the prizefighters, those that would fight him in the ring with gloves on or off, although he had no boxing experience at all. But Micky is the gamest of them all. They couldn't even stop him by shooting him. So who was the hardest man in Britain? I don't think there's an answer to that question. I've only mentioned a few people that could have a fight. There is also Joe Stratford, Vic Dark, Brian Outen, Matthew Thomas, John Cooney, the gypsy fighter Bartley Gorman, plus hundreds more, some I don't even know.

I feel that if, by magic, all the people mentioned in this book could be matched up with each fighter in their prime you'd get a different result every time, as every fight is different. You need a lot of luck. They can get lucky and catch you out or vice versa. The police started calling me and Micky and Paul the Goodfellas, as they knew not one of us would swallow or back down off of no one. As Joe Pesci wouldn't swallow off of the mafia in the film *Goodfellas*, and none of us have ever been beaten in a street fight.

AFTERWORD

I think the final words for this book should be about Reg Kray. Everyone knows it is the biggest travesty in British history. Thirty-two years, and for what crime? For killing Jack 'The Hat' McVitie. I knew Jack. I didn't like him. He was a right violent loudmouth, who loved hurting people. He told everyone what he thought of the Krays and what he was going to do to them. He made it abundantly clear he thought the Krays were just mugs. I know that he spent some money that Reg had sent him to pick up – on purpose, to make a fool out of Reg. It was obvious to everyone including Jack that a confrontation was becoming inevitable. Jack was calling it on. Reg just got in first or else Jack would have killed him.

What Reg done wrong was he trusted his allies. That was his downfall, as it has been with so many men far greater than Reg. Throughout the pages of history, even Jesus had his Judas. One after the other they fell, one by one betraying him. But Reg kept staunch and strong. I know from experience that Reg could have said what he knew about other people and got a lighter sentence for him and his brother, but both of them upheld the code they had always lived by. The code of honour. So they both paid the full price.

Both twins died while still incarcerate. After all those years Reg never divulged any of the secrets he knew about people. And Reg knew loads of people who went on to become national celebrities. Although so many of these so-called friends have sensationalised their stories by talking and writing badly of Reg, and indeed Ron, they never retaliated and stooped to saying what they knew. They have never once spoken out of turn about anyone. Reg paid his debt to society in full. In prison he helped everyone with advice in whatever way he could. I know he got at least 25 young men jobs to go to when they left. Reg has rung one of his pals and got them employment.

And Mike Tyson obviously feels the same. One of the biggest cons this country has ever seen was when Mike Tyson came over here and fought Julius Francis. If you can say fought, it was like racing a Ferrari with a mini car. Everyone knew Julius had no chance. It came on the radio that only seven people in this country had a bet on Julius to win. It was just an exercise to get Tyson and Frank Warren loads of money. Julius even advertised the *Daily Mirror* on the souls of his boxing boots. It was a gross mismatch, which shouldn't have been allowed to take place

Anyhow, the morning after the fight, it was shown in the television room at Wayland prison. The room was full to capacity. Reg Kray walked in, his place had been saved, a chair right at the front.

Then, after the bout, Tyson said that he supported Reggie Kray fully. He had just had the fight with Julius, everyone was trying to interview him and he thought of Reg. I think it was a wonderful gesture. Every con in the television room gave Reg a clap when Tyson had finished talking, as a sign of respect for Reggie. It was nice to see and hear, and it let Reg know that not only Iron Mike Tyson but all of us was behind him as well. Rest in peace, old pal.

No one wants to go to prison but I personally think prison life taught me a lot. On the downside since I have been away I have lost some good friends: Bartley Gorman, Micky Roman, Georgie Woods, Danny O'Leary, Reggie Kray, Terry Mc Carthy, my uncle Terrible Ted, my father's lifelong partner Teddy, Barry Keeley, Jerry Upton, to name just a few. But it has also made me realise what good friends I've got in Billy McCrudden, the Daltrey family, Tony Weedon, Richard Brittain, Danny Donnegan, my cousin Ted, Pat plus two of Reggie's pals – Jacqui Williams and Tania. They both really supported Reg and myself. Sid Carr proved to be a star. Also the big, good-looking ginger geezer and his mob from Essex and two of the Smythe family, who had major problems of their own but still made plenty of time for me. Their poor relative Bill lost his life in Chelmsford prison and last but no means least, Nick Paul, a fine sportsman, a real East End boy who hasn't stopped helping me. I respect him greatly. He his not only my parole officer, he has proved to be a very fair man, who deserves to be respected.

It goes without saying also a big thank you to my mum and dad, my wonderful children Sharon and Danny and my wife Rebecca. But it's all over now, so it's back to London to even more experiences I hope. If I have upset anyone with my writings I am very sorry, but I have written it as I saw it.

'We are all born owning many qualities –
some we may never know we possess. It all depends
what kind of run god gives us.'
Big Mick Johnson – Rochester Prison, 2000